CHRONOLOGICA:
The Incredible Years That Defined History

BLOOMSBURY

LONDON · OXFORD · NEW YORK · NEW DELHI · SYDNEY

Bloomsbury Publishing
An imprint of Bloomsbury Publishing Plc

50 Bedford Square
London
WC1B 3DP
UK

1385 Broadway
New York
NY 10018
USA

www.bloomsbury.com

WHITAKER'S, the W Trident logo and the Diana logo are trademarks
of Bloomsbury Publishing Plc

First published in Great Britain in November 2016 by Bloomsbury Publishing Plc

British Library Cataloguing-in-Publication Data
A catalogue record for this book is available from the British Library.

ISBN: HB: 978-1-4729-3294-5
       ePub: 978-1-4729-3295-2

2 4 6 8 10 9 7 5 3 1

Printed and bound in China by C&C Offset Printing Co., Ltd

To find out more about our authors and books visit www.bloomsbury.com. Here you will find extracts, author
interviews, details of forthcoming events and the option to sign up for our newsletters.

Contents

Contents

Contents

Contents

ABOUT *WHITAKER'S* – THE TEAM BEHIND CHRONOLOGICA

CHRONOLOGICA is written and compiled by the team behind *Whitaker's Almanack* – one of the oldest annual reference books in the UK. Jam-packed full of facts and figures on topics including: Politics, Kings and Queens, World Geography, Art, Music, Science and Sport. The first edition was published on 10 December 1868 and was such a success that it had to be reprinted immediately!

In 1878 a copy of *Whitaker's* was included in a time capsule buried beneath the monument Cleopatra's Needle on the Embankment in London, together with a set of contemporary coins and a copy of *The Times* newspaper.

On 29 December 1940, a wartime bombing raid struck the *Whitaker's* editorial offices in Warwick Lane, obliterating almost all the archive and reference library used to compile the book. This prompted Prime Minister Winston Churchill to write to Sir Cuthbert Whitaker seeking assurances that the publication of *Whitaker's* would not be interrupted: a measure of the book's importance.

Whitaker's Almanack is mentioned in many famous works of literature, including Bram Stoker's *Dracula* and Ian Fleming's James Bond novel *Moonraker*. A copy of *Whitaker's* is even used by Sherlock Holmes to decode a message in Sir Arthur Conan Doyle's fourth and final Holmes mystery *The Valley of Fear*.

We hope you enjoy the fascinating journey through time which is **CHRONOLOGICA: The Incredible Years That Defined History.**

The Whitaker's Team

50 Bedford Square
London WC1B 3DP
whitakersalmanackteam@bloomsbury.com
www.whitakersalmanack.com

EDITORIAL STAFF
Project Editor: Oli Lurie
Editorial Assistant: Pari Thomson
Executive Editor: Ruth Northey

753 BC

THE MYTH OF ROMULUS AND REMUS

Romulus and Remus were twin boys and the pivotal characters of Rome's foundation myth. According to the myth their mother was princess Rhea Silvia, daughter of Numitor, King of Alba Longa and their father was Mars, the Roman god of war. Before the twins were born, Numitor's brother Amulius seized power, killed Numitor's male heirs and forced Rhea Silvia to become a priestess to the goddess Vesta.

Following the birth of the boys Amulius had Rhea Silvia thrown into the river Tiber where she was caught beneath the waves by the river god who married her. The twin boys were set adrift on the river in a reed basket which floated downstream until the basket was caught in the branches of a fig tree where they were found by a she-wolf who suckled them until they were found by a shepherd and his wife who raised the boys as their own.

The twins proved to be natural leaders and each acquired many followers. When they discovered their true origins, the twins raised an army and marched on Alba Longa slaying Amulius and restoring Numitor to the throne.

Rather than wait to inherit Alba Longa, Romulus and Remus chose to found a new city. The twins disputed which hill their city should be built on, Romulus favouring the Palatine, Remus choosing the Aventine. On the hill favoured by Remus there were six vultures, but on the hill preferred by Romulus there were 12. Romulus took this as a sign from the gods and founded the new city, named it Rome, after himself, and started to build a wall around the Palatine Hill. However, Remus was jealous and began to make fun of Romulus' wall. At one point Remus jumped over the wall to show how easy it was to cross. Romulus became angry, the twins fought and Remus was killed.

With Remus dead, Romulus continued to build his city and created its first army and senate. The image of the she-wolf suckling the divinely fathered twins has become an iconic representation of the city and its founding legend.

THE FOUNDING OF ROME

Disregarding the myth of Romulus and Remus, Greek writers of the fifth century BC credited the foundation of Rome to the Trojan legend Aeneas. The Greeks believed that Aeneas had travelled to Italy and settled near Rome, following the fall of Troy in 1184 BC from which he was the only hero to have survived the Greek invasion, according to Homer's epic poem, the *Iliad*. Aeneas married Lavinia, the daughter of a local king named Latinus upon his arrival in central Italy and from their marriage a kingdom of Alba Longa was established, which eventually resulted in the monarchy of King Numitor, whereby the story evolved over time so that by the first century BC the stories of Aeneas and Romulus and Remus combined into the account of Rome's foundation.

Upon Rome's foundation in 753 BC, Romulus was believed to have offered refuge to exiles and refugees who were not welcome in other settlements. However, as Rome lacked female citizens, Romulus devised a plan in which he invited Rome's neighbouring community, the Sabines, to a festival but his invitation was a trick and on his order the men of Rome abducted the Sabine women. After a war broke out between the two communities, the Sabine women now resident in Rome, persuaded the Sabine's not to seize the new city and instead a pact was agreed whereby Romulus and the Sabine king, Titus Tatius, jointly ruled.

A Roman scholar by the name of Marcus Terrentius Varro had proposed that the exact foundation date of Rome was 21 April 753 BC, after he estimated the length of the reign of the seven Roman kings starting with Romulus up to the expulsion of the last tyrant king, Tarquin the Proud and the establishment in 509 BC of the Roman Republic.

Archaeological discoveries on the Palatine Hill, chosen by Romulus as the founding location of Rome, included fortification walls which dated to the mid-8th century BC, which corresponds to Varro's belief that the foundation of Rome was 753 BC.

490 BC

THE BATTLE OF MARATHON

During the Greco-Persian Wars, which began in 499 BC and lasted until 449 BC, the Persian King Darius the Great, made an attempt to conquer Greece and take revenge against Athens, which had supported a regional revolt against Persian rule. The first Persian invasion of Greece began in 492 BC and the Persian army quickly subjugated Thrace and Macedon and when Darius sent ambassadors across Greek regions to call for their surrender, only Athens and Sparta refused to accept and instead executed Darius' messengers. In 490 BC, under the command of Datis and Artaphernes, a Persian invasion force reached Greece and captured Eritrea, which was destroyed and its citizens enslaved. Subsequently, the Persians landed in the region of Attica, preparing for an assault on Athens.

The Persians landed at the bay of Marathon, approximately 25 miles from Athens itself. The Athenians, led by the general Miltiades, an Olympic chariot-racer, were supported by the city of Plataea and numbered 10,000 men while the Persians far outnumbered the Greek defending army, numbering 20,000 soldiers. With the Spartans refusing to assist Athens due to their peaceful festival of Carneia, the Athenians elected to stand firm at Marathon and blocked the exits from the mountainous land. Miltiades devised a plan to attack the Persians on the wings before closing in towards the Persian centre. The tactics worked and the Persian army collapsed, with the surviving soldiers retreating to their ships. The Greek historian Herodotus estimated that 6,400 Persians had been killed and incredibly just 192 Athenians died, with much of the credit due to the fighting skills of the hoplites – citizen-soldiers of Athens, armed with spears and round shields.

Upon hearing that the fleeing ships were instead destined for Athens, the Athenians quickly marched back to the city to prevent the ships landing and on seeing the city refortified, the Persians lost hope and returned home. Although it is recorded that the Persian commander Artaphernes survived the war, conflicting reports about Datis state that he may or may not have been killed at Marathon. Darius the Great began to plan another war against the Greeks, personally in command of his armies but when a revolt broke out in Egypt, which was part of the Persian Empire, the expedition was delayed and his health began to deteriorate. He died in October 486 BC and was succeeded by his son Xerxes I who, like his father, would seek to conquer Greece.

PHEIDIPPIDES, THE LEGENDARY RUNNER OF MARATHON

Legend has it that a Greek long-distance runner called Pheidippides (also referred to as Philippides) was sent from the city of Athens to Sparta to call for reinforcements before the Battle of Marathon. Renowned warriors, the Spartans had been a crucial component of Greek armies in previous battles and were desperately needed, given how outnumbered the Greeks were by the Persian force. The distance between the two cities was a staggering 140 miles, which Pheidippides is said to have completed in about two days. After winning a historic victory at the Battle of Marathon, the Greek army, exhausted from the battle and their heavy equipment, marched as quickly as possible back carrying to Athens to intercept the Persian fleet, which was sailing towards Athens. The triumphant Greeks reached Athens to witness the Persian ships sailing away. The city had been saved.

Over time, this account has become confused with another story about another remarkable feat of running. According to Plutarch, an Ancient Greek historian, a Greek messenger was sent from Marathon to Athens, a distance of around 25 miles (40 km), to bring news of the Greek victory. The runner is said to have run the distance without stopping and heroically delivered the message, believed to be either 'we have won' or 'hail, we are the winners', to the Athenian assembly before tragically collapsing and dying of exhaustion. This moment was captured in a famous painting by French painter Luc-Olivier Merson in 1869.

In preparation for the first modern Olympic Games, which were to be held in 1896 in Athens, Frenchman Michel Bréal, made a suggestion to include a 'Marathon' race. He suggested that this special race should follow the route from Marathon to Athens taken by the legendary runner in 490 BC. Bréal's friend Pierre de Coubertin, who founded the International Olympic Committee and was instrumental in organising the 1896 Olympics, liked his friend's idea, and so the Marathon became an Olympic event. Fittingly, the winner of the first Olympic Marathon event was Greek – a water carrier called Spyridon Louis.

Early versions of the Olympic Marathon were run over distances of 25–26 miles. It wasn't until the London Olympics of 1908 that the fixed distance of 26 miles 285 yards was instituted. This distance was decided upon by the British Olympic Committee so that the race could start from Windsor Castle and finish outside the royal box at White City Stadium in London. The dramatic finish of the 1908 Olympic marathon is credited as the reason marathon races became so popular. Over 500 marathons are now organised worldwide each year.

356 BC

ALEXANDER THE GREAT

Alexander the Great, the king of Macedonia, was a legendary leader and conqueror who united the Greek city-states and defeated the Persian Empire.

Born in Pella, Macedonia in 356 BC, he was the son of King Philip II and was taught by the great philosopher Aristotle. The young Alexander was famed for taming a magnificent horse called Bucephalus when he was just ten years old, and he took part in his first military expedition, against invading Thracian tribes, at the age of 16. After his father was assassinated in 336 BC, Alexander became king with the support of the army, and executed many possible rivals, including some half-siblings. He quickly took control of the Greek states, known as the Corinthian League, asserting his power in Thessaly, defeating an Illyrian invasion of Macedonia, and crushing a revolt in Thebes with a brutal massacre.

Philip II had long planned an invasion of Asia, and the Corinthian League now granted Alexander full military power in a campaign against the Persian Empire, with an army of about 30,000 foot soldiers and 5,000 cavalry. In spring 334 BC, he marched through Troy, before defeating Persian King Darius III's army near the Granicus River. He declared himself 'great king' of Persia and the whole of Asia, at the age of 25, and went on to marry a Persian princess called Roxana.

Over the next eight years, he founded over 70 cities, leading his army a further 11,000 miles and creating an empire that spanned three continents and covered around two million square miles. He conquered Syria and most of the Levant, captured Tyre after a long siege in 332 BC, and founded the great city of Alexandria in Egypt, where he was welcomed as a liberator and hailed as the son of the god Amun. He was determined to continue expanding, and marched on to northern India, where his army finally refused to go any further. On their return south, Alexander was wounded several times, and died of a fever in Babylon in 323 BC.

At the time of his death, his territory stretched from Greece to Egypt, from the Danube to the Ganges, a vast area united by a common Greek language and culture. Although his empire was later torn apart, this 'Hellenistic' influence remained powerful for centuries. Alexander is remembered as a military genius who never lost a battle, a man of legendary ambition, recklessness and power.

THE TEMPLE OF ARTEMIS BURNS DOWN

In 356 BC, the great Temple of Artemis was deliberately burned down by a madman called Herostratus.

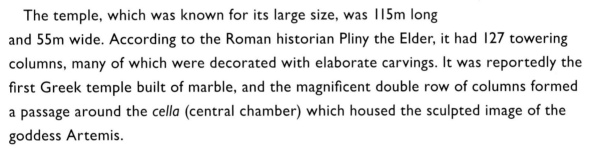

For centuries before the first temple was built, there had been a sacred site at Ephesus, an ancient Greek port city now on the west coast of modern-day Turkey. The original Temple of Artemis had been destroyed by a flood in the 7th century BC, and the new temple, also known as the Artemesium, was rebuilt from around 550 BC by the Cretan architect Chersiphron and his son Metagenes. It was partly funded by the hugely wealthy Croesus, who was the king of Lydia and the city's ruler, and it was decorated by some of the most famous artists in the ancient world.

The temple, which was known for its large size, was 115m long and 55m wide. According to the Roman historian Pliny the Elder, it had 127 towering columns, many of which were decorated with elaborate carvings. It was reportedly the first Greek temple built of marble, and the magnificent double row of columns formed a passage around the *cella* (central chamber) which housed the sculpted image of the goddess Artemis.

The temple was visited by merchants, kings and worshippers, who came to pay homage to Artemis, the Greek goddess of purity, childbirth and the hunt. Many left offerings in the form of jewellery and other precious objects, and archaeologists have discovered over a thousand items from this era on the site, including silver and gold coins.

Herostratus destroyed the temple by setting fire to its wooden roof beams, hoping that the act would make his name famous throughout the ancient world. Instead, he was sentenced to death, and the people of Ephesus were forbidden from mentioning his name. According to Greek and Roman legend, the structure burned down on the same night as Alexander the Great was born, and the goddess was too preoccupied attending to his birth to save her temple. It was eventually rebuilt on an even larger scale from 323 BC, and stood for almost 600 years until it was destroyed by the Goths in 268 AD.

280 BC

THE THEORY OF ARISTARCHUS OF SAMOS

Until the closing period of the Middle Ages, the civilisations of the world generally agreed that the Earth was at the centre of the universe and that the Sun and all other planets revolved around it. In 310 BC, a Greek astronomer and mathematician was born by the name of Aristarchus of Samos, who would become the first person to claim that the Sun was at the centre of the known universe and that the Earth itself rotated around the Sun.

Prior to the theory of Aristarchus, a Greek philosopher named Philolaus of Croton who lived between 470 BC and 385 BC claimed that a Central Fire, which was not the Sun, occupied the centre of the universe and all stars and planets, including the Earth, rotated around it. Aristarchus, however, claimed the Central Fire was the Sun itself and that the stars in the sky were incredibly distant suns which did not move. The astronomer also observed that the universe was much bigger than previously believed. Although Aristarchus' text has been lost, it was recorded by the famed Greek inventor Archimedes in his book *The Sand Reckoner*.

It wasn't until Nicolaus Copernicus, a mathematician of the Renaissance, expressed his theory that the Sun was at the centre of the Solar System – an astronomical concept named heliocentrism – that Aristarchus' ideas were established to be correct.

Aristarchus additionally calculated the size of the Earth and distances of the Moon and the Sun. From his calculations, the Greek astronomer deduced that the Sun was approximately six or seven times wider than the Earth. It is suggested that Aristarchus himself abandoned his theories as other Greek astronomers of the time rejected his model, based on the fact they believed all planets had a circular orbit, which conflicted with his proposals. Instead, his heliocrentic views were rejected and the geocentric theories of Ptloemy that the Earth was at the centre of the universe, prevailed.

THE COLOSSUS OF RHODES IS BUILT

The Colossus of Rhodes only stood for 54 years before it was toppled in a devastating earthquake, but it was incredible enough to be considered one of the Seven Wonders of the Ancient World. It was built to celebrate the island of Rhodes victory following the Siege of Rhodes in 305 BC. In 2015, architects announced plans to rebuild the Colossus at a height of 135m, which unlike the original Wonder, would straddle two piers of the island's harbour.

In 305 BC, a Macedonian army led by Demetrius I, the son of a Macedonian general of Alexander the Great, invaded Rhodes. When the siege failed, the citizens of Rhodes celebrated the victory and employed the architect Charos of Lindos to construct a great statue of their patron, Helios, god of the sun. The construction started in 292 BC and the builders used siege equipment left behind by the Macedonians. The Colossus stood on a 15m-high white marble pedestal near the harbour's entrance. There have been many debates about where exactly the Colossus of Rhodes stood but a common misconception is that the statue straddled the harbour to allow ships through the port. Paintings and descriptions of the Colossus frequently depict it with a posture of legs placed either side of the harbour mouth but this image is almost definitely incorrect as the people of Rhodes would not have been able to engineer the pose. Even William Shakespeare's play *Julius Caesar* describes the eponymous Roman general as having huge legs to walk under 'Like a Colossus'.

It is understood that Charos the architect did not live to see the completed Colossus of Rhodes in 280 BC with one myth being that he committed suicide after being informed of a mistake in the structure. The Colossus itself was 30m tall and formed with a skeleton of iron bars covered in brass plates for the skin. Some sources explain that the statue of Helios actually stood on a breakwater in the harbour. Wherever it was, in 226 BC it came down during an earthquake which destroyed much of the harbour. However, after breaking at the knees it lay in pieces for eight centuries and although offers were made to rebuild it, the collapse of the Colossus was seen as a bad omen. When the Roman philosopher Pliny the Elder visited the toppled statue, he remarked that each finger was larger than most statues.

THE LIGHTHOUSE OF ALEXANDRIA IS BUILT

The Lighthouse of Alexandria was the most famous lighthouse in the ancient world. Commissioned by the Egyptian ruler Ptolemy I, it was completed in 280 BC, during the reign of his son Ptolemy II. The lighthouse was designed by the Greek architect Sostratos, and built from limestone on a small island called Pharos, near the city of Alexandria. One of the Seven Wonders of the Ancient World, it provided a model for all the lighthouses which came after it.

The lighthouse, also known as the Pharos of Alexandria, was reported to be around 110m high, and was one of the tallest structures in the world at the time. Contemporary descriptions, as well as images of the lighthouse on ancient Alexandrian coins, tell us that it had three levels: a square base, an octagonal middle, and a cylindrical tower, with a ramp spiralling around the outside. From the top of the tower, a mirror flashed during the day and a fire burned at night, to warn ships that they were approaching land. A gigantic statue also stood at the top, which was probably an image of Alexander the Great or Ptolemy II.

The lighthouse was badly damaged in a series of earthquakes between 956 AD and 1323. It fell into disrepair, and in 1480 the Egyptian Sultan Qu'it Bay used the stones from its ruins to build a fort. In 1994, the remains of the lighthouse were rediscovered by the archaeologist Jean-Yves Empereur, who discovered hundreds of huge stone blocks beneath the water around Alexandria's eastern harbour, as well as a giant statue. They were believed to have fallen from the lighthouse during the earthquakes.

14 AD

THE DEATH OF THE FIRST ROMAN EMPEROR

Arguably the most important Roman in history, the first emperor of Rome (although he never claimed the title himself) died in 14 AD, having expanded the Roman borders and brought a period of peace and prosperity to Rome after many years of civil war. Augustus was born as Gaius Octavius in Rome in 63 BC. His great-uncle, who adopted him, was the Roman general and dictator Julius Caesar and when Caesar was assassinated in 43 BC by his political rivals, Octavian, as Gaius Octavius was now known, was revealed in Caesar's will to be his heir.

Following years of civil war during the later years of the Roman Republic, Octavian established a power-sharing agreement with the politicians Mark Antony and Marcus Lepidus, which was known as the Second Triumvirate. However, tensions grew after Mark Antony was given control in the east of the Empire, including Egypt. When Mark Antony divorced Octavian's sister Octavia and began a relationship with Cleopatra, the last pharaoh of Egypt, Octavian declared war. The future Roman emperor defeated Antony and Cleopatra in a naval battle at Actium in 31 BC, ending a series of internal conflicts and bringing peace.

Augustus' building projects in Rome included the Temple of Caesar, Mausoleum of Augustus and the original Pantheon – in fact, he claimed to have built or restored 82 temples in one year. As the Roman biographer Suetonius recorded, Augustus declared 'I found Rome a city of clay, but I left it of marble'. Literature flourished under his rule and Augustus was the patron of illustrious poets such as Virgil, author of the *Aeneid*, and Horace.

While bringing peace to Rome, he expanded the empire's borders, making Rome safe from barbarians. Roman possessions in Africa and Asia Minor (the ancient name for an area of Turkey) increased under Augustus' leadership but a defeat at the Battle of the Teutoburg Forest in 9 AD stopped further expansion into Germania.

Augustus may have lived a long time ago, in a different world to ours, but changes he made still impact our lives. For example, taking inspiration from his great-uncle who had renamed the seventh month of the year July – after Julius – Augustus renamed the eighth month of the year from Sextilius to August.

On 19 August 14 AD, Augustus died, which led to a succession crisis. He had been hoping for a direct blood-relative, ideally a son to become emperor. However, a series of deaths and tragedies left only his adopted son Tiberius to rule as Caesar.

TIBERIUS BECOMES EMPEROR OF ROME

Unlike many megalomaniacs of the Roman Empire, Tiberius was reluctant to succeed Augustus as the second Emperor of the Roman Empire and was described by the historian Pliny the Elder as 'the gloomiest of men'. Incredibly, just 12 years into his reign, Tiberius removed himself from the city and settled on the comparatively isolated island of Capri, leaving Rome in the hands of the fearsome and conniving prefect Sejanus. Although he was famed for being one of Rome's greatest generals and with his brother Drusus helped expand the frontiers of Rome into modern day Germany during his military career, his perceived role in the death of Germanicus and unwillingness as emperor left him as an unpopular Caesar.

Born Tiberius Claudius Nero on 16 November 42 BC, Tiberius' mother Livia Drusilla divorced his father and married Augustus in 39 BC, making Tiberius the step-son of the future first Emperor of Rome. It is the combination of Tiberius' Claudian heritage merged with his marriage to Augustus' daughter Julia the Elder, which historians declared as the beginning of the Julio-Claudian dynasty. Following a succession crisis due to the deaths of Augustus' two sons Gaius and Lucius, it was determined that his adopted son Tiberius was to be the next emperor but he had retired to Rhodes in 6 BC and while his motives remain unknown, it is possible he was angry at the emperor for being forced to divorce his wife Vispania Agrippina who he loved.

However, Tiberius did succeed Augustus upon the emperor's death and the Senate declared him as Princeps on 18 September 14 AD. At first, his rule was steady and he continued the good work of Augustus despite being unpopular with the Senate. When his adopted son Germanicus, the celebrated military general, died in Syria, Tiberius was embroiled in the controversy and he started to lose interest in the organisation of the empire. He became more of a recluse when his own son Drusus died in 23 AD and he put his trust in Lucius Aelius Sejanus. The leader of the Praetorian Guard in Rome, Sejanus instigated the 'treason trials' of the city, leading to the convictions and executions of many aristocrats. However, realising Sejanus would stop at nothing to gain power, Tiberius ordered his death along with his supporters.

In 27 AD, Tiberius had departed for Capri and would not return to the city of his birth and many rumours spread about evil deeds which took place on the island. When Tiberius died aged 78 on 16 March 37 AD he was succeeded by Caligula.

GERMANICUS BEGINS ROMAN CAMPAIGN IN GERMANY

Much of what is known about Germanicus comes from the Roman senator Tacitus who recorded the events of the Roman Empire from the reigns of Tiberius to Nero. As a member of the ruling Julio-Claudian dynasty of Rome, Germanicus was the great-nephew of the first emperor Augustus, nephew of the second emperor Tiberius, father of Caligula, the third emperor, older brother of Claudius, the fourth emperor and grandfather of Nero, the fifth emperor of Rome and last of the Julio-Claudian dynasty. However, he himself was never Caesar due to his premature death while on a military campaign in Antioch, Syria on 10 October 19 AD. His military expertise, capture of two lost legionary eagles and early death made him a legendary figure throughout the empire.

Born on 24 May 15 BC as Nero Claudius Drusus, he was given the title Germanicus when it was bestowed to his father posthumously after successful military campaigns in Germania – the land in present-day Northern Europe which was then occupied by the Germanic people. After marrying Augustus' granddaughter Agrippina the Elder, the couple had nine children, one of which was Caligula, which meant 'Little Boots', so called because he joined his father on military campaigns in Germania.

After serving in a political capacity as a Quaestor and serving in the military in Illyricum and the Rhine, Germanicus was appointed as Consul in 12 AD. The Consul was the highest-elected politician of Rome and two men served in the role for one year. As the commander of the campaigns in Gaul and the Rhine he was a popular leader and prevented any revolts that broke out after the death of Augustus in 14 AD. Although many people yearned for him to become the new emperor, Germanicus was loyal to his adoptive father and inflicted defeats of Germanic tribes during three campaigns from 14 AD to 16 AD. During this time he recaptured two of the three legionary eagles which had been lost by the Roman General Publius Quinctilius Varus at the Battle of the Teutoburg Forest in 9 AD and defeated the Germanic chieftain Arminius, responsible for the slaughter of Varus' forces. Germanicus returned home to receive a Triumph through the city, the last ever awarded to a man who was not Caesar.

In 19 AD Germanicus died while in Syria, where he had conflicted with the governor Gnaeus Calpurnius Piso. It was alleged that Germanicus had been poisoned by Piso's wife and Tiberius was behind the plot as he became jealous of the soldier's popularity.

68 AD

EMPEROR NERO COMMITS SUICIDE

The fifth Roman Emperor Nero was one of the most infamous in the empire's history. Emperor during the Great Fire of Rome and Boudica's uprising in Britain, Nero is a fascinating example of brutal and immoral leadership.

Born on 15 December 37 AD in Antium, near Rome, Lucius Domitius Ahenobarbus (Nero) was the son of Gnaeus Domitius Ahenobarbus and Agrippina the Younger, who was the sister of the sister of the reigning Emperor Caligula and the great-granddaughter of Augustus. Agrippina seeked for her son to obtain power and when her husband died she married the new Emperor Claudius in 49 AD, which was objected to at the time, possibly as Agrippina was the emperor's niece. Claudius had his own son, Britannicus (named after the emperor's conquest of Britain) but as he was younger than Nero, Agrippina hoped that Claudius would favour his new step-son to be his successor. However, Claudius preferred his biological son and realising this, Agrippina poisoned Claudius, allegedly with poisonous mushrooms and Nero succeeded to the throne as the last emperor of the Julio-Claudian dynasty in 54 AD.

Shortly after rising to power, Nero had Britannicus executed to prevent any threat from him or his supporters. Power-hungry, Agrippina attempted to rule alongside her son and at the beginning of his emperorship, her image was portrayed alongside his on coins. However, a megalomaniac himself, Nero had his mother killed in 59 AD. The first years of his reign were fairly successful as he was advised by two men, Burrus and the philosopher Seneca but when the former died and the philosopher retired from the royal household, Nero's reign became less fair and the legions and people of Rome began to grow tired of the cruel emperor.

In 64 AD the Great Fire of Rome occurred, which was one of the most famous events of the city's history. The fire began on 18 July and lasted six days before being brought under control. Roman biographers such as Suetonius and Tacitus differ on their theories why the fire broke out. Some argued Nero started the fire himself to destroy the city and build his new palace, the Domus Aurea (Golden House) while other historians claimed the fire was an accident. It is recited that Nero fiddled while Rome burnt, which can mean either that the emperor played his lyre or that he fidgeted, unsure what to do in order to save the city, which is a condemnation of his leadership. Nero blamed the Christian people for the fire and they were persecuted for the act.

By the year 68 AD Nero had been forced to flee from Rome after uprisings in Britain by Boudica and in Judea. A rebellion led by Galba moved against the emperor and when Nero requested a gladiator kill him before he could be murdered by rebels, none came forward, leading the emperor to question 'Have I neither friend nor foe?' Nero had been declared a public enemy by the Senate and when Galba's men approached his hideout villa on 9 June 68 AD, Nero ordered his secretary Epaphroditos to kill him. By the time his enemies broke into the room, the emperor was dead.

YEAR OF THE FOUR EMPERORS BEGINS

Upon the death of Nero, the last Roman Emperor of the Julio-Claudian dynasty, a civil war erupted which became known as the Year of the Four Emperors. Beginning immediately after Nero's death, Galba, the governor of Hispania Tarraconensis, became the sixth Emperor of Rome following a rebellion led by him against Nero. Galba was the final emperor to rule who had been born in the first century BC. His reign began on the 9 June 68 AD but by the beginning of the following year, he would be dead.

Galba was a notoriously cruel ruler and increased taxes against areas of the empire which failed to acknowledge him as the new emperor. As he was quite old, he left much of the organisation of Rome in the hands of three of his favourite Romans, whose influence over the emperor made him unpopular with the people of Rome. Following a mutiny by two legions in Germania, who refused to swear loyalty to Galba, they toppled statues of him and cried out for a new ruler. When the governor of Lusitania, Otho, a former friend of Nero, was overlooked as Galba's successor, he gained the support of the Praetorian Guard – the bodyguards of the emperor – and when Galba travelled to meet with the mutineers he was killed on 15 January 69 AD, offering his neck 'for the good of the Romans'.

On that same day, Otho became the new emperor but by 16 April 69 AD he too was dead. When a commander of the army of Germania Inferior, by the name of Vitellius, was proclaimed emperor of the area, he became so popular that his armies marched on

Rome to install him as Caesar. When the original plan emerged, it had been Galba on the throne, but the new emperor wished to avoid a civil war and offered peace to Vitellius. Following a defeat at the Battle of Bedriacum, Otho stabbed himself in the heart with a dagger, wishing to save Rome from further conflict. So overwhelmed were some of his soldiers that they threw themselves on his funeral pyre to die alongside him.

When news reached the Senate of Otho's death, they proclaimed Vitellius to be the 8th Emperor of Rome. Like Galba and Otho before him, his was to be a brief rule and on 22 December 69 AD, Vitellius was slain. The new emperor held many banquets, feasts and parades which almost bankrupt the palace. When money-lenders started to request their debts be repaid, the emperor had them tortured and executed. At the same time, Vespasian, a commander who had besieged Jerusalem, was declared emperor by his legions on 1 July 69 AD. They began to march towards Italy to depose Vitellius, who like Otho, attempted to offer a truce to the enemy. Vitellius went into hiding but he was caught and thrown into the Tiber and Vespasian was declared as the new emperor. The Year of the Four Emperors was concluded and Vespasian ruled for ten years, during which time the Colosseum was built and in 79 AD he was succeeded by his son Titus.

105 AD

PAPER IS INVENTED IN CHINA

Cai Lun (62–121 AD) was a eunuch and court official employed by the imperial palace of the Eastern Han dynasty in 75 AD. Among Cai's duties, he was in charge of the manufacture of weaponry and instruments. In 105 AD, he conceived a remarkable invention, creating sheets of paper from pulped tree bark, old cloth rags, hemp remnants and fishing nets. At the time, writing was either performed on bamboo tablets, which were quite heavy or on cloth made from pure silk, which wasn't in abundant supply and was expensive to produce. Cai's creation wasn't only a far superior writing surface; it was also much cheaper than silk to produce, very light in weight and much more plentiful in supply.

Cai brought his discovery to the emperor, who praised him, honouring him with the title of Marquis and bestowing upon him great riches. Cai's support for Empress Zhang would eventually lead to his undoing. The empress had become jealous of one of her husband's imperial consorts, Consort Song, who was falsely accused of committing witchcraft. Emperor Zhang ordered Cai Lun to imprison and interrogate Consort Song, and she committed suicide in prison. In 121 AD, Consort Song's grandson, An, became Emperor. Unable to forgive Cai Lun's part in his grandmother's untimely end, Cai was sent to prison where he committed suicide by drinking poison.

Cai's apprentice Zuo Bo, made significant improvements to Cai's pioneering papermaking process. Before long, their techniques were quickly adopted across China, and from there, paper eventually spread across the world. Legend has it that two Chinese prisoners of war, captured during the Battle of Talas in 751 AD, revealed the secret of papermaking. A paper mill soon appeared in Samarkand (in modern-day Uzbekistan) and another was built in Baghdad before 793 AD. By the 13th century, paper mills, powered by water, had started to appear in parts of Europe. Paper was for a while called 'bagdatikos', in reference to Baghdad's involvement in paper's introduction to the West.

Meanwhile, Cai's fame endured in China and he was lauded in traditional ancestor worship. Evidence of this appears in Fie Zhu's writing of the Song Dynasty (960–1279) some eight centuries later. He described a temple that had been built in Cai Lun's honour in Chengdu. Hundreds of families, who were working in the papermaking industry that Cai Lun had started, made the trip to pay their respects to the famous inventor.

TRAJAN'S BRIDGE IS CONSTRUCTED

For 1,000 years, Trajan's Bridge was the longest arch bridge in the world in terms of both span and length. The bridge stretched across the lower Danube after the Roman Emperor Trajan had ordered its construction for use by Roman legions fighting in Dacia, a territory which today is part of several eastern European countries. Although the bridge was only functional for a few decades, the sheer size of the structure made it a major architectural achievement.

As the Emperor of Rome from 98 to 117 AD, Trajan directed the largest territorial expansion of any Roman ruler. Trajan's Column celebrates the emperor's conquests in the Dacian Wars of which the bridge played a vital role. The column was built in 113 AD by the architect Apollodorus of Damascus who was a favourite of the emperor and had been previously instructed to build Trajan's Bridge in 103 AD. Also known as the 'Bridge of Apollodorus over the Danube', the segmental arch bridge was 1,135m long, 15m wide and 19m high from the river's surface. It was completed in 105 AD with each of the wooden arches supporting the bridge spanning 38m. Its main use was for Roman troops to cross into Dacia during the wars from 101 to 106 AD. At either end of the bridge stood a Roman castrum (fort) so that access to the bridge was only possible after passing through a camp.

Built near the present-day cities of Drobeta-Turnu Severin in Romania and Kladovo in Serbia, the bridge was actually pulled apart by the Emperor Hadrian who succeeded Trajan, so as to stop enemies crossing back into Roman territory. By 1982, twelve of the original twenty pillars of the bridge were located underwater by archaeologists. As for Apollodorus, the architect was exiled and then executed by Hadrian after he had mocked the emperor's artistic talents.

597 AD

THE FIRST ARCHBISHOP OF CANTERBURY

In the fifth and sixth centuries, the Roman state of Britain began to be influenced by pagans, known as Anglo-Saxons. They created the kingdom of Kent and when Æthelbert became king in 589 AD he became the first British king to convert to Christianity. He had married Bertha, the daughter of Charibert, king of the Franks and importantly, a Christian. The role played by Bertha, who took her chaplain Liudhard with her to England, cannot be underestimated. The oldest church in the English-speaking world, St Martin's Church in Canterbury, was her private chapel and the site of Æthelbert's baptism. Realising Kent was becoming a stronghold of Christianity in Britain, with links to Europe through its location, Pope Gregory I dispatched the Benedictine Monk, Augustine, to England.

In 597 AD, a group of 40 monks landed alongside Augustine at the Isle of Thanet in Kent. Æthelbert, who had not yet converted, allowed the monks to settle in Canterbury but it is alleged he was sceptical of the travellers and he was suspicious of their 'sorcery'. In the year 601 AD, the pope had written to Æthelbert as a Christian king but it was some time before the entire royal court had converted and the influence of Augustine was gradual. Augustine, who is known as the 'Apostle to the English' was consecrated as a bishop, establishing the seat at Canterbury and on Christmas Day 597 AD converted thousands of Kentish citizens during a mass baptism.

Augustine of Canterbury died in 604 AD and was revered as Saint Augustine. Shortly before his death, he consecrated Laurence of Canterbury as his successor, who had also been sent by the pope to Christianise the island. Laurence faced a crisis following the death of Æthelbert in 616 AD when the new king, Eadbald, did not immediately convert to Christianity. However, the Kentish king was convinced to convert like his father and the role of the Archbishop of Canterbury continued.

ÆTHELBERT'S CODE OF LAWS

Believed to be the first instance of a document written in the Germanic-language of English, the *Law of Æthelbert* was a set of legal rulings which originated in the Kingdom of the Kentish, before the Kingdom of England had even formed. The King of Kent from approximately 589 to his death in 616 AD was Æthelbert, who was the first of any English king to convert to Christianity and who became a saint after relinquishing his paganist heritage and helping to establish Christianity in Canterbury.

The exact date when the *Law of Æthelbert* was written is still uncertain but it was believed to be composed in the late sixth century with the year 597 AD a commonly suggested date. The document was the first law code to be written in any Germanic-language and is centred around compensation and punishment for personal injury, in addition to maintaining social wellbeing. The compensation aspect of the document is decided in accordance with rank, beginning with the king and ending with a slave, and because of the king's new religion, protection for the church was also included.

When King Alfred the Great, who ruled Wessex from 871 to 899 AD, wrote his own law, he refered to the *Law of Æthelbert*. However, the original document was lost or destroyed and it only exists as part of the *Textus Roffensis*, also known as the 'Rochester Book'. It is a medieval manuscript written around the year 1122 and also included the 1100 coronation charter of King Henry I.

Chapters of the *Law of Æthelbert* include 'Offences against women', 'Compensation for the semi-free' and 'Offences against the church'. As the first written code of laws, the timing of its release coincided with the king's new religion and his desire to convert the Kingdom of the Kentish into an enlightened society. The 'Rochester Book' is preserved in the Medway Archives in Kent.

1040

MACBETH KILLS KING DUNCAN I OF SCOTLAND

Duncan I, whose real name was Donnchad mac Crinain and who was nicknamed 'The Diseased' was King of Alba (Scots), reigning from 1034 to 1040. Duncan was born around the turn of the millennium in 1001 and succeeded his grandfather King Malcolm II upon his death.

His role in history would almost be forgotten were it not for William Shakespeare who wrote the tragedy *Macbeth* sometime between 1599 and 1606. Unlike Shakespeare's elderly King Duncan however, the real Duncan I was a fairly young ruler. Macbeth himself, whose full name was Mac Bethad mac Findlaich was the king's 'dux' (duke) which was a title originating from the Roman translation for 'leader of war'. In 1039, Duncan led a large Scottish army to besiege Durham but the assault failed. The following year he travelled north with his loyal forces to Moray, where Macbeth resided, to suppress a rebellion there. Unfortunately for Duncan he was murdered at Bothnagowan, near Elgin by Macbeth and his followers from Moray. The king was buried in Elgin but was dug up and relocated to the Isle of Iona.

As for Macbeth, he became King of Scots until 15 August 1057 where he was himself killed by the slain Duncan's son who later ruled the kingdom as Malcolm III.

Unlike the real life event, Shakespeare recorded Macbeth killing the king in his sleep. The play is believed to have first been performed in 1611 at the Globe Theatre and printed in the *First Folio* of 1623. In theatre, thespians believe the play to carry a curse and do not directly refer to it as *Macbeth* but instead call it *The Scottish Play*.

THE WORLD'S OLDEST EXISTING BREWERY OPENS

It is incredible to think that the world's oldest brewery obtained a licence to make beer in 1040. Still operating today and nearing its 1,000 year anniversary, the Bavarian State Brewery Weihenstephan in Germany can trace its history as far back as 725 AD when a Benedictine monk, Saint Corbinian, founded a monastery alongside twelve other monks on Nährberg Hill in Weihenstephan, north of modern-day Munich in Germany.

The monks did not know it at the time but they had settled in a location which would become famous as a brewery and the first historical mention of hops, a key ingredient in the production of beer, dates back to 768 AD when a landowner was required to pay a tax to the monastery for the hop garden in the monastery's vicinity. In 955 AD, the monastery was ransacked and demolished by Hungarian forces but the monks restored the building, allowing the possibility of a brewery to continue. History was made in 1040 when Abbot Arnold was granted a licence to brew and sell beer from the City of Freising and the Weihenstephan Monastery Brewery was founded.

It wasn't exactly a success instantly because the monastery burned down four times between 1085 and 1463, while plagues, famines and an earthquake also temporarily stopped production of beer. Plunderers such as the Bavarian Emperor Ludwig in 1336 destroyed the monastery but each time it was knocked down, the monks rebuilt it and continued to improve the beer. In 1803 the abbey was dissolved and the brewery was put under the ownership of Bavaria but in 1852, Weihenstephan became the world's centre for brewing and in 1921 the name of the brewery became the Bavarian State Brewery Weihenstephan. It continues brewing to this day.

FIRST RECORD OF CHINA INVENTING FIREWORKS

A popular legend is that fireworks were discovered by chance in China during the second century BC when saltpeter (also known as potassium nitrate) was accidentally dropped into a cooking fire. The result was a mysterious, colourful flame. Later experiments involved mixing saltpeter with sulphur and charcoal, which created a more powerful reaction, burning with considerable force and producing even more colourful flames. This mixture was an early form of gunpowder, one of the 'Four Great Inventions' of China, along with the compass, papermaking and printing.

However, the first documentary evidence relaying to fireworks appeared in a Chinese manuscript from 1040 in which several different recipes for fireworks appear. One of these involved demonstrating how to wrap gunpowder inside paper and adding chemicals in order to create a 'fire pill'. A number of the recipes are similar to the ingredients used to manufacture fireworks today.

Impressive firework displays were held during China's Song Dynasty (960–1279) and common people were able to buy fireworks from market stalls. In 1100, Emperor Huizong of Song was treated to a firework spectacle as part of a military demonstration. The loud explosions emanating from this new discovery were believed to frighten away evil spirits.

1066

THE BATTLE OF STAMFORD BRIDGE

Although the Battle of Stamford Bridge was a decisive English victory and is debatably the event which caused the demise of the Vikings, its success is often overlooked as the Battle of Hastings took place less than three weeks later. However, it is impossible to evaluate Hastings without considering the Battle of Stamford Bridge and how King Harold II's victory against the Viking invaders soon resulted in his demise.

When the King of the English Edward the Confessor fell into a coma at the end of 1065, he had not named his successor to the throne. When he briefly awoke in 1066 he selected Harold Godwinson before dying on 5 January. The following day Harold was crowned King of England and became the last Anglo-Saxon king. William II, Duke of Normandy believed he had a rightful claim to the throne and so prepared an army to invade England. Harold II heard of this plan and established troops on the Isle of Wight in preparation but William's invading force did not leave port for many months. While Harold II began his return to London, the Viking invasion began in the north.

Harald Hadrada, King of Norway since 1046 had joined forces with King Harold II's brother, Tostig, who had been exiled the previous year. With 300 ships and 9,000 men, Hadrada (meaning 'hard ruler' and whose real name was Harald Sigurdsson) sailed up the River Ouse in Yorkshire before defeating an English army at the Battle of Fulford near York. The city surrendered and Hadrada gained the people's support while the English king began a 185 mile journey north, which his army completed in just four days.

The English army surprised the Vikings at Stamford Bridge, where Harold II had learned hostages and supplies were being taken. Around 15,000 English soldiers fought the invading force, where across a bridge near the River Derwent, Harold II's forces killed 6,000 men while suffering heavy losses themselves. The King of Norway was killed after being shot through his windpipe with an arrow, while Tostig was also killed. The surviving invaders surrendered and returned home, promising to never attack the land again but just three days later, William II and his army landed on the south coast of England.

THE BATTLE OF HASTINGS

William II, Duke of Normandy landed with an army of around 7,000 soldiers near Pevensey on the south coast of England. He had been promised the English throne by his cousin King Edward the Confessor, when he visited England in 1051. But when Harold Godwinson was named as the new English king by Edward on his deathbed, William was angered and planned to take the throne by force. He was to become William the Conqueror, the first Norman king of England.

King Harold II had of course just supressed the invasion of Harold Hadrada at Stamford Bridge and faced a long march south to repel this new threat. Exhausted from the journey, the English army of approximately 6,000 soldiers established a base on Senlac Hill, to give themselves the advantage of high ground against William's army.

Although called the Battle of Hastings, the battle actually took place 6.5 miles northwest of Hastings, near the present day town of Battle. The clash began at 9 o'clock on the morning of 14 October 1066, just three weeks after the English victory at Stamford Bridge. Celebrated in the 70m long Bayeux Tapestry, it is one of the most well-known battles of the Middle Ages. At first, the Norman army struggled to break down the English defences, even though many more of the invading army were on horseback and had more archers than the defending army. Interestingly, the sides broke for lunch but when William staged a retreat, known as a 'feigned flight' in which to coax the English from their defensive positions, the English army accordingly chased the Normans, but William's tactics worked and the English army were exposed and cut down. As for Harold II, the Bayeux Tapestry depicts him being hit in the eye by an arrow, but modern historians believe it is more likely he was bludgeoned to death. The battle ended at dusk.

The Norman conquest of England had begun, with many changes to occur to culture and language. Modern English we speak today can be traced to a blend of the Norman language used by William the Conqueror and Anglo-Saxon English.

KING WILLIAM I IS CROWNED

Following William the Conqueror's success at the Battle of Hastings, he and his Norman army made their way to London but first had to suppress uprisings against his invasion, including that of Edgar, the Ætheling, who was the disputed King of the English from October to December 1066. With victories in Dover, Canterbury and finally Winchester, where the royal treasury was secured, he finally reached London at Southwark in November.

William I was crowned King of England on Christmas Day 1066, the first monarch to be crowned at Westminster Abbey. The streets of London leading to the ceremony were lined with soldiers and William rode through the celebrations accompanied by 260 of his chiefs, priests and monks, many of whom were English. Geoffrey, the Bishop of Coutances, asked the Normans in their language if they believed William should inherit the title of King of England and similarly the Archbishop of York asked the English in attendance the same question. Both parties agreed he should become king.

William's reign included a threatened invasion by the Danes and trouble with his son but also saw him build many castles across England including the White Tower at the Tower of London in 1078 while he also compiled the *Domesday Book*, listing every landholder in England alongside a survey of their land. He died while on a campaign in Normandy on 9 September 1087 and his son William II inherited the English throne.

1099

THE FIRST CRUSADE AND THE SIEGE OF JERUSALEM

The First Crusade began in the year 1096 when Pope Urban II called for Christians from Western Europe to aid the Byzantine Emperor Alexios Comenus who was under threat from the Seljuq Turks. It was alleged that Christians in Jerusalem were being persecuted by the Seljuq Turks after the dynasty had taken control of the holy city in 1071 and so the pope ordered the capture of Jerusalem.

While the first 'crusaders' to travel to the area were mostly peasants, and were crushed at Constantinople by the Seljuq Turks, a larger force began to head towards Jerusalem in 1096. This consisted of the Kingdom of France, the Holy Roman Empire, Duchy of Apulia and the Kingdom of England. As they travelled east, the Roman Catholic military expedition defeated several Turkish armies and captured many towns before beginning a six-month siege at Antioch beginning in October 1097. When a traitor let them in to the city a massacre began and the city was ransacked. When the siege was over, the crusaders began their final journey to Jerusalem.

The Christian army, whose numbers had been reduced by the constant warmongering, arrived at the holy city on 7 June 1099 and began another siege after discovering the city to be greatly fortified. Jerusalem was now held by the Fatimid Caliphate who had captured it from the Seljuq dynasty in 1098. On 13 July, the crusaders finished the construction of three large siege towers which enabled them to clamber across the city's walls. When the Gate of Saint Stephen was forced open, the 1,300 knights and 11,000 infantry of the crusading forces surged in to the city, killing thousands of the occupiers. It is alleged that the Crusaders cut open the stomach of the dead Muslims believing that they swallowed their gold to keep it hidden and when the bodies were burnt, many Crusaders kept watch for liquid gold. When Egyptian soldiers confronted the new occupants of the city shortly after, they too were defeated and the Muslim opposition to the first Crusade was broken. Godfrey of Bouillon, a Frankish knight, was appointed the first ruler of the Kingdom of Jerusalem after its establishment but he refused to accept the title of King as he believed that belonged to Jesus Christ and instead was named Advocate of the Holy Sepulchre.

While the Kingdom of Jerusalem lasted until 1291 when the city was destructed, there were Nine Crusades in total with the last ending in 1272 when the future King Edward I, son of the English King Henry III, withdrew from his crusade to return home.

EL CID, HERO OF SPAIN

He was born in Vivar in the Kingdom of Castile in 1040 and named Rodrigo Diaz de Vivar. Although that name has been forgotten during the millennium since his birth, his nickname of El Cid is renowned in Spanish history. A military leader of Castile and a celebrated general of the Moors, who gave him the familiar name, El Cid is one of the most distinguished heroes of Spain.

Brought up in the court of King Ferdinand I of Castile, before Spain was a united country, El Cid was elected to be the commander of the royal troops when Sancho II succeeded his father. During this period of history, the Moors, who were Muslims of North African and Arabic descent, had settled in Spain, Sicily and Malta and were at war with the kingdoms of Spain, including Castile. In 1057, El Cid joined Sancho II in a war against the Moorish kingdom of Zaragoza. The young soldier, who would later serve Zaragoza, negotiated terms for the king, al-Muqtadir, to be a tributary of Sancho II. When the old king, Ferdinand I, had died he left his kingdoms to his sons and Alfonso VI was given rule over Leon. Sancho wished to have the kingdom for himself and dispatched El Cid to defeat Alfonso VI which he achieved at the Battle of Golpejera. It was around this time that El Cid killed a knight in single combat to receive his other moniker of El Campeador, which means 'Outstanding Warrior'.

In 1072, Sancho II died and with no heir, his brother Alfonso, the same man El Cid had defeated in battle, succeeded him. El Cid was removed from his esteemed military role and his influence declined but he was not banished from the kingdom and actually married Alfonso's niece Jimena, which linked him to the royal household. However, during a campaign against the Moorish king of Sevilla in 1079, El Cid began a feud with Count Garcia Ordonez, the new commander of the royal troops and a battle broke out in which El Cid's troops defeated the army of Ordonez and the Count was captured. In 1081, El Cid was quickly exiled from the kingdom.

As an exile, El Cid became a general for the Moorish rulers of Zaragoza, who believed their hiring of such a great warrior was a triumph. For almost a decade El Cid served the kingdom and in 1082 El Cid defeated the Moorish king of Lerida and his Christian allies, including the Count of Barcelona. The Moors named him El Cid, or 'the Lord' at this time. Two years later he overpowered a Christian army of Aragon. When Alfonso VI's kingdom was invaded by Almoravids from North Africa, the king reluctantly recalled the great warrior to his home. Although he returned to Castile to fight for the king he became Prince of Valencia in 1094 and ruled over the area with the support of both Christians and Muslims. He lived peacefully in the principality for five years but when the Almoravids who he had previously been at war with besieged his city, a famine broke out which possibly caused his death on 10 June 1999. A legendary story says the body of El Cid was fitted with his armour and placed on a horse which rode into battle against the besiegers, boosting the morale of his men to continue the fight.

1215

THE MAGNA CARTA IS SEALED BY KING JOHN

In 1214, a mercenary army raised by King John of England was defeated by the French at the Battle of Bouvines in northern France. This army had been paid for largely by a tax known as 'scutage', a payment made to the king instead of providing knights for military service. This medieval tax was very unpopular with the barons of the kingdom.

John's reign was also marked by his strained relationship with the Church. In 1206 King John had rejected the election of Stephen Langton as Archbishop of Canterbury, and in 1208 John was excommunicated by Pope Innocent III. A party of rebel barons, together with Archbishop Langton and the Pope's representative, urged the king to 'to abolish all the evil customs by which the kingdom of England has been unjustly oppressed'. The demands of the barons were recorded in a document known as the Articles of the Barons.

In early 1215, the dispute escalated when John refused to meet the barons' demands. In May, many barons renounced their oaths of allegiance to the king, choosing Robert Fitzwalter (1162–1235) as their leader. Later that month the rebel barons led by Robert Fitzwalter captured the city of London forcing John to negotiate with them.

To resolve the political crisis he faced, King John granted the Charter of Liberties, now known as the Magna Carta (The Great Charter), at Runnymede, on the River Thames near Windsor on 15 June 1215. The Magna Carta was authenticated with the 'Great Seal' rather than the actual signature of the king. On 19 June the rebel barons made their formal peace with the king and renewed their oaths of allegiance to him.

It is thought that at least 13 copies of the Magna Carta were made to be dispatched across the kingdom, but of these originals only four copies still survive: one in Lincoln Cathedral; one in Salisbury Cathedral; and two at the British Library. Magna Carta established for the first time the principle that everybody, including the king, was subject to the law. Most famously, the 39th clause gave all 'free men' the right to justice and a fair trial. Some of Magna Carta's core principles are echoed in the United States Bill of Rights (1791), as well as in the Universal Declaration of Human Rights (1948) and the European Convention on Human Rights (1950).

GENGHIS KHAN'S MONGOL ARMY CAPTURES BEIJING

In 12th-century Mongolia, a boy called Temujin was born around 1162 to Yesugei, the khan or leader of a minor Mongol clan, the Borijin. At the time, the grasslands (steppes) north of the Great Wall of China were occupied by tribes and clans involved in constantly shifting alliances and rivalries. Temujin took command of his clan and with a great instinct for warfare began to kill leaders of rival groups and threaten or win others into his service. By his mid-forties in 1206, Temujin was known as Genghis Khan ('unshakeable ruler').

Genghis Khan led a succession of campaigns. Mongol armies travelled and fought on horseback and took huge numbers of reserve horses with them. They had no supply train to delay them, could survive on little food and lived off the land, pillaging as they went and eating some of their horses if they needed to.

By 1213 the Mongols had overrun all the territory north of the Great Wall of China, which had previously been controlled by the Jurchen Jin Dynasty (1115–1234). Genghis now broke through the Wall and attacked northern China. In the spring of 1214 they descended on the Jurched capital at Zongdu (present-day Beijing). There had been a coup and the newly installed Emperor Xuanzong did not feel secure enough to face a prolonged siege. He offered Genghis substantial rewards if the Mongols would withdraw and acknowledged the Mongol chief as his overlord.

Satisfied, Genghis Khan left to return to Mongolia, but the Emperor soon broke the agreement, moving his court to the city of Kaifeng, far to the south. Genghis was infuriated by the Emperor's deceit and in 1215 he again marched on Beijing. He finally took Beijing on 1 June 1215, ruthlessly ransacking the city and massacring its inhabitants.

Genghis Khan went on to extend his empire over northern China, invade Afghanistan and conquer Georgia, Russia and northern Persia. By the time of his death in 1227 Genghis Khan's empire stretched from the Pacific to the Black Sea and covered an area larger than the Roman Empire at its height.

1312

KING EDWARD III

Edward of Windsor was born on 13 November 1312 at Windsor Castle. His father was King Edward II of England and his mother was Queen Isabella, the daughter of the French King Philip IV and she would become the sister of three French kings in succession. Isabella, known as the 'She-Wolf of France' was just 16-years-old when her son Edward was born.

When he was 14, his mother and her lover, the powerful English nobleman Roger Mortimer, led a rebellion against the English king, who was deposed and shortly after died. The young Edward was crowned King of England but his mother ruled in his place, alongside Mortimer. In 1330, King Edward III, as he was now titled, had Mortimer executed at Tyburn, accused of assuming royal power and then engineered a successful military campaign against Scotland – a task his father was unable to accomplish – before turning his attention to France.

The king of France was Philip VI and Edward III believed that he himself had more right to the French throne as the old king's grandson, whereas Philip VI was only his cousin. Edward's claim to the throne was the event which instigated the Hundred Years' War between England and France, which altered the course of history and witnessed events such as the Battle of Agincourt. In 1337, Edward assumed the title of king of France and landed in Normandy with his eldest son Edward, the Black Prince in July 1346. They defeated King Philip VI with a victory at Crécy and captured Calais, which was to be established as a base for later campaigns. When the war once again commenced in 1355, the Black Prince won a decisive victory at Poitiers and even captured the French King John II, known as 'the Good'. The Treaty of Bretigny in 1360 saw England controlling one-quarter of France and ended the first chapter of the Hundred Years' War.

When he was granted the French region of Aquitaine, Edward III relinquished his claim to the throne, but when the French proclaimed war once more in 1369, Edward was too old to campaign and left the task to his sons who lost much of the territory Edward had gained. Besides his military victories, King Edward III established the Order of the Garter, still one of the most prestigious honours in the United Kingdom.

Although he was known as a gifted soldier and inspiring king and is claimed to be one of the greatest English monarchs, contemporary ideas of Edward III are not always so favourable, with some historians stating he was more interested in adventure than stabilising the country. During his reign, half the population died when the Black Death came to England in 1348. It returned twice more during his reign and the king himself lost a daughter. He died on 21 June 1377, aged 64 and was succeeded by his grandson Richard II, the son of the Black Prince.

THE KNIGHTS TEMPLAR ARE DISBANDED

The Knights Templar, also known as the Poor Fellow-Soldiers of Christ and of the Temple of Solomon was established when the Pope and the Roman Catholic Church endorsed the organisation in 1129. The 'Order' came into existence when a French knight named Hugues de Payens proposed to create a new monastic order to protect the pilgrims in the Kingdom of Jerusalem, following the successful capture of the Holy City during the Crusades. Members of the Knights Templar comprised much of the most skilled military during the Crusades and also controlled a large proportion of the economic activity across Christendom of Europe and the Holy Land. However, when rumours spread of heretical activities of the Order, they were disbanded in 1312.

At its most powerful, the Knights Templar had around 20,000 members and their presence was ensured across Europe including in England, Portugal and Italy. When the Grand Master and founder of the Order, de Payens, visited England in 1128 to raise money and recruit men for the Crusades, the English Knights Templar was established and until its dissolution, had connections with English kings including Richard I and Henry II who both appeared to trust the Order and some members were present as King John signed the Magna Carta.

The Knights Templar were recognisable by their dress of a white mantle (a cape worn to the floor across the person's front and back) which was emblazoned with a red cross. Many of the members also had long beards, which many shaved off during their persecution to avoid detection. Members who were not soldiers instead managed the economic divisions of the Order and financed the construction of forts to support the Crusades. When a member joined the Order they handed in all their wealth through which the Knights Templar established a banking system and were pioneers in the form of modern banking. The piety, poverty and chastity vows which new members committed to for life are recognised by the symbol of the Order, a horse ridden by two knights, to represent poverty, as the first Grand Master at one stage could not afford to ride his own horse.

When the Holy Land was lost, the support of the Order began to diminish and a suspicion arose about the Knights Templar and especially their secret initiation ceremony. In 1307, many members of the Order were arrested and tortured, forced into confessing their guilt and likely fabricated accusations by the Inquisition. Members found guilty were burned at the stake. The initiation ritual was alleged to have included spitting on the Cross, denying Jesus Christ, worshipping idols and homosexual practices, in addition to fraud and corruption.

King Philip IV of France who was in debt to the Order, used this opportunity to have the organisation disbanded and threatened military action against them but Pope Clement V agreed to his demands and at the Council of Vienne in 1312 he dissolved the Order.

1368

THE CONSTRUCTION OF THE GREAT WALL OF CHINA

The Great Wall of China was one of the largest construction projects ever attempted. It is not one entire length of wall, however, instead consisting of many individual walls. The earliest of these walls were built in the 7th century BC in the state of Chu and was known as the 'Square Wall'. It was located in the northern region of the capital province to protect its most important settlements. Other states followed suit in the following three centuries. In 221 BC, Shihuangdi, the first emperor of the Qin Dynasty, unified China and set about deconstructing the fortifications established in previously separate states. He initiated a ten-year wall-building program in the north and linked existing portions of wall. However, the wall was untended after his death and fell into disrepair.

It was the Ming Dynasty's work on the wall from 1368, known as the Ming Great Wall, which forms the best-preserved, most extensive and most visible part of the wall today. In the middle of the 14th century, Zhu Yuanzhang, who would go on to become the first emperor of the Ming Dynasty, forced the Mongol Yuan dynasty out of China and into the Central Asian steppes. After capturing the Yuan capital Khanbaliq (modern-day Beijing), which had been founded by Kublai Khan in 1264, Zhu established the Ming Dynasty in 1368, and became known as the Hongwu Emperor. Initially the Hongwu Emperor's defensive policy relied on fast-moving armies patrolling the northern frontier close to the steppe. An inner line of forts provided a defensive wall to retreat to, which formed the precursor to the Ming Great Wall. The Hongwu Emperor altered his policy from 1373 onwards and focused on shoring up his defences, bringing in garrisons at 130 strategic places around Beijing.

From the late 15th century, the Ming Great Wall was divided into north and south lines, which were called the Inner and Outer Walls. Strategic fortresses, called 'passes', and reinforced gates were situated along the wall. The Zijing, Juyong and Daoma passes, located closest to Beijing, were known as the Three Inner Passes. Three Outer Passes – Piantou, Ningwu and Yanmen, and were positioned further to the west. These six passes were heavily fortified during the Ming Dynasty, providing crucial defensive protection for the capital.

The Ming Great Wall, as it is known, spans 5,500 miles from Dandong in the east to Jiayu Pass. Roughly a quarter of the wall's length consists of natural features, including mountains and rivers. There are a number of moats and ditches, but the vast majority – around 70 per cent – of the wall is manmade.

THE MING DYNASTY IS ESTABLISHED IN CHINA

Zhu Yuanzhang was born in 1328 in Zhongli Village and during his early life, many of his older siblings were given up by his parents, unable to support or feed them. When Zhu was 16, the Huai River burst its banks and caused a severe flood which lead to a plague spreading throughout the land. Apart from one brother, his entire family was wiped out by the plague and so Zhu travelled to become a novice monk at a Buddhist monastery. At the same time, soldiers of the Yuan Dynasty, which ruled imperial China, were fighting Buddhist rebels known as the Red Turbans. During one of these skirmishes, the monastery was burned down and Zhu joined the rebels. This decision marked the beginning of the Ming Dynasty, which would rule until 1644 and would see the rebuilding of the Great Wall of China, the construction of the Forbidden City, trade routes developing across the globe and the rise in art, literarure, music and poetry across China.

After Zhu joined the Red Turbans, he married the daughter of one of the rebel commanders and rose to power to mastermind the defeat of the Mongol-led Yuan Dynasty with the capture of the city of Nanjing. Zhu named himself as Hongwu Emperor and called his new dynasty Ming, which means 'bright'. The rebuilding and fortification of the Great Wall of China began almost immediately and the emperor also began the construction of a wall around the new capital of Nanjing, to keep invaders out, which was a common theme of ancient and imperial China. A supposed 200,000 workers helped build the wall, much of which stands today.

In 1402, Yongle, the son of Hongwu, became emperor and reigned over many important advances of the Ming Dynasty. Between 1411 and 1415 the Grand Canal, which had been in existence since the 5th century BC, was rebuilt entirely. The canal, which runs from Beijing to Hangzhou, links the Yellow River and Yangtze River and was declared a UNESCO World Heritage Site in 2014. Yongle moved the Chinese capital to Yan and renamed it as Beijing. In the centre of Beijing, the emperor arranged for the establishment of the Forbidden City, which would remain as the Chinese imperial palace until the end of the Qing Dynasty in 1912. The construction of the Forbidden City lasted from 1406 to 1420 and spread over 180 acres, incorporating 980 buildings and surrounded by a ten-metre-high defensive wall. The translation of the Chinese name of Zijin Cheng is actually 'Purple Forbidden City' supposedly named after the colour of the city walls and the night sky.

During the reign of Yongle, a eunuch by the name of Zheng He rose to fame as an explorer who opened up many trade routes for the Ming Dynasty. He had been born in 1371 before being captured by Ming troops who castrated him so that he was able to serve in the imperial palace, which was a tradition of imperial China. There, Zheng He became an adviser to the young Yongle and when he became emperor, Yongle promoted his adviser to the position of admiral. Between 1405 and 1433, Zheng He commanded seven maritime expeditions which employed 27,800 men, sailing to Southeast Asia, India, the Middle East and even to Africa. Around 36 different states established trade agreements with China and Zheng He is now considered a hero of Chinese history, but the succeeding Hongxi Emperor ended the trade voyages as he believed they were expensive.

During the Ming Dynasty's rule, art flourished with blue and white porcelain being an especially popular product. When the Portuguese explorer Vasco da Gama sailed for China in 1497, the king had requested that he bring back not just spices but also porcelain. The product is one of the most enduring symbols worldwide of the dynasty.

By the early 17th century, the major threat to the Ming Dynasty was northeast of the Great Wall of China in Manchuria. To defend themselves against the Manchus, the government raised taxes and neglected many provinces. When he lost his job as a postal messenger due to the economic hardships instigated by the tax levies, Li Zicheng joined a group of roving bandits and became a leader in a peasant rebellion. In 1644, his army captured Beijing, finding the final Ming Chongzhen Emperor hanging from a tree outside the walls of the Forbidden City. A surviving Ming general, Wu Sangui, joined forces with the Manchus as a last resort and they defeated the rebel army, to begin the Qing Dynasty.

1415

POPE GREGORY XII RESIGNS

Angelo Corraro was born in May 1326 in Venice and while little is known of his early life, in 1380 he became Bishop of Castello. A decade later he was made Titular Patriarch of Constantinople. His rise through the church continued and he became Supreme Pontiff, or Pope, on 30 November 1406 and took the name Gregory XII. His resignation in 1415 ended the Western Schism and it would be another 598 years until another Pope resigned from his position.

The Western Schism occurred between 1378 and 1417 and split the Roman Catholic Church as three men claimed to be the true Pope. Soon after he was elected as Pope, Gregory XII offered to meet the Antipope Benedict XIII at Savona but the meeting was delayed as both popes and their supporters grew distrustful of one another and feared of being held prisoner. When Gregory XII's cardinals became dissatisfied at the failure to settle the matter of the Western Schism, Gregory gathered his cardinals at Lucca but several cardinals abandoned him and sought out Benedict XIII hoping to negotiate with him to stand down as pope, alongside Gregory XII in order to elect a new pope. However, when the cardinals summoned a Council of Pisa, neither Pope nor Antipope attended.

In June 1409, the Council of Pisa did depose both men as heretical and scandalous and they elected Alexander V as the new Pope that same month. While Gregory attempted to use his influence to denounce Benedict XIII and Alexander V for the same reasons he had been condemned at Pisa, his declaration was largely ignored. At the Council of Constance, where Jan Hus was sentenced to death, the Western Schism was ended when the resignation of Gregory and John XXIII (the successor of Alexander V) was announced, while Benedict XIII was excommunicated by the church after refusing to stand down. After a two year vacancy, Pope Martin V was elected.

On 28 February 2013, Pope Benedict XVI announced his resignation, claiming a 'lack of strength of mind and body' had made his role impossible and replaced Gregory XII as the last pope to resign.

JAN HUS IS BURNED AT THE STAKE

Jan Hus, who is commonly known in English as John Huss, was born in 1370 in Bohemia. Hus was a religious reformer who was influential in the Christian church before Martin Luther and John Calvin. During his life he was involved in the Western Schism of 1378 to 1417, when three men claimed to be the pope, motivated by political factors rather than religion. At In 1415, after being convicted of supporting the teachings of the Catholic dissident John Wycliffe, Hus was convicted of heresy and burned at the stake.

Hus studied at the University of Prague, later becoming dean of the university's philosophy department in 1401. The university was struggling against the German masters who were opposed to church reforms and the Czech masters who were readers of the English religious reformer John Wycliffe. Hus was influenced by Wycliffe's teachings and agreed with his proposals for reformation of the Roman Catholic clergy. In 1403, Hus became the adviser to Zbynek Zajic, the Archbishop of Prague and the reform movement's influence grew. At the same time, Wycliffe's proposals were condemned as heretic by the masters at the university. The archbishop Hus had advised began to warm towards the opponents of reform and had two of the members of the reformists sent to Rome, where they returned as key opponents of the reformation. Hus was outnumbered in his views.

When the Western Schism occurred, Hus was excommunicated by Zajic after he had refused to obey orders of the new Pope Alexander V. King Sigismund of Hungary invited Hus to attend the Council of Constance to explain his views to the council and possibly help solve the crisis. Hus was reluctant to attend but when he was promised safety at the council, Hus accepted the invitation. However, when he arrived in Constance, his safety was not actually guaranteed and the Hungarian king had him arrested. He was tried before the council and declared a heretic supporter of Wycliffe. When the council insisted Hus recant to save his life, but when he refused he was sentenced to death on 6 July 1415 and burned at the stake. Following his death, the outraged Bohemians distanced themselves from Papal rulings and went to war with the Roman church in the Hussite Wars.

THE BATTLE OF AGINCOURT

The Battle of Agincourt, fought in northern France between the armies of King Henry V of England and King Charles VI of France, is one of the most famous battles in English history. Immortalised by William Shakespeare's play *Henry V*, the battle occurred on 25 October 1415, during King Henry's campaign in France, which took place during the Hundred Years' War.

Henry had succeeded his father, Henry IV, as King of England in 1413 and resolved to reignite the war against the French, believing that he had a rightful claim to the French throne. After raising funds and gathering military support, Henry crossed the English Channel in 1415 and following a successful siege of the French port of Harfleur, King Henry marched his troops to Calais. However, before they reached Calais, the English army was intercepted by a French army, led by the Constable of France, Charles d'Albret. With just a comparatively small force of 6,000 to 9,000 men, the English became dispirited at the overwhelming number of French soldiers, which has been approximated to be between 12,000 to 36,000 men.

Henry, undercover, made his way around his army's camp at night, offering words of encouragement to keep the English spirits up. The following day, 25 October, was St Crispin's Day and saw an English army line up against the French army at Agincourt. Within two hours of the battle commencing, a victory to King Henry V became clear, with great success coming from the English archers, whose longbows were stronger than previous generations, able to unleash armour-piercing arrow heads at a range of 250 yards. Historians have estimated that up to 1,000 arrows a second may have been let loose by the English archers during the battle, such was their skill and speed. Legend has it, the two-fingered 'V' sign originated from these archers, who displayed their bow-pulling fingers to antagonise the French.

Around 400 English soldiers died in the battle, while up to 8,000 of the French army died, including Charles d'Albret. King Henry V had his victory and would remain in France for three-and-a-half-years, during which time he met King Charles VI and married his daughter, Catherine of Valois, to effectively make him heir apparent to the French throne. However, in 1422, Henry died after contracting dysentery during another military campaign. Catherine of Valois was remarried, to Owen Tudor and their grandson became Henry VII, the first Tudor King of England.

1431

VLAD THE IMPALER (DRACULA)

Vlad Tepes, or Vlad the Impaler, is believed by many scholars to have been the inspiration for the vampire Dracula of Bram Stoker's Gothic horror novel. The second son of Vlad II of Wallachia, he was born in the winter of 1431 in Transylvania in the Kingdom of Hungary (today part of Romania), and gained notoriety in 15th century Europe for his cruel methods of punishing his enemies.

The name Dracula, meaning 'son of Dracul', was derived from his father's membership of the Order of the Dragon ('*draco*' in Latin) – a group created to defend Christian Europe against the Ottoman Empire. Vlad II was assassinated by nobles in 1447, and Dracula launched a series of campaigns to regain his father's position. He succeeded briefly in 1448, and was quickly deposed, but eventually seized and held power from 1456 until 1462. Halfway through his reign, the pope declared a new crusade against the Ottomans, and Dracula – now Vlad III – found himself at war with Sultan Mehmed II. It was during at this time that he committed many of his infamous atrocities and earned his nickname: his preferred method of execution was to impale his enemies on stakes in the ground. As he retreated from a battle in 1462, he left the banks of the Danube filled with thousands of impaled victims as a warning to the Ottoman invaders – a 90,000 strong force which included Vlad's own brother Radu.

That year, defeated by the Ottoman advance, Dracula evaded capture only to be betrayed and imprisoned by his ally Matthias Corvinus, the King of Hungary. He was eventually released and managed to regain the Wallachian throne in 1476. His third reign lasted only a few months before his death, but his reputation for tyranny and torture has endured.

JOAN OF ARC IS EXECUTED

Joan of Arc was burned at the stake in the marketplace of Rouen, France on 29 May 1431, at the age of 19, before a crowd of an estimated 10,000 spectators. France was in the midst of the Hundred Years' War against England, and she had been captured after being thrown from her horse during the French attack on English-held Burgundy in 1430. Despite protesting her innocence, she was tried as a heretic by pro-English church officials, and charged with crimes including witchcraft, heresy and cross-dressing.

Born in 1412 in Domrémy, France, Joan of Arc (Jeanne d'Arc) grew up in a poor farming family, and began to have mystical visions at a young age. These encouraged her to take a vow of chastity and to seek an audience with the future Charles VII of France, offering her aid in driving out the English. In 1429, Joan cropped her hair and dressed in men's clothes to make the 11-day journey across English territory to Charles's court at Chinon. Initially suspicious of her claims of being able to save France, Charles was won over during a private meeting, and his clergymen were convinced by her piety and humility. She was given a horse and armour and sent to accompany Charles to the English siege at Orléans. Despite being wounded by an arrow to the shoulder during the battle, she later returned to encourage the final assault which succeeded in lifting the siege. She claimed that her actions were divinely inspired, and earned the nickname 'The Maid of Orléans'.

In 1456, 25 years after her death, a second trial declared Joan's innocence and proclaimed her a martyr. She became a semi-legendary figure and French national heroine, and was made a saint in 1920.

HENRY VI IS CROWNED KING OF FRANCE

Following the Treaty of Troyes in 1420, King Henry V of England, who was on the cusp of conquering France, was recognised as the heir apparent to the French throne, occupied by King Charles VI. When Henry V married the king's daughter, Catherine of Valois that same year, they had a son, Henry, who was born at Windsor Castle in England on 6 December 1421. Nine months later, he would become the youngest person to succeed to the English throne and seven weeks after, became the titular King of France upon the death of Charles VI.

A regency council was summoned to govern England until Henry VI was fit to rule the kingdom for himself and his uncle John, Duke of Bedford led the regency. When the late French king's biological son Charles VII became the new French king on 17 July 1429, Henry VI was quickly crowned as the King of England at Westminster Abbey on 6 November 1429 and two years later he was crowned as the King of France at Notre Dame de Paris on 26 December 1431, aged just ten-years-old.

Henry VI was not a strong ruler and internal power struggles in the royal court resulted in the king losing influence. In 1445 he married Charles VII's niece, Margaret of Anjou, hoping the marriage would cement a peace between England and France but the Hundred Years' War he had inherited from his father continued and after the French heroine Joan of Arc devastated English forces, vital territories such as Normandy were lost. By 1453, all English possessions in France, apart from Calais, were retaken by the French and the Hundred Years' War was proclaimed to be over. While Charles VII became known as 'the Victorious', the English King Henry VI suffered a mental breakdown. Following England's defeat, rich landowners in the country complained of the financial loss from the forfeiture of French land which became one of the causes for the War of the Roses beginning in 1455. Henry's reign ended in 1461 when he was deposed by Richard of York but despite being imprisoned in the Tower of London in 1465, he was restored as king in 1470. On the edge of insanity, Henry VI was again dethroned by Edward IV who became king. On 21 May 1471, Henry was murdered in the Tower of London.

THE HUNDRED YEARS' WAR ENDS

The Hundred Years' War is a misleading title for one of the longest conflicts in world history, as it actually lasted for 116 years, from 1337 to 1453. Fought between the House of Plantagenet, which ruled England, and the House of Valois, which ruled France, the war occurred for two major reasons: the significance of the duchy of Gascony, which was a fief of the French crown, although it belonged to England; and the English King Edward III's claim to the French throne, following the death of the last king of the House of Capet, Charles IV. The conflict, which was the major contest of the Middle Ages engulfed the region with the French support including Genoa, Bohemia and Scotland and the English allies including Portugal, Flanders and Burgundy. The Hundred Years' War was a key period in the rise of the national identity and patriotism of both kingdoms and although there was no final treaty or definite victor, France gained the most from the conflict.

Historians have divided the war into three phases: the Edwardian War which lasted from 1337 to 1360; the Caroline War which took place from 1369 to 1389; and finally the Lancastrian War which began in 1415 and ended with the conclusion of the war in 1453 and the retaining of the French throne by the House of Valois. Following the Norman Conquests which saw William the Conqueror become King of England in 1066, the English kings were vassals to the French kings for their possessions in France. For three centuries, the French kings had striven to reduce the English territories in France to the stage that England were only left with the duchy of Gascony, for which they wanted complete control. In 1328, the French King Charles IV died, becoming the final ruler of the House of Capet and the English King Edward III was declared the inheritor of the French throne by his mother Isabella of France. She was the daughter of the French King Philip IV and overlooked herself in favour of her son, but the French court did not approve the decision.

The French Kingdom had greater military and financial resources than England, but the English army was well-trained and had advanced military equipment, such as the devastating longbows used at the Battle of Agincourt in 1415. In the early periods of the conflict, England won decisive victories at sea at Sluys and on land at Crécy and Poitiers. By 1360, the French King John accepted a Treaty of Calais which gave England the total rule of Gascony, which then occupied one third of France. By 1380, however, the king's son Charles V had reconquered much of the lost territory. King Henry V rekindled the war with the famous victory at Agincourt. He was named as the next king of France in the Treaty of Troyes in 1420 but died shortly after. With the military prowess of Joan of Arc, who lifted the siege of Orleans in 1429, the French began to get the upper hand in the war and following the Battle of Castillon in 1453, England lost the duchy of Gascony. Though the war was never formally ended, the English were unable to match the might of the French troops. The only area still held by England was the port of Calais but that was finally won back by the French in 1558.

THE FALL OF CONSTANTINOPLE

On the evening of 28 May 1453, a final sombre ceremony was held inside the city walls of Constantinople, the capital of the Byzantine Empire. For 52 days, a massive army of the Ottoman Empire, led by Sultan Mehmed I, had laid siege to Constantinople, present-day Istanbul. The Sultan had offered terms to Constantine XI, the Byzantine Emperor, offering him and his citizens safe passage from the city if they surrendered their home, but the emperor refused. The following day, the army of Mehmed II began its final assault which marked the end of the Roman Empire and the conclusion of the Middle Ages.

Constantinople had been designated as the new capital of the Roman Empire by the Emperor Constantine the Great in 330 AD. The Western Roman Empire had collapsed in 476 AD when Romulus Augustulus was deposed by Flavius Odoacer, the first King of Italy. The Fall of Constantinople arguably instigated the Renaissance period as many Byzantine scholars, architects, artists, philosophers and scientists fled the city for Western Europe. Meanwhile, a debate raged about the establishment of a 'Third Rome' with Russia claiming Moscow should be the centre of a New Rome and rival factions argued their cause. Even in the 20th century, the Italian dictator Benito Mussolini claimed that his fascist state and plans for a new empire were the 'Third Rome'. Following the sacking of the city, Mehmed II had declared himself 'Caesar of Rome' which implied he hoped to continue the notion of a Roman Empire. However, he was instead called Mehmed the Conqueror and the political institution he established endured until the creation of Turkey in 1922.

As for Constantine XI, he led the defence of Constantinople having refused to surrender and with the support of Genoan, Venetian and Greek troops, fought gallantly against the invading army. The Byzantines were far outnumbered by the Ottomans, who had a huge naval force, an army estimated to be around 200,000 men and importantly 70 cannons which were used to smash down the heavily fortified city walls. The Byzantine army on the other hand totalled approximately 10,000 men. While almost half of them were killed during the siege, around 30,000 citizens of Constantinople were enslaved. There were no witnesses to Constantine's death and his body was never identified, therefore he has become a 'sleeping hero' in Greek mythology, known as the 'Marble King' waiting to be resurrected to reconquer the city.

1455

THE GUTENBERG BIBLE IS PRINTED

Johannes Gutenberg was a German inventor who changed the course of history in the 1450s by developing the mechanical moveable type printing press. His machine was a system of letters and characters that could be repositioned to reproduce a document. This revolutionised the availability of the written word, because books would no longer need to be copied out by hand. Moveable type had actually been already invented in the Far East, but Gutenberg's invention made it possible to print many

copies quickly. The technology spread quickly around the world and played a crucial role in the Renaissance and the Reformation. Books were no longer the preserve of the elite, but would become available to the middle classes too.

In 1455, Gutenberg finished what became known as the Gutenberg Bible. Written in Latin, it was also called the 42-line Bible, on account of the number of lines per page. Historians have estimated that around 180 copies were printed, which sounds minute, but given that there were around 30,000 books in the whole of Europe, it is a significant number. Around 135 of the 180 copies were printed on paper, while the remainder were printed on vellum, a type of parchment made from the skin of calves. These vellum copies were very heavy and took around 170 calfskins just to produce a single copy.

In 1456, a business dispute led to Gutenberg being sued by his business partner Johann Fust. Gutenberg stood accused of misusing a large sum of money loaned by Fust to help set up his printing operation. Gutenberg lost the lawsuit and had to hand over his equipment to Fust, along with half of the printed Bibles. His endeavours did finally receive some recognition in 1465 and was awarded the title 'Hoffman' (gentleman of the court), which gave him a stipend as well as a large allowance of grain and wine.

Forty-nine copies of the Gutenberg Bible have survived, and are located in libraries, museums and galleries around the world. Only 21 of these are complete versions, seven of which are in the UK. The two copies of the Gutenberg Bible currently owned by Russia were looted from Leipzig during the Soviet Occupation of Germany in 1945.

THE WARS OF THE ROSES BEGINS

The Wars of the Roses began with the First Battle of St Albans on 22 May 1455, when Richard of York defeated the army of Henry VI. Richard put Henry VI in prison and became the 'Lord Protector' of England.

The Wars of the Roses were fought between two rival families who both laid claim to the throne of England: the House of Lancaster and the House of York. It was a series of battles, often fairly small and sometimes years apart which were fought over 30 years, from 1455 to 1487. The name 'Wars of the Roses' came from the heraldic symbols, or badges, of the two warring houses: the House of Lancaster was represented by a red rose and the House of York by a white rose. The two houses were both branches of the royal House of Plantagenet.

St Albans was the opening battle in the Wars of the Roses. Richard, Duke of York had been Lord Protector while King Henry VI, had suffered a bout of insanity. The king recovered in early 1455 and lost no time in taking back his power base by excluding the former Lord Protector Richard Neville, Earl of Warwick from court.

Richard and the Earl of Warwick assembled their private armies in the north and led a force of around 3,000 on a march toward London. Henry VI's 2,000-strong Lancastrian army moved from London to intercept the Yorkist army, halting in the town of St Albans where they set up defensive barricades, and waited.

Following several hours of failed negotiations the slightly larger Yorkist force launched a frontal assault on the town. In the fighting that followed through the narrow streets of St Albans, the Yorkists first suffered heavy casualties. Then a small group of soldiers, led by the Earl of Warwick, cleverly outflanked the Lancastrian defences by picking their way through small back lanes and gardens until they reached the market square where the main body of Henry's army were being held in reserve. Warwick's longbowmen reigned arrows onto Henry's personal bodyguard, killing a number of important Lancastrian noblemen, including the Duke of Buckingham.

The wounded Henry VI was later escorted back to London by York and Warwick. Richard, Duke of York was restored as Lord Protector of England, effectively ruling the country. Henry's wife Queen Margaret, along with their young son Edward of Westminster, fled into exile.

1483

THE SISTINE CHAPEL OPENS

The Sistine Chapel was constructed in the Vatican Palace complex between 1473 and 1481. It is named in honour of Pope Sixtus IV, who commissioned the architect Giovanni dei Dolci to design it. It is a rectangular chapel featuring six arched windows on its side walls and a flattened barrel-vaulted ceiling. The side walls of the chapel were decorated with beautiful frescoes depicting the Life of Christ and the Life of Moses, which were painted by some of the foremost Renaissance painters, including Sandro Botticelli. The frescoes were completed in 1482, but it wasn't until 15 August 1483, on the Feast of the Assumption, that Pope Sixtus IV consecrated the chapel. During this opening ceremony, the chapel held its first mass and the Pope dedicated the chapel to the Virgin Mary.

The Sistine Chapel's most famous artworks are the frescoes on the ceiling and sanctuary wall, which were painted by Michelangelo between 1508 and 1512. The ceiling frescoes feature nine scenes from the Book of Genesis, including the iconic *Creation of Adam*. Aside from being a major tourist attraction, the Sistine Chapel is the site of the papal conclave, the meeting of cardinals that elect a new Pope.

THE FIRST EXECUTION AT THE TOWER OF LONDON

On 13 June 1483, William Hastings became the first person to be executed at the Tower of London. He was accused of treason by Richard, Duke of Gloucester, and beheaded in the Tower's courtyard.

Born around 1431, Hastings was a follower of the House of York, and loyal courtier of his distant cousin, the future King Edward IV. He fought alongside Edward at the Battle of Mortimer's Cross, and was present when he was proclaimed king in London on 4 March 1461. Hastings became one of England's most important figures, taking on the roles of Lord Chamberlain and Master of the Mint. He was made the first Baron Hastings in 1461, and helped defeat the Earl of Warwick's Rebellion (1469–71).

After Edward's death in 1483, the king's young son was crowned Edward V, while the Duke of Gloucester was made Lord Protector. Richard's unexpected decision to execute Hastings may have been caused by a desire to destroy supporters of the new king, and seize the throne for himself. Hastings was buried in Windsor Castle's chapel, near the tomb of Edward IV.

THE MYSTERY OF THE PRINCES IN THE TOWER

The 'Princes in the Tower' were Edward, born in 1470 and his brother Richard, born in 1473. Their parents were Edward IV and his wife, Elizabeth Woodville. Shortly after Edward was crowned Edward V, he and his brother disappeared and were never seen alive again.

The reasons behind the princes' disappearances were probably entirely due to the power struggles of the time, which had resulted in the princes' father, Edward IV, winning the struggle against the House of Lancaster to establish the House of York on the English throne.

With the support of the powerful Earl of Warwick, known as 'the Kingmaker', Edward IV won a series of battles, culminating in overthrowing the Lancastrian king, Henry VI, at the Battle of Towton in 1461. Henry VI fled the country with his remaining supporters and Edward was crowned King Edward IV. In 1464 Edward IV secretly married Elizabeth Woodville, a commoner. This angered his chief supporter and adviser the Earl of Warwick who had wanted Edward to marry someone else. Warwick, alongside many others, was furious at the favours now shown to Elizabeth and her relatives. Warwick first tried to supplant Edward with Edward's younger brother. When this failed, Warwick fled to France, where he joined forces with Henry VI.

The Lancastrian army invaded England in September 1470 and restored Henry VI to the throne in October. Edward IV fled to the Netherlands until March 1471, when he returned to England, defeating the Lancastrians at Tewkesbury in May. The heir to the House of Lancaster, Edward of Westminster, was executed after the battle and, a few days later, Henry VI was also put to death, ending the direct Lancastrian line of succession.

A period of comparative peace followed, but this was short-lived as King Edward IV died unexpectedly on 9 April 1483 and his eldest son, who was just 12-years-old, was proclaimed Edward V. As Edward was under age, his uncle, Richard, Duke of Gloucester, who was third in line to the throne after the two princes, was named as protector. As Edward travelled towards London to be prepared for his coronation, he was met by Richard. He arrived at the Tower of London on 19 May 1483 – at that time the traditional residence for monarchs prior to their coronation. Meanwhile the dowager Queen, Elizabeth Woodville, sought sanctuary in Westminster Abbey with her remaining children, including her younger son Richard, Duke of York, who was second in line to the throne.

Plans continued for Edward's coronation, but the date was postponed from 4 May to 25 June. On 16 June Richard was taken from the Abbey, joining his brother in the Tower. At this point the date of Edward's coronation was indefinitely postponed. Both princes were declared illegitimate, removing them from the line of succession, on the basis that their father's marriage to Elizabeth Woodville was invalid as Edward was already contracted to marry someone else.

On Sunday 22 June, a sermon was preached at St Paul's Cross claiming Richard to be the only legitimate heir of the House of York. On 25 June a group of lords, knights and gentlemen petitioned Richard to take the throne and the following day Richard officially began his reign.

It is unclear what happened to the boys after they were both lodged in the Tower, but it is widely assumed that they were murdered on the orders of their uncle Richard in an attempt to secure his hold on the throne. Alternatively, other parties, such as Henry Tudor (later King Henry VII) may have been responsible and it has also been suggested that one or both princes may have escaped assassination. If they were murdered, t is presumed that this occurred some time in the summer of 1483, as after this date the princes were not seen again.

Richard, Duke of Gloucester was crowned Richard III in July 1483.

THOMAS CROMWELL, CHIEF MINISTER TO HENRY VIII

Thomas Cromwell was born in Putney, London around 1485. Thomas' father, Walter, worked as a fuller, a blacksmith and a brewer, while his name appears on the local court lists for various misdemeanours, including watering down beer and assaulting his neighbour. The young Cromwell was, on his own later admission, also something of a ruffian.

In 1500, Cromwell ran away to the continent and in 1505, entered the service of Francesco Frescobaldi, a Florentine banker, later travelling to Belgium and becoming a trader in his own right.

By 1515 Cromwell had returned to England and now fluent in French and Italian, with a good knowledge of Latin, he began to practice law. He married Elizabeth Wykys, a widow, with whom he went on to have three children: Gregory, Anne and Grace but his wife and two daughters died of the 'sweating sickness' in 1528. Around 1517 Cromwell's knowledge of Italian language and culture secured him a position with Cardinal Wolsey, King Henry VIII's powerful First Minister. Under the Cardinal's patronage, Cromwell gained access to the court and in 1523 he became an MP.

By 1529 Cromwell was Cardinal Wolsey's secretary and most senior adviser. Henry VIII was seeking a divorce from his first wife Catherine of Aragon in order to marry Anne Boleyn. Wolsey tried unsuccessfully to get permission from the Pope but his failure resulted in him being stripped of his government office and accused of treason. On the journey to London to stand trial Wolsey fell ill and died on 29 November 1530. In 1533, Cromwell persuaded parliament to make Henry head of the Church of England, after which Henry annulled his marriage to Catherine and married Anne Boleyn. In April 1534, the king made Cromwell his Principal Secretary and Chief Minister.

But by 1536, Anne had failed to have a son and Henry, desperate for a male heir, had fallen in love with Jane Seymour. Cromwell, despite bringing about the King's marriage to Anne in the first place, was asked to come up with a plan to replace Anne with Jane. Cromwell intimidated and tortured those close to Anne into making false confessions and when Anne was tried for treason and adultery, she was found guilty and executed in 1536. Henry VIII married Jane a week later and Cromwell's success saw him secured as Henry's right-hand man.

In 1537 Jane Seymour died after giving birth to Henry VIII's longed-for son and heir Edward VI. In 1539 Cromwell was tasked with finding a suitable fourth wife for the king. Seeking an alliance with the princes of Germany, Cromwell suggested Anne of Cleves but when she arrived in England, Henry was disappointed by her looks and was reluctant to marry her. Cromwell's persuasion for the king to proceed with the marriage proved to be a fatal misjudgement.

Henry's marriage to Anne of Cleves was a disaster and in order to get it annulled the King was forced to give evidence of a personal nature in court which left him embarrassed and furious with Cromwell for convincing him to marry Anne. Cromwell's enemies at court seized the opportunity to move against him and he was charged with treason and corruption before being executed at the Tower of London on 28 July 1540.

THE BATTLE OF BOSWORTH

The Battle of Bosworth was one of the last major battles of the Wars of the Roses between the Houses of York and Lancaster. King Richard III and his army of approximately 15,000 men fought against Henry Tudor, Earl of Richmond and his 11,000-strong army on a large battlefield. The battle was fiercely fought – in fact archaeologists suggest that more cannon shot was discovered on the battlefield than on any other medieval battlefield.

The battle began early on the day of 22 August 1485 and was over before midday. Although it is now known as the Battle of Bosworth, at the time it was called the Battle of Redemore, which means 'place of reeds'. It was only in the early-16th century that it was given the name we use today. The site of the battle is a controversial debate but was recently revealed to be around two miles from where originally thought.

During the battle, it is said that King Richard was without a horse but when he was offered one to flee to safety he declared 'This day I will die as a king or win', at which point he charged towards Henry Tudor's standards alongside 200 loyal Yorkists. The king was killed in the melee, his 26 month reign coming to a bloody end, and his army defeated. Henry Tudor was crowned as the new king, under an oak tree, following the battle. The death of King Richard III and the coronation of King Henry VII marked the end of the Middle Ages in England and instigated the Early Modern era and the reign of the Tudors.

The Battle of Bosworth is particularly well remembered in William Shakespeare's history *Richard III*. Shakespeare portrays the king as a plotting and vindictive character while also giving him unflattering physical features such as a hunchback and a limp. The confirmation in 2013 of Richard III's bones buried beneath a car park in Leicester proved that many abnormalities given to the slain king were imprecise while the skeleton had evidence of 10 injuries – 8 of which were to the king's skull. The legacy of the battle is still manifest in the 21st century.

1494

CHRISTOPHER COLUMBUS'S FIRST SIGHTING OF JAMAICA

Christopher Columbus (1451–1506) was an Italian explorer who made four historic voyages across the Atlantic Ocean to the Americas between 1492 and 1498. He was celebrated as the 'discoverer' of the New World, although the Viking explorer Leif Erikson had in fact reached Canada five centuries previously. Although Columbus was not the first European to visit the Americas, his voyages had a lasting impact, ushering in an era of colonisation and conquest.

Columbus's plan was to reach the East Indies by sailing west rather than the traditional eastern route. He took three ships – Niña, Pinta and Santa Maria – on his first voyage, which left Palos de la Frontera in southwestern Spain on 3 August 1492. However, his estimation of the circumference of the earth was woefully inaccurate, and upon reaching what actually turned out to be the Bahamas, he was convinced that he had landed at Japan. His next stop was Cuba, which he incorrectly calculated must be China. He travelled on to Hispaniola (modern-day Haiti and the Dominican Republic) before leaving for Spain, via the Azores.

Columbus's second voyage reached the Lesser Antilles islands in the Caribbean including Dominica, Guadeloupe, Antigua and Montserrat. From there he travelled to the Greater Antilles, returning to Hispaniola on 22 November. He departed Hispaniola on 24 April 1494 and travelled to Cuba again on 30 April before spotting what we now know as Jamaica on 5 May. Columbus named it St. Jago, in honour of the patron saint of Spain. Columbus famously declared the island 'the fairest my eyes have ever seen'. At the time, the island was inhabited by Arawak Indians, and it is the Arawak word Xaymaca (meaning 'land of wood and water') which is where the word 'Jamaica' derives.

THE TREATY OF TORDESILLAS

During the exploration of the New World in the late-15th century, the Italian explorer Christopher Columbus discovered Cuba and Hispaniola (the island now shared by the Dominican Republic and Haiti). After Columbus had claimed the new land for the Crown of Castile in Spain, Ferdinand II of Aragon and his wife Queen Isabella I of Castile wrote to Pope Alexander VI, who was originally from Valencia, to support them in claiming the new territory for their kingdom. King John II of Portugal had been furious with the New World being claimed as Spanish as he declared that a previous treaty had resulted in all land of the area being Portuguese. The resulting Treaty of Tordesillas established the future of the New World.

On 4 May 1493, the pope suggested a new line of demarcation from the North to South Pole in which all land 100 leagues (320 miles) to the west and south of the Cape Verde Islands, which were owned by the Portuguese, should belong to Castile. When the pope then suggested giving all new land east of the line to Spain, King John II grew unhappy with the terms and approached King Ferdinand and Queen Isabella directly. On 7 June 1494, they agreed on a new demarcation line, this time to be 370 leagues (1,185 miles) west of the Portuguese-owned Cape Verde Islands and although it gave the Spanish claim to the land west of the line, it allowed Portugal to discover new land to the east of the line. This agreement became the Treaty of Tordesillas and was signed by Spain on 2 July 1494 and Portugal on 5 September that same year. By 1529, the Treaty of Zaragoza similarly divided the land on the other side of the world between Spain and Portugal.

Although the Treaty of Tordesillas was not sanctioned by the new Pope Julius II until 1506, it was agreed upon as an official contract by the two kingdoms before then. While other European powers were absent from the negotiations, many nations ignored the treaty and explored the world for their own expansion. As the New World was mostly undiscovered, it was quite unknown exactly what the two kingdoms would occupy but historians claim Portugal knew of the protuberance of Brazil in South America which jutted out into Portuguese territory and by 1500 the explorer Pedro Alvares Cabral had landed in Brazil to claim the land. Portuguese settlers expanded the territory of Brazil past the demarcation line which was not strictly enforced and this is the reason Brazil's national language is Portuguese and not Spanish which is used across the rest of the continent.

1497

AMERIGO VESPUCCI DEPARTS FOR THE AMERICAS

Amerigo Vespucci was born on 9 March 1454 in Florence, Italy and was educated by his uncle, a Dominican friar, before beginning a career as a merchant. He was employed as a clerk at the House of Medici and became a favourite of Lorenzo de Medici. He then began a period of his life at sea and partook in up to four voyages for which America was named in his honour.

When King Manuel I of Portugal invited Vespucci on a voyage to explore the east coast of South America, the keen merchant accepted and became an observer during voyages between 1499 and 1502. There is a debate around whether the voyage which Vespucci wrote about in 1497 actually took place after a letter allegedly written by the explorer to an Italian magistrate in 1504 was claimed to be a forgery. Historians have argued that the voyage to the New World from 1497 to 1498 did not take place and the letters were not written by Vespucci. However, the second voyage during which the Florentine discovered the mouth of the Amazon River is known to have occurred. A third voyage is claimed to be accurate while a fourth in 1501 has been questioned by historians.

Nevertheless, the expeditions became famous due to these letters describing the voyages and their discoveries. As part of a voyage which explored South America and discovered it was a new land, and not part of Asia as originally believed by Christopher Columbus, the new land mass was named America when a German cartographer, Martin Waldseemuller, produced a new map to illustrate the new land. As he had read the letters of Vespucci, he named the land of the New World, America, after the explorer's Latin name, Americus.

In Vespucci's later life he became a Spanish citizen and he ran a navigator school in Seville. He died on 22 February 1512.

VASCO DA GAMA SETS SAIL FOR INDIA

Little is known of the early life of the Portuguese explorer Vasco da Gama, who would become the first man to sail directly from Europe to India. He was born around 1460 in southwestern Portugal into a noble family and in 1492 he was sent to the port city of Setubal and to the Algarve on the orders of the Portuguese King John II to seize French ships which had attacked Portuguese vessels.

Seeking a route from Western Europe to the East, the new Portuguese King Manuel I appointed da Gama to command a fleet in search of a maritime passage to India. The explorer departed in July 1497, hoping to navigate a successful path which would allow Portugal to break the Muslim control of trade with India and the East. The fleet sailed down the west coast of Africa before veering out into the Atlantic Ocean and then arced back to the southern tip of Africa. Da Gama rounded the Cape of Good Hope and sailed up the east coast of the continent, which is a route still sailed by ships. On the journey, an Arabic navigator was helped on board and he assisted da Gama in finding India, which the fleet reached in May 1498, landing at Calicut, which is now Kozhikode. The voyage successfully became the first to complete a non-land crossing from Europe to Asia.

Having found India, da Gama returned to his homeland and the king dispatched another fleet to secure a trading station in the new land. After hearing of a massacre in Calicut, da Gama returned to India in 1502, where he forced the ruler to agree a peace with the Portuguese settlers. On his return to Portugal, da Gama created a trading post in Mozambique, which became colonised by the Portuguese in 1505. The nation's official language is still Portuguese.

Back in Portugal, the explorer became the advisor to the king regarding issues in India and in 1524, he was sent back to India as the Portuguese viceroy and sent back there to suppress corruption which had broken out. When da Gama arrived in Cochin, he became ill and died on 24 December 1524. It was not until 1539 that his body was returned to Portugal for burial.

THE CORNISH REBELLION TAKES PLACE

The primary cause of the rebellion was Henry VII's tax levy to pay for a war against the Scots. The terms of the levy violated the Stannary Charter of 1305 which prohibited taxes of this nature from being raised in Cornwall. Cornwall had already contributed significantly to the Scottish expedition, even though it was not affected by any border incursions.

Michael Joseph An Gof, a blacksmith from St Keverne, and Thomas Flamank, a lawyer from Bodmin, led around 15,000 rebels through Devon to Wells, where they were joined by Lord Audley. An Gof remained in command of the rebel army and Lord Audley joined Flamank as 'leader' of the expedition.

They continued on to Winchester from where they headed to Kent on an unsuccessful mission to seek recruits. Some of the men lost heart when the men of Kent did not rise with them and quietly returned to Cornwall.

The Cornish army arrived in Guildford on 13 June. Henry VII had been concentrating on Scotland and had been caught slightly unawares by the scale and speed of the approach of the Cornish revolt. Nevertheless, he had dispatched 500 troops under the command of Lord Daubeny to meet the rebels. Daubeny's royal force clashed with the Cornish army just outside Guildford on 14 June but did not stop the rebels from continuing to London. Around 10,000 Cornish rebels arrived at Blackheath outside London on 16 June and pitched their final camp.

The Battle of Deptford Bridge (also known as the Battle of Blackheath) took place on 17 June 1497 and was the culminating event of the Cornish Rebellion. Henry VII had mustered an army of some 25,000 men to the 10,000 Cornish, who also lacked the supporting cavalry and artillery arms essential to the professional forces of the time. Probably fairly unsurprisingly the King's men routed the Cornish rebels.

By 2pm, Henry VII had returned to the City in triumph. An Gof and Flamank were both sentenced to be hung, drawn and quartered. However at the King's 'mercy' they were allowed to hang until dead before being decapitated. They were executed on 27 June at Tyburn. Lord Audley, as a peer of the realm, was beheaded on 28 June at Tower Hill. Their heads were then displayed on pike-staffs on London Bridge.

1514

NICOLAUS COPERNICUS CLAIMS THE SUN IS AT THE CENTRE OF THE SOLAR SYSTEM

Nicolaus Copernicus (1473–1543) was a Polish astronomer born to wealthy merchant parents. His father died when Nicolaus was between 10 and 12, and thereafter, he was cared for by his uncle Lucas Watzenrode. Lucas became the Bishop of Warmia a few years later, and his wealth and influence enabled him to take care of Nicolaus' education. Copernicus studied liberal arts, which included astronomy, at the University of Cracow. He left before completing his degree and continued his studies at the University of Bologna, where he spent some time living in the same house as the university's principal astronomer, Domenico Maria de Novara. He went on to study medicine, which included an astrology component, at the University of Padua between 1501 and 1503. He also began work on a revolutionary new model of the universe that would turn contemporary scientific thinking on its head.

The dominant theory of the time was called the Ptolemaic System, which had been formulated by the Greco-Egyptian mathematician Ptolemy around the year 150. Ptolemy has asserted that the Earth was a static object located at the centre of the universe and that the Sun, Moon, planets and stars travelled in a circular orbit around the Earth. Copernicus's revolutionary idea, which he formulated between 1508 and 1514, was that the Sun rather than the Earth was the centre of the universe, known as a 'heliocentric' system. He also proposed that the Earth is not a stationary object, but rather it turns twice a day on its axis. He included his heliocentric hypothesis in a forty-page manuscript called Commentariolus ('Little Commentary').

His theory in its final form was published nearly 30 years later in 1543. He had actually finished the work over 10 years previously, but was apprehensive about the contempt 'to which he would expose himself on account of the novelty and incomprehensibility of his theses'. Copernicus wrote about his fear of being vilified in the dedication to his masterpiece, which he addressed to His Holiness Pope Paul III. As legend goes,

Copernicus suffered a stroke shortly afterwards and went into a coma. He is said to have woken up, and looked at the final printed copy of his book before dying.

It was a full sixty years until the Catholic Church officially criticised Copernicus's theory. In 1633, the Italian astronomer Galileo Galilei was tried and convicted of heresy for 'following the position of Copernicus, which is contrary to the true sense and authority of Holy Scripture'. Copernicus had ruffled feathers, but had made a hugely significant contribution to the scientific revolution.

HENRY GRACE À DIEU

Larger than the famed ship *Mary Rose*, King Henry VIII's great ship *Henry Grace à Dieu* was the biggest and most formidable warship in Europe when launched in 1514. Constructed at the Woolwich dockyards on the Thames, the ship which was also known as 'Great Harry' played a vital role in the naval life of the English king.

In 1504, the Scottish King James IV ordered the construction of a large ship named *Michael*, which when launched in 1511 was far larger than the English warship *Mary Rose*. Jealous and troubled by the accomplishment, Henry VIII ordered the construction of *Henry Grace à Dieu*, which means 'Henry Grace of God'. The construction of the carrack began in 1512 and by 1514 the ship was launched, weighing over 1,000 tons. The 165m-long ship contained 43 cannons but early on in Great Harry's career, it was clear that the ship was too top heavy and its poor stability meant the weaponry on board was ineffective. Therefore in 1536 the ship was revamped with the weight and height of the ship reduced so that the handling of the vessel was improved.

Henry Grace à Dieu was involved in the Battle of the Solent against the French in 1545 which provided an indecisive result but did witness the *Mary Rose* sinking to its doom. The fate of the ship is unknown, but it is commonly believed to have been discarded on the Thames when no longer valid for service.

Henry VIII enlarged the Royal Navy during a period when naval dominance was becoming crucial. There were only 6 warships when he was crowned but, by the time of his death, there was a fleet of 57 Royal Navy warships which later played a vital role against the Spanish Armada.

1517

MARTIN LUTHER POSTS HIS NINETY-FIVE THESES

The legend is that Martin Luther nailed a copy of his *Ninety-Five Theses* on to the door of the All Saints' Church in Wittenburg, Germany which instigated the Protestant Reformation on 31 October 1517. Although the image of Luther nailing his Theses to the church door is iconic, it is almost certainly a fabrication and it is more likely that he simply hung the text on the door or passed the document around. But who was Martin Luther and why was his *Ninety-Five Theses* so important in religious history?

Martin Luther was born in Eisleben, Germany on 10 November 1483 and became a monk, although his father Hans had hoped his son would become a lawyer. Luther had turned to religion after being caught in a thunderstorm in which he was almost struck by lightning. He considered the episode to be a sign from God and stopped his study of law to go to an Augustinian monastery. Over the next few years he carried on his studies and in 1512 he became a professor of biblical studies after obtaining a doctorate.

The Augustine teachings which Luther followed stated that the Bible, not the Church, was the definitive religious authority and that people could not simply gain salvation by their own acts but only God's divine grace could grant salvation. By the beginning of the 16th century in Europe, a group of theologians began to doubt the teachings of the Roman Catholic Church which practiced bestowing 'indulgences' to offer absolution to sinners.

Luther was against the granting of indulgences and the Catholic Church's belief that redemption was possible through works of righteousness. He composed the *Ninety-Five Theses*, which were officially called the *Disputation on the Power and Efficacy of Indulgences*. This list of questions and proposals, which is considered to be the founding text of the Protestant Reformation, reinforced his two central beliefs and criticised the act of granting indulgences. Soon, the *Ninety-Five Theses* spread across Germany and to Rome and by 1518 the pope had condemned Luther and stated his 'scandalous' document conflicted with the ideas of the Church. In 1520, Pope Leo X issued a papal bull declaring that the ideas of Luther were heretical. Luther refused to retract his theses and was excommunicated.

On 17 April 1521, Luther was summoned to the 'Diet of Worms' (an imperial council) in Germany where he remained defiant and famously stated 'Here I stand. I can do no other.' When the Holy Roman Emperor Charles V demanded that Luther's writings be burned, the reformist was forced into hiding. By the end of Luther's life, his teaching were not just religious but also political but he was not heavily involved in the rebellions which broke out. Luther's later views included the pope being the antichrist and he additionally called for the expulsion of Jews from the empire. He died on 18 February 1546.

THE SWEATING SICKNESS RETURNS TO ENGLAND

The Sweating Sickness, which was also known as the English Sweat, was a disease that ravaged England on five separate occasions from 1485 to 1551. Although it is not certain what exactly caused the epidemics – theories such as high levels of dirt, insects, lice and ticks have been cited – a type of hantavirus, carried by rodents, seems the most likely explanation for the deaths which spread across the land.

Each outbreak of the Sweating Sickness, besides the second in 1508, had a high death count and most of what is known of the epidemic was written by a physician named John Caius who recorded the symptoms in 1552 while he was in Shrewsbury. According to Caius, the sufferer would get a headache, followed by giddiness and then severe prostration. Soon after, the victim would be overwhelmed by sweat, delirium and a quick pulse. Most victims died between three and 18 hours after the first headache set in. Unlike some diseases, people who survived once often suffered again from the sickness. Although the epidemic mainly devastated England, there was an outbreak in Europe in 1528, affecting Scandinavia, Lithuania, Poland and Russia. However, the populaces of France and Italy were almost completely unharmed.

The 1517 outbreak was extremely severe and emerged in Calais, which at the time was under English rule. The university cities of Cambridge and Oxford suffered greatly and in towns across England, up to half the population succumbed to the English Sweat.

1519

FERDINAND MAGELLAN BEGINS THE FIRST CIRCUMNAVIGATION OF THE EARTH

Ferdinand Magellan was born in 1480 in Sabrosa, Portugal into a noble family. After Vasco da Gama had navigated a maritime route from Western Europe to Asia, Magellan wished to seek a naval route from Portugal to the Spice Islands in the East but by the use of a western passage. His epic circumnavigation of the Earth, which began in 1519 with 260 men and five ships, would conclude in Spain in 1522 with just 18 men still on board and Magellan long dead.

Having served in the Portuguese navy during his younger days, Magellan approached King Manuel I of Portugal to receive support for a mission to journey west towards the Spice Islands of Indonesia. At that period, spices were one of the most valuable commodities, but the king refused to support Magellan's voyage. So the eager explorer approached the Spanish King Charles I for his support, having renounced his Portuguese nationality. Spain was the main rival to Portugal in controlling the spice trade and the Spanish king happily supported Magellan's proposal. Charles I was the grandson of King Ferdinand and Queen Isabella who had likewise supported the historical expedition of Columbus.

Magellan bid farewell to his family and departed from Spain in August 1519, on board the lead ship *Trinidad*. The fleet began by crossing the Atlantic Ocean and reached South America just over one month later. Hoping to discover a legendary strait that would allow them to pass through the continent, they sailed close to the coastline. One ship sailed ahead and was shipwrecked in a storm but its crew were saved. In October 1520, another storm forced the ships close to land but believing they were about to be wrecked, the crew sighted the famous strait through the land which became known as the Strait of Magellan. However, the crew of *San Antonio* became distrustful of the voyage and returned to Spain, leaving three ships on the journey.

One month after entering the strait, the ships entered a massive ocean which was calm and quiet. Magellan named this ocean the Pacific, meaning 'peaceful'. Magellan believed that the journey across the Pacific would not be too long but it took three months and 20 days, during which many of the crew died of hunger and scurvy.

Upon finally reaching land on the island of Cebu in the Philippines, Magellan was killed in a fight between the islanders of Cebu and their neighbours. He died on 27 April 1521 after being shot with a poison arrow. Another ship was lost but the remaining two continued and reached the Spice Islands on 5 November 1521. Loaded with spices but just 18 men, the remaining ship *Victoria* arrived at Seville, Spain in September 1522. The first European to actually circumnavigate the globe was Juan Sebastian de Elcano, Magellan's deputy who took control after his leader's death. Although it was already doubted, Magellan's voyage discredited the theory that the Earth was flat.

THE DEATH OF LEONARDO DA VINCI

Leonardo di ser Piero da Vinci was born in the Tuscan town of Vinci, Italy on 15 April 1452. The brother of 17 half-siblings, he received no formal schooling but was to become one of the leading individuals of the Renaissance, often described as the 'Renaissance Man'. A polymath whose interests included painting, sculpting, drawing, architecture, science, music, history and anatomy, da Vinci was also a prominent inventor and has been credited with introducing the concepts of the tank, parachute and even helicopter.

His most famous art works include the *Mona Lisa*, *The Last Supper* and the *Vitruvian Man*, with his work celebrated in galleries and museums around the world. However, during his lifetime, his studies which filled 13,000 pages of notes and drawings – including observations of the world he made on his travels, but also everyday notes such as a grocery list and more innovative ideas such as a description of shoes for walking on water – were never published. He was also the first person to explain why the sky is blue!

Da Vinci was a notoriously slow painter and many of his works were unfinished at the time of his death, such as *St. Jerome in the Wilderness*, which hangs in the Vatican Museums in Rome. However, he did complete many works with the *Mona Lisa* being arguably the most famous and most visited painting in the world. Only measuring

67

77cm × 53cm, the oil painting, also known as *La Gioconda* (which translates as 'happy') is thought to be of Lisa Gherardini, commissioned by her husband and painted by da Vinci between 1503 and 1506. In 2005, researchers at the University of Amsterdam claimed that the subject of the portrait is 83 per cent happy, 9 per cent disgusted, 6 per cent fearful and 2 per cent angry. It was stolen from the Louvre by an Italian patriot in 1911, it was returned to the museum in 1914 and its fame expanded outside the art world.

Da Vinci's other famous works include his late-15th century *The Last Supper*, in the Santa Maria delle Grazie church in Milan, which depicts the Last Supper of Jesus with his disciples – a mural measuring 4.4m × 8.8m. Da Vinci was also a master of line drawing and his *Vitruvian Man*, a study of the proportions of the male body as described by the Roman architect Vitruvius, was created by the artist in 1490. Writing by da Vinci shows he was left handed and wrote from right to left!

After King Francis I of France captured Milan in October 1515, da Vinci became a friend of the king and lived in Amboise, France after Francis had made him Premier Painter and Engineer and Architect to the King. Francis at one time commissioned Leonardo to make a mechanical walking lion which contained lilies in its chest.

When da Vinci died on 2 May 1519, aged 67, it is said that the king held the Italian's head in his arms. Of the 'Renaissance Man', Francis said 'there had never been another man born in the world who knew as much as Leonardo.'

1520

SULEIMAN THE MAGNIFICENT BECOMES SULTAN OF THE OTTOMAN EMPIRE

In December 2015, archaeologists revealed that they had discovered what they believed to be the remains of the tomb of Suleiman the Magnificent. Built on the spot where the Ottoman Sultan died on 7 September 1566, it is believed his heart and organs were buried in the tomb but his body was taken back to Constantinople. The discovery reminded the world of Suleiman I, the longest-reigning Ottoman Sultan whose rule saw the expansion and Golden Age of the Ottoman Empire.

Born on 6 November 1494 in Trabzon, along the coast of the Black Sea, he was inspired as a young man by the conquests of Alexander the Great and wished to build an empire similar to his hero. He ascended to the throne upon the death of his father Selim I and following the ceremony of the girding of the sword on 30 September 1520, he became the 10th Sultan of the empire. Ruling as Suleiman I, he began to fulfil his desire and expanded the boundaries of the empire, leading his troops in battle to conquer Belgrade, Rhodes and much of Hungary. He also organised the conquests of the Balkans, the Middle East and North Africa as far as Algeria. Under his rule, the Ottoman Empire encompassed the important cities of Jerusalem, Mecca, Medina, Baghdad and Damascus and his naval fleet controlled the Mediterranean and Red Sea. He was given the epithet 'Magnificent' for his role in the territorial gains of the empire.

As a patron of the arts and allegedly a distinguished poet himself, Suleiman ushered in the Golden Age of the empire as culture such as literature, art and poetry flourished. His legislative changes across the empire which amended laws in taxation, crime, education and welfare earned him the title 'Lawgiver'.

His 46-year-reign was the longest of any Ottoman Emperor but came to an end on 7 September 1566 during a siege of the Hungarian fortress of Szigetvar. The death of the 71-year-old Sultan was kept secret for 48 days so the morale of the troops was not damaged and his son Selim II succeeded him. Suleiman is regarded as one of the mightiest

Sultans of the empire and William Shakespeare even wrote of him towards the end of the 16th century in his play *The Merchant of Venice*.

THE FIELD OF THE CLOTH OF GOLD

Kings Henry VIII of England and Francis I of France met near Calais between 7 and 24 June 1520, for a gathering designed to increase the bond of friendship between their countries. Magnificent temporary palaces and pavilions were built for the two kings, and the tents and sumptuous costumes displayed so much cloth of gold, a precious fabric woven with silk and gold thread, that the meeting was named after it. Henry VIII arrived with Queen Catherine of Aragon, his advisor Cardinal Wolsey, and 6,000 nobles, attendants and servants. His lavishly decorated palace was erected at Guines, and covered almost 2.5 acres, with over 2,800 tents, an ornate chapel, a great hall, and a gilded fountain that spouted spiced wine, claret and water through different channels.

Francis was camped with his retinue near Ardres, and the monarchs met at a midway point called Val D'Or ('the Golden Vale'). The days were filled with elaborate banquets, music, dancing and entertainment, as well as archery and jousting tournaments in which both kings participated. Henry unexpectedly challenged Francis to a wrestling match, which ended when the French king threw him to the ground and bested him. Nevertheless, the atmosphere was cordial, despite the fact that 'many persons present could not understand each other'. In a chapel service on the penultimate day, the French and English chaplains took it in turns to sing mass.

Above all, the meeting provided an opportunity for the kings to outshine each other with dazzling displays of wealth and culture. Henry's ceremonial armour and horse's caparison alone were decorated with 2,000 ounces of gold and 1,100 large pearls. However, the political outcome was negligible, and did little to improve relations between the two countries. Soon afterwards, Henry formed an alliance with Spain, France's enemy, and by 1522, France and England were at war.

1533

ATAHUALPA, THE LAST INCA EMPEROR, IS EXECUTED

Atahualpa was the last true emperor of the Incas. The word 'Inca' itself means 'King' so technically Inca only ever referred to one man. The Inca Empire had stretched across much of South America including Peru, Ecuador, Columbia and Bolivia but the Spanish Conquest of the Inca Empire between 1532 and 1572 saw the end of the empire and the ascendency of Spain's influence over the continent.

The last emperor was born around 1500 as the son of the Sapa Inca Huayna Capac, whose death in 1527 sparked a civil war between Atahualpa and his half-brother Huascar who both wished to succeed their father. Atahualpa ruled the northern region while Huascar took the south. In 1532 Huascar was captured by Atahualpa's army at the Battle of Quipaipan and Atahualpa's reign began, unaware of the encroaching danger of the Spanish.

The conquistador Francisco Pizarro had departed Spain in order to conquer portions of South America, enthused by the earlier conquests of Hernan Cortes. In 1532 he headed for the western coast of the continent, supported by just over 160 men. While celebrating the capture of his brother at the Konoj hot springs near Cajamarca, word reached Atahualpa that a small invading party was nearby but hearing of the size of the group, the Inca was indifferent. He went to meet the Spanish, alongside 6,000 men and stopped frequently to drink so by the time he arrived at Cajamarca he was drunk. When he reached Cajamarca no Spanish were in sight but it was a trap and when Pizarro gave the order, the Spanish infantry and cavalry attacked, massacring thousands of the local men.

Atahualpa was captured but when he understood the Spanish desire for gold, he ensured they received it from across the empire so as to preserve his life. Although it is believed the Spanish grew fond of Atahualpa for his bravery and wit, they realised the threat of keeping him alive was too dangerous and so after a quick trial in which they found him guilty of revolt and practicing idolatry, they strangled the Inca on 26 July 1533. He had been baptised as a Catholic before his execution so that he could not be executed by burning as the Incas believed that the soul would not pass on to the afterlife if the body was burned.

KING HENRY VIII IS EXCOMMUNICATED

On 11 July 1533, Pope Clement VII declared his sentence on the annulment of King Henry VIII's marriage to Catherine of Aragon and his subsequent marriage to Anne Boleyn.

Pope Clement's sentence refused to acknowledge Henry's divorce from Catherine or his marriage to Anne and announced that the King would be excommunicated from the Roman Catholic Church by September 1533, if he did not abandon Anne and restore Catherine to her position of Queen. Henry ignored the Pope's sentence.

Interestingly the official 'papal bull' of excommunication was not actually issued until 1538. Pope Clement VII died on 25 September 1534 having not got round to issuing the paperwork. Pope Clement's successor, Paul III, drew up the 'bull' on 30 August 1535, which was finally issued in November 1538. By this time Anne Boleyn had been executed two years previously and Henry's 3rd wife Jane Seymour had died the year before.

QUEEN ELIZABETH I IS BORN

On 7 September 1533, Anne Boleyn, King Henry VIII's second wife, gave birth to a daughter at Greenwich Palace. She was named Elizabeth after her two grandmothers, Elizabeth of York (the former queen consort of King Henry VII) and Elizabeth Howard. After her mother was arrested and executed on trumped-up charges of adultery and treason, Elizabeth was declared illegitimate by an Act of Parliament in June 1536.

Elizabeth ascended the throne on 17 November 1558, aged 25, succeeding her childless half-sister Mary. Elizabeth's reign lasted over 44 years, which was characterised by religious tolerance, political and military successes, and a period of cultural accomplishment, including the plays of Christopher Marlowe and William Shakespeare. Her shrewd Religious Settlement, made during the year of her accession, helped to tackle the country's religious divisions and reasserted the Church of England's independence from Rome. Her clever choice of councillors and advisers protected her at a time when many enemies, both foreign and domestic, were actively attempting to assassinate her.

Despite considering the prospect of a strategic marriage to secure the succession of the Tudor dynasty and strengthen England's isolated position, she never married. Her childhood friend and later courtier, Robert Dudley, who she made the Earl of Leicester in 1564, occupied a unique place in her affections, but their attachment never led to marriage.

Despite Elizabeth's patient and skilful diplomacy towards the French and Spanish, by the mid-1580s, it was evident that a major military conflict with Spain was imminent. This came in 1588 with the Spanish Armada, a huge fleet assembled to invade England, but it was defeated in one of history's greatest naval victories. Elizabeth delivered a famous rousing speech to troops stationed at Tilbury, defending her ability as a female leader, 'I know I have the body but of a weak and feeble woman; but I have the heart and stomach of a king, and of a king of England too.'

Elizabeth died on 24 March 1603, having successfully unified England and reasserted the country's reputation as a major European power. She had won the respect and adoration of her subjects and her legacy endures to this day.

1536

ANNE BOLEYN IS EXECUTED

Anne Boleyn, the second wife of King Henry VIII, was executed on charges of incest, adultery and treason at the Tower of London. From the scaffolds she made a short speech to the crowd, 'I am come hither to accuse no man, nor to speak anything of that, whereof I am accused and condemned to die, but I pray God save the king and send him long to reign over you, for a gentler nor a more merciful prince was there never: and to me he was ever a good, a gentle and sovereign lord,' she said, adding, 'I take my leave of the world and of you all, and I heartily desire you all to pray for me. O Lord have mercy on me, to God I commend my soul.' At which point she was beheaded by a swordsman.

Anne Boleyn was born, most likely, between 1501 and 1507, although the exact date is unknown. Anne was the daughter of Sir Thomas Boleyn and his wife, Lady Elizabeth Howard, daughter of the Duke of Norfolk. After living in France for a time during her youth, Anne returned to England in 1522 and was appointed to the English court as lady-in-waiting to Catherine of Aragon, Henry VIII's first wife.

By the mid-1520s, Anne had become one of the most admired ladies of the court and in 1523 she was betrothed to Lord Henry Percy. However she had also caught the attention of the King and her engagement to Lord Percy was ended by Cardinal Thomas Wolsey on Henry's orders.

Anne initially rejected Henry's advances, shrewdly refusing to become another of his mistresses, despite the fact this would have also brought her power and wealth. Love letters from the king to Anne, written between 1527 and 1528, survive to this day. Henry petitioned the Pope to annul his marriage to Catherine, on the basis that she had previously been married to his older brother (who had died) and so was technically his sister-in-law, in order that he could marry Anne.

Pope Clement VII refused to annul Henry's marriage to Catherine. Despite this, in January 1533, Henry VIII and Anne were married in a secret ceremony conducted by Thomas Cranmer, Archbishop of Canterbury. Henry then broke with the Catholic

Church passing the Act of Supremacy, declaring himself Supreme Head of the Church of England and giving himself the authority to annul his own marriage. In June 1533 Anne was crowned Queen of England in a lavish ceremony at Westminster Abbey.

Henry and Anne's daughter Elizabeth (the future Queen Elizabeth I) was born on 7 September 1533. Two more pregnancies ended in stillbirth, but Henry was still desperate for a male heir and he blamed Anne for this misfortune. Around this time he took on Anne's lady-in-waiting Jane Seymour as his mistress and began to plot to get rid of Anne.

In April 1536, Sir Francis Weston, William Brereton, Mark Smeaton, Sir Henry Norris and Anne's own brother Lord Rochford were arrested on suspicion of having had relations with the Queen. Anne was investigated by a secret commission which included her father, her uncle the Duke of Norfolk and Thomas Cromwell, Henry's chief adviser. On 2 May 1536 Anne was arrested on charges of adultery with five men including her own brother, Lord George Rochford. At the trial, presided over by the Duke of Norfolk, Anne was accused of adultery and witchcraft. She was convicted and imprisoned in the Tower of London.

Within 24 hours of Anne's execution on 19 May, Henry VIII and Jane Seymour were betrothed and then married just 11 days later on 30 May 1536 at the Palace of Whitehall.

BUENOS AIRES IS FOUNDED BY PEDRO DE MENDOZA

During the Age of Discovery when European powers began the exploration of unconquered territories, the Spanish colonisation of the Americas which began with the discoveries of Christopher Columbus in 1492, saw the Spanish Empire expand through Central America, the Caribbean and South America. In 1536 Buenos Aires, which is now the capital city of Argentina, was founded by Pedro de Mendoza.

Mendonza was a Spanish conquistador, or 'conqueror' who was born in 1487 to a noble family in Granada. As Mendoza rose through the Spanish court of King Charles I, who was also the Holy Roman Emperor under the title of Charles V, he served as an officer during Spain's campaigns in Italy and in 1529 he volunteered to command an exploration of South America, which he funded through his own finances. By 1534, as he prepared a fleet to sail for the New World, he was appointed as the Governor of the area of South America known as New Andalusia. Mendoza was ordered to lead his expedition towards the Río de la Plata, known in English as River Plate, which forms the border between Argentina and Uruguay and flows into the Atlantic Ocean.

On 24 August 1535, Mendoza departed Spain with 2,000 men aboard a fleet of 13 ships. Although three ships joined the fleet at the Canary Islands, two ships were lost at sea during the voyage. Mendoza was suffering with syphilis during the voyage and his illness resulted in poor leadership. When his lieutenant Juan de Osorio attempted to depose Mendoza, he was executed for treachery. Towards the close of the year, the fleet reached the Río de la Plata and on 3 February 1536, Mendoza founded Buenos Aires.

Mendoza called the new settlement 'Holy Mary of the Fair Winds' and he began to establish roads and forts, which had been ordered by Charles V. Mendoza was still ill and spent much of his time in bed and while the 3,000 natives of the region originally befriended the Spanish, they soon moved away from the new settlement. Mendoza was angered by the natives resentment of the conquistadors and a war ensued in which the new governor's brother was killed alongside many Spanish soldiers, but the natives retreated. When the settlers ran out of food and a famine broke out, they began to eat snakes, lizards, rats and even boots. Cannibalism was also reported to have occurred and to make matters worse, the natives regrouped and attacked the new city.

Unwell and disheartened, Mendoza headed back to Spain but he died during the journey on 23 June 1537. The settlers of Buenos Aires vacated the future Argentine capital in 1542 and relocated to the new city of Asunción, now the capital of Paraguay. In 1580, Buenos Aires was established for the second time, as the Spanish conquest of South America continued.

1547

EDWARD VI BECOMES KING OF ENGLAND AND IRELAND

When King Henry VIII died on 28 January 1547, his only legitimate son, Edward, became King Edward VI of England and Ireland, with his coronation taking place one month later on 20 February. He was the first monarch raised as a Protestant but his reign only lasted six years and was to be dominated by rebellions in England and battles for power within the royal household.

Edward was born on 12 October 1537 at Hampton Court Palace. His mother, Jane Seymour, who was the third wife of Henry VIII, died just 12 days after Edward's birth. Although he was intellectually mature, such as being fluent in Greek and Latin, Edward was physically not strong and suffered poor health.

Edward's uncle, Edward Seymour, Duke of Somerset, the brother of Jane Seymour, led the Regency Council which governed the realm during the king's reign and established himself as Protector. Alongside the Archbishop of Canterbury, Thomas Cranmer, Somerset began reforming England into a Protestant nation, with the support of the king. When the new Protestant Book of Common Prayer was issued in 1549 however, a peasant's revolt in Cornwall and Devon broke out and a rebellion led by the farmer Robert Kett in Norfolk against social and economic inequalities also upset Edward's reign.

When the Duke of Somerset was arrested and replaced in his role by General John Dudley, 1st Duke of Northumberland, Somerset was executed, with the king writing a brief entry in his diary: 'Today, the Duke of Somerset had his head cut off on Tower Hill'. It had been Northumberland who had crushed the uprising in Norfolk and when the king began to deteriorate in health due to tuberculosis, he used his political influence to persuade Edward to make his daughter-in-law, Lady Jane Grey, his successor.

King Edward VI died on 6 July 1553 and was indeed succeeded by Jane, who would become known as the 'nine-day Queen', as just nine days into her reign she was replaced by Mary, the half-brother of Edward.

EXECUTION BY BOILING IS OUTLAWED IN ENGLAND

Richard Roose was a cook in the household of John Fisher, the Bishop of Rochester. According to the bishop's biographer Richard Hall, Roose entered the kitchen one day and put poison into the porridge which was being made ready for Fisher's dinner. The bishop, however, was not hungry and so the poisoned porridge was served to his guests and servants who ate the meal unaware of the danger. Hall records that Mr Bennet Curwen and an 'old widow' died suddenly and the others who dined on the porridge never regained their health. When Roose was found guilty of the crime, the English Parliament passed an 'Acte for Poysoning' making murder by poisoning a crime of high treason. It was decided that the punishment for the crime would be Death by Boiling. Roose was boiled to death on 5 April 1531 at Smithfield in London and in the words of one witness Roose 'roared mighty loud' but noted that the crowd who watched Roose's execution preferred the method of the 'headsman' referring to the usual practice of beheading.

In 1535, Fisher himself was executed by order of King Henry VIII who had passed the law to permit execution by boiling. Fisher had refused to accept Henry as Supreme Head of the Church of England and there is a theory that Anne Boleyn's family had appointed the cook to poison the bishop who was in opposition to her marriage to the king. Rather than being boiled alive, Fisher was beheaded on Tower Hill.

Though the punishment was carried out again on a woman named Margaret Davy in 1542 who had been found guilty of poisoning, it was repealed during the reign of King Edward VI in 1547.

IVAN THE TERRIBLE BECOMES THE FIRST TSAR OF RUSSIA

On 16 January Ivan, son of Grand Prince Vasily III of Moscow and his second wife, Elena Glinskaya, was crowned 'Ivan IV, Tsar and Grand Prince of All Russia'. The title 'Tsar' was derived from the Latin 'Caesar' and essentially means 'Emperor'. Ivan IV was the grandson of Ivan the Great and part of the Rurik dynasty.

Ivan's father had died on 4 December 1533, immediately after his father's death, the three-year-old Ivan was proclaimed grand prince of Moscow. His mother ruled in Ivan's name until her death (allegedly by poison) in 1538. The deaths of both of Ivan's parents reignited the power struggles between the nobles who tried to control the young prince and, through him, the realm. The years 1538–47 were therefore a time of murderous strife among the 'boyars' – the highest rank of the nobility in Russia.

Following his coronation, in February 1547, Ivan married Anastasia Romanovna, great-aunt of the first tsar of the Romanov dynasty. He married several more times after her death in 1560, but this first marriage seems to have been the happiest.

Ivan IV's power became absolute after he succeeded in conquering the remaining independent principalities. He also organised the *Streltsi* – military rulers – to govern his districts and the *Oprichniki* – a personal army or police force – to suppress the boyars.

Ivan confiscated the property of the boyars and granted state property to those who served him. Since his soldiers were tenured to the state for life, their land grants became hereditary and they formed a new ruling elite.

In 1582, after the Livonian War with Poland and Sweden, Russia lost her far northern territories and her access to the Baltic. In the same year, the Tsar killed his son, Ivan, in a fit of rage.

Ivan's achievements were many. Politically he made Russia an important European power. Ivan also encouraged Russia's cultural development, especially through printing, establishing Russia's first publishing house The Moscow Print Yard in 1553.

Ultimately Ivan's reign of terror resulted in the weakening of all levels of the aristocracy, including the military rulers he had originally sponsored. The long and unsuccessful Livonian War overextended the state's resources and brought Russia to a state of almost total economic ruin by the time of Ivan's death in 1584.

1572

THE ST BARTHOLOMEW'S DAY MASSACRE

King Charles IX of France, influenced by his mother, Catherine de Medici, ordered the assassination of Huguenot Protestant leaders in Paris, starting a massacre that resulted in the killing of tens of thousands of Huguenots across France.

The Massacre of Saint Bartholomew's Day was the culmination of a series of events. On 18 August 1572 the Peace of Saint-Germain put an end to three years of religious civil war between Catholics and Protestants (Huguenots) in France. This peace was precarious since a faction of Catholics, led by the Guise family, refused to accept it. In September 1571 Huguenot leader Admiral Gaspard de Coligny was readmitted to the King's council. Many were shocked by the return of a Protestant to the court, but Catherine de Medici and her son Charles IX, conscious of the kingdom's financial difficulties, were determined not to let war break out again.

To cement the peace between the two religious parties, Catherine planned to marry her daughter Margaret to the Protestant prince Henry of Navarre (the future King Henry IV). The royal marriage was arranged for 18 August 1572 despite the objection of both the Pope and the powerful King Philip II of Spain.

The impending marriage led to the gathering of a large number of Protestants in Paris. After the wedding, Coligny and other leading Huguenots discussed terms of the Peace of St. Germain with the King. On 22 August, an attempt was made on Coligny's life as he made his way back to his house from the Louvre. He was shot from an upstairs window, and seriously wounded. The assassin escaped, and it is difficult to determine who was responsible, but the most likely culprits were: the Guise Family; The Duke of Alba, Governor of The Netherlands – Coligny planned to lead a campaign to free the Dutch from Spanish control; and Catherine de Medici herself who was becoming increasingly worried at the influence Coligny had over her son, fearing he would lead her son into war with Spain.

The attempted assassination of Coligny triggered a crisis. Aware of the danger of reprisals from the Protestants, the King and his court visited the wounded Coligny and promised to seek out and punish those responsible for his attempted murder.

On the evening of 23 August, Catherine went to discuss the crisis with the King. Although records of the meeting do not survive, it is believed that Catherine convinced her son that the Huguenots were on the brink of rebellion and Charles took the decision to eliminate the Protestant leaders. Shortly after the meeting between Catherine and the King, the municipal authorities of Paris were summoned, ordered to shut the city gates and to arm the Catholic citizens of the city in order to prevent any attempt at a Protestant uprising.

A list of those to be assassinated was drawn up. Top of the list was Coligny, who was brutally beaten and thrown out of his bedroom window just before dawn on 24 August.

Once the killing started, mobs of Catholic Parisians, apparently overcome with bloodlust, began a general massacre of Huguenots. Charles issued a royal order on 25 August to halt the killing, but his pleas went unheeded as the massacres spread.

The mass slaughters continued well into October, reaching the provinces of Rouen, Lyon, Bourdeaux, and Orleans. An estimated 3,000 French Protestants were killed in Paris, and as many as 70,000 across France.

THE EXECUTION OF TÚPAC AMARU

Following the execution of the last Sapa Inca Atahualpa in 1533, during the Spanish expedition led by Francisco Pizarro, a Neo-Inca State was established by the slain Inca's brother Manco Inca Yupanqui in 1537. Although the Inca Empire had been mostly conquered by the Spanish, a small independent state was founded in Vilcabamba by the Inca royal family. Though the surviving Incans originally collaborated with the conquistadors, a war continued until the final Inca leader Túpac Amaru was executed in 1572.

At first, Manco Inca Yupanqui allied the Incas to the Spanish forces but after he was mistreated, he instigated a new war against the invaders. By 1540 he had settled his followers in Vilcabamba but four years later he was killed in a Spanish onslaught. His son succeeded him but he also died in 1561 after accepting Spanish rule. When his brother died in 1571, his younger brother, Túpac Amaru, became the final Sapa Inca of the Neo-Inca State.

A new war began and the Spanish crossed into Vilcabamba on 24 June 1572 to find the city deserted and Túpac Amaru, the nephew of Atahualpa, gone, which effectively resulted in the end of the new Inca Empire. Although many of the escapees were caught, Túpac and his wife escaped but as she was heavily pregnant, their getaway was slow. Eventually, the Spanish who were led in their pursuit by Martín García Óñez de Loyola, found Túpac and his wife warming themselves at a campfire and arrested them.

Túpac was sentenced to death for the murder of Spanish priests in Vilcabamba. Though the Spanish King Philip II condemned the decision to execute Túpac, as the accused was an independent king, the sentence was carried out. On 24 September 1572, Túpac was ridden to the Cathedral of Santo Domingo in the centre of Cuzco, on a mule with a rope around his neck. As Túpac climbed a scaffold where he would be killed, many of his supporters wailed for their leader and 'deafened the skies' according to witnesses. When Túpac Amaru raised his hands to request silence he stated 'Mother Earth, witness how my enemies shed my blood.' The descendants of the Sapa Inca were expelled to other parts of the continent as the empire came to an end.

1600

KING CHARLES I IS BORN

Charles I was born in Dunfernline Palace, Fife on 19 November 1600, the second son of James VI of Scotland and Anne of Denmark. In 1603, on the death of Elizabeth I, his father also inherited the English and Irish Crown. Charles' older brother Henry died in 1612 leaving Charles as heir, and in 1625 he became the first monarch to inherit all three crowns, becoming King of England, Scotland and Ireland. Three months after his accession he married Henrietta Maria of France.

At the start of Charles' reign his friendship with George Villiers, Duke of Buckingham, was deeply unpopular. Buckingham had a lot of enemies among the nobility who were concerned that he had too much influence over the King – Buckingham was assassinated in 1628.

Charles was also directly in conflict with parliament. Firstly parliament disagreed with his military spending. In addition, many of his Protestant subjects, particularly the Puritans, were suspicious of Charles' marriage to a Catholic.

Charles dissolved parliament three times between 1625 and 1629. In 1629, he dismissed parliament and resolved to rule alone. Charles now had a problem. He was very short of money, but under the terms of the Magna Carta, taxes could not be imposed without the agreement of parliament. This didn't stop Charles, who continued taxing, revived ancient levies and also introduced new taxes, including his deeply unpopular 'Ship Money' which taxed the general public to support the Royal Navy. At the same time, religious oppression in the kingdom drove many Puritans and Catholics to emigrate to the North American colonies.

Unrest in Scotland – because Charles attempted to force a new prayer book on the country – put an end to his personal rule. He was forced to call parliament to obtain funds to fight the Scots. In November 1641, an uprising in Ireland caused further political tension. Charles attempted to have five members of parliament arrested and in 1642 Civil War began.

The Royalists were defeated in 1645–6 by a combination of parliament's alliance with the Scots and the formation of the New Model Army. In 1646, Charles surrendered to the Scots, who handed him over to parliament. He escaped to the Isle of Wight in 1647 and encouraged discontented Scots to invade. This 'Second Civil War' was over within a year with another royalist defeat by the parliamentarian General Oliver Cromwell.

Convinced that there would never be peace while the king lived, a 'rump' of radical MPs, including Cromwell, put the King on trial for treason. Charles I was found guilty and executed on 30 January 1649 outside the Banqueting House on Whitehall, London.

THE ERUPTION OF HUAYNAPUTINA

The eruption of the Volcano Huaynaputina occurred at 5pm on 19 February 1600. It was the largest recorded volcanic eruption in South American history and killed over 1,500 people when ash from the eruption buried ten nearby villages. As a result of the eruption, the Northern Hemisphere experienced its coldest year for six centuries in 1601 which caused a famine in Russia.

The volcano is in the Andes mountain range, lying in Peru at an elevation of 4,850m. It is a Stratovolcano, making it the same type as other devastating volcanoes such as Vesuvius and Krakatoa. The name Huaynaputina means 'Young Volcano' and not much is known of the volcanic activity before the Spanish colonisation of the continent began in the 16th century. It is believed that the local people made ritual human sacrifices to the volcano and when a booming noise was reported to be emanating from Huaynaputina a few days before the major eruption, natives prepared human and animal sacrifices to appease its anger but ash and gas were spewed from its crater during the ceremony.

The main eruption on 19 February 1600 sent ash into the air and loud explosions were heard, while lava poured down the mountain towards the villages. The eruptions continued for almost a month and when it exploded, devastation was caused by the volcanic mudflows and thick ash which devoured nearby villages. Recovery from the eruption in terms of agriculture and the human population took almost two centuries.

THE EAST INDIA COMPANY IS ESTABLISHED

Soon after the Spanish Armada was defeated in 1588, a group of London merchants presented a petition to Queen Elizabeth I seeking permission to sail to the Indian Ocean. Permission was granted and on 10 April 1591, on one of the earliest English overseas expeditions to India, three ships sailed from Torbay around the Cape of Good Hope to the Arabian Sea. One ship, *Edward Bonventure*, then sailed on to the Malay Peninsula and subsequently returned to England in 1594.

On 22 September 1599, another group of merchants met with the intention of sailing to the West Indies and on 31 December 1600, the Queen granted a Royal Charter to George, Earl of Cumberland, and 215 Knights, Aldermen and Freemen. The Company named on the Charter was the 'Company of Merchants of London trading with the East Indies'. The charter granted the company a 15-year monopoly on all English trade with the East – all countries 'east of the Cape of Good Hope and west of the Straits of Magellan'.

On 13 February 1601, four ships commanded by Sir James Lancaster set sail on the first East India Company voyage; destined for the pepper producing islands of Sumatra and Java.

Initially, the company struggled in the spice trade because of the competition from the already well-established Dutch East India Company. On the first voyage of 1601 the company opened a factory in Bantam and imports of pepper from Java were an important part of the East India Company's trade for twenty years. The factory in Bantam remained open until 1683.

The East India Company eventually expanded to account for half of the world's trade, particularly in basic commodities including cotton, indigo dye, salt, saltpetre (used to make gunpowder), silk and tea. The company also established the early beginnings of the British Empire in India.

1603

SIR WALTER RALEIGH IS TRIED FOR TREASON

Sir Walter Raleigh was an English explorer, writer, soldier and favourite courtier of Queen Elizabeth I. However, in July 1603, only a few months after her death, he was arrested and charged with treason for involvement in the main plot against Elizabeth's successor, King James I. Although Raleigh was found guilty, the king spared his life, and he remained imprisoned in the Tower of London until he was pardoned in 1616.

Raleigh was born around 1552 and grew up in a Protestant family in Dorset. He fought in the service of Elizabeth in Ireland, and was appointed captain of the Queen's Guard in 1586. However, he lost royal favour after secretly marrying Elizabeth Throckmorton, one of the Queen's ladies-in-waiting, and they were both imprisoned in the Tower in June 1592. After his release, he launched his first expedition to Venezuela and Guyana in search of gold. Although the expedition failed to locate any mines, he was able to regain favour with Elizabeth through his later involvement in the Capture of Cadiz in 1596, and his command as Rear Admiral on a naval campaign to the Azores in 1597. After Raleigh's release from prison in 1616, he was granted royal permission to mount a second expedition to Venezuela to hunt for 'El Dorado', the legendary city of gold. During the expedition, a detachment of Raleigh's soldiers, under the command of his friend Lawrence Keymis, attacked and pillaged a Spanish outpost, violating English peace treaties with Spain. As a result, Raleigh's death sentence was reinstated when he returned to England, and he was beheaded at Westminster Palace in 1618.

THE REIGN OF KING JAMES I BEGINS

On 25 July James VI of Scotland, aged 37, was crowned James I of England at Westminster Abbey; thereby conjoining the Scottish and English Crowns.

Born on 19 June 1566 at Edinburgh Castle in Scotland to Mary, Queen of Scots and her second husband Henry Stewart, Lord Darnley, he was descended through the Scottish kings from Robert the Bruce and was the great-grandson of Margaret Tudor, sister of Henry VIII.

James's father, Lord Darnley, was found murdered just eight months after James was born. His mother then married James Hepburn, Earl of Bothwell, a union which was deeply unpopular and alienated her subjects and advisers who forced her to renounce the Scottish throne in favour of her infant son. James became King James VI of Scotland aged just 13 months in July 1567 and was crowned at Stirling.

Mary fled to England but as she was a Catholic she was seen as a threat to her Protestant cousin Elizabeth I and was imprisoned for 19 years before being executed for treason after being linked to various Catholic plots against Elizabeth.

James was well educated – fluent in Latin and French and competent in Italian. In 1589 he was married to Anne, daughter of Frederick II of Denmark and Norway and by the time he ascended the throne as James I he had three children who had survived infancy: Henry (later Prince of Wales), Elizabeth (later wife of Frederick V, Elector Palatine) and Charles (Charles I).

James I succeeded the last Tudor monarch Elizabeth I on her death in 1603. Elizabeth had died unmarried and childless and James was her nearest blood relative and the first monarch of the House of Stuart. James reigned for 22 years as James I and was succeeded by his second son, Charles in 1625.

1605

MIGUEL DE CERVANTES' *DON QUIXOTE* IS PUBLISHED

Miguel de Cervantes was born on 29 September 1547 near Madrid in Spain and was a soldier, tax collector and purchasing agent before writing one of the most celebrated works of fiction in history, *Don Quixote*, cited as the first modern European novel. Fully titled *The Ingenious Gentleman Don Quixote of La Mancha*, it was originally published in two volumes, firstly in 1605 and then 1615 and is regularly discussed as one of the most prominent novels of the Spanish Golden Age.

To just list Cervantes career prior to the publication of *Don Quixote* would be a disservice to his intriguing life. In 1569 he had moved to Rome and was employed as a cardinal's chamber assistant before he joined the army to fight against the Ottoman Empire for control of the Mediterranean. However, in 1575 he was taken prisoner by Ottoman pirates and held in captivity for five years. He returned home when his family paid a ransom for his release. Cervantes then worked as a purchasing agent for the Spanish Armada – a fleet of 130 ships which sailed for England in 1588 in the hope of dethroning Queen Elizabeth I. Following this he became a tax collector for the government but irregularities in Cervantes' accounts saw him thrown in jail in Seville for three years, where he had the idea for *Don Quixote*.

The 1605 novel follows the journeys of a nobleman named Alonso Quixano who loses his sanity and departs to revive chivalry, alongside a farmer called Sancho Panza. The novel proved to be so popular that an unknown writer named Alonso Fernandez de Avellaneda published an unauthorised second part. As he had previously promised an official continuation to his successful novel, Cervantes published a second part in 1615. In the first part of the book, the central character fails to see the world in reality and some of the scenes of his adventures such as an attack on a flock of sheep and the protagonist fighting windmills that he imagines are giants are celebrated slices of literature.

While it was believed Cervantes died on 23 April 1616, the same day as William Shakespeare, he had actually died the previous day, as a result of diabetes. On 17 March 2015, researchers who were looking for the lost bones of Cervantes believed they had discovered the author's remains at the Covenant of the Barefoot Trinitarians.

THE GUNPOWDER PLOT

The Gunpowder Plot was the failed attempt of a group of English Catholics to blow up the Houses of Parliament and kill the Protestant King James I.

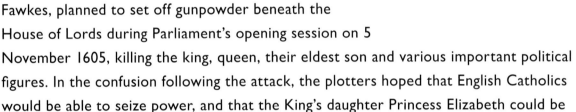

The plotters, led by Robert Catesby, were angered by the king's persecution of Roman Catholics in England. The country had endured several decades of religious turmoil, with Henry VIII setting up the Church of England, Mary I reverting to Catholicism, and Elizabeth I finally restoring Protestantism. Catesby, together with fellow conspirators Thomas Wintour, Thomas Percy, John Wright and Guy Fawkes, planned to set off gunpowder beneath the House of Lords during Parliament's opening session on 5 November 1605, killing the king, queen, their eldest son and various important political figures. In the confusion following the attack, the plotters hoped that English Catholics would be able to seize power, and that the King's daughter Princess Elizabeth could be married to a Catholic monarch.

They rented a cellar under Parliament and filled it with around 36 barrels of gunpowder. The plan was for Fawkes to light the fuse and escape across the Thames. However, the plot was discovered when an anonymous letter was sent to the MP Lord Monteagle, warning him to stay away from the opening of Parliament – probably from Monteagle's brother-in-law, Lord Tresham, a new member of the conspiracy.

The letter was shown to the king, and on the night of 4 November 1605, a royal search party discovered Fawkes in the cellar with matches in his pockets, and the gunpowder barrels hidden under piles of wood and coal. He was tortured and forced to reveal the names of the other conspirators, and they were all arrested.

1606

AUSTRALIA IS FIRST SIGHTED BY WILLEM JANSZOON

Willem Janszoon was a Dutch navigator who was born in 1570. Little is known about his early life but later he served as a governor in the Dutch East Indies and was an admiral in the Dutch defence fleet. His greatest achievement was as the captain of the *Duykfen*, the first European ship to reach Australia.

In Janszoon's early career at sea, he was a mate on board the *Hollandia* in the service of the Oude Compagnie, a predecessor of the Dutch East India Company. In 1598, he was a crew member of the second fleet sent by the Dutch to the Dutch East Indies (present day Indonesia) and he returned to the region again in 1601. Janszoon sailed back to the Dutch East Indies for a third time on 18 December 1603 as captain of the *Duyfken* (which means 'Little Dove'), but when the other ships of the fleet left the island of Java, Janszoon was sent to search the undiscovered world for new trade and economic prospects.

On 18 November 1605, the *Little Dove* set sail from the Java town of Banten and on 26 February 1606 the ship made landfall at the Pennefather River on the shore of Cape York, Queensland in Australia. Janszoon called the Pennefather the 'River with the Bush' and believed the new land he had found to be a southern extension of New Guinea. With his crew, he charted 220 miles of coastline and journeyed south to Cape Keerweer before encountering Indigenous Australians. According to an account from the time, the two parties were respectful of each other at first and the Dutch presented gifts of tobacco and soap but allegedly when the local women were taken and the Dutch made the Indigenous Australians do their hunting, violence broke out and the Dutch retreated home.

In Janszoon's later life he served as the Governor of Banda in the Dutch East Indies from 1623 to 1627 and was believed to have died in 1630. As for the *Duyfken*, it was damaged beyond repair after battling three Spanish ships. Captain James Cook would reach the eastern coastline of Australia in 1770 but it was Janszoon who made history as the first European to see Australia.

THE GUNPOWDER PLOT TRIAL BEGINS

After the Gunpowder Plot was discovered and Guy Fawkes was arrested, he was forced to confess, along with his fellow conspirators Thomas Wintour and Thomas Bates. The trails began on 26 January 1606, and the seven prisoners – who also included Everard Digby, John Grant and Ambrose Rookwood – were taken from the Tower of London to the Court of the Star Chamber. The King and his family were among those who watched the trial, which began with a speech by Sir Edward Philips, who described the wickedness of the plot in great detail.

The Attorney-General Sir Edward Coke then spoke, placing heavy blame for the plot on three Jesuit priests, Fathers Garnet, Tesimond and Gerard. Coke condemned each of the plotters to death, before their confessions were read out. Although Fawkes pleaded not guilty, while Bates and Wintour begged for mercy, the jury declared the seven conspirators guilty of high treason.

GUY FAWKES IS EXECUTED

On 30 January 1606, Everard Digby, Robert Wintour, John Grant and Thomas Bates were dragged through the streets of London to St Paul's Churchyard before being hung, drawn and quartered. The following day, Guy Fawkes, together with Thomas Wintour, Ambrose Rookwood and Robert Keyes was executed in the Old Palace Yard at Westminster directly opposite the Houses the Parliament, the building they had planned to blow up.

The plot increased Protestant suspicions of English Catholics, and those who refused to attend Anglican services were fined and punished. After the executions, Parliament declared 5 November, the day the conspirators had chosen for their plot, as an annual day of public thanksgiving. Known as Guy Fawkes Day, it is still celebrated with fireworks and bonfires, and straw 'guys' – figures meant to represent Fawkes – are often burnt.

1613

LONDON'S GLOBE THEATRE IS DESTROYED

On 29 June 1613, the Globe Theatre caught fire during a performance of William Shakespeare's play *Henry VIII*. A theatrical cannon, set off during the play, accidentally set fire to the wooden beams and straw thatch. A contemporary description of the event claims that although the theatre was destroyed, no one was hurt except a man whose burning breeches were put out with a bottle of ale.

The Globe Theatre was built in 1599 by Shakespeare's acting company, the Lord Chamberlain's Men, in Southwark, on the south side of the River Thames. When the lease of their previous playhouse, The Theatre, expired, they dismantled it and used the beams to make the skeleton of The Globe. Evidence suggests that it was a circular, three storey open-air structure with covered balconies, which could fit an audience of about 3,000 – including 2,000 'groundlings' who could stand in the 'pit' around the central stage. It was the first theatre to be built for and fully financed by a single acting company. Owned by Shakespeare and four other actors, The Globe quickly became a success, and many of the playwright's works were first performed there, including *Hamlet* (1600–2), *Twelfth Night* (1602), and *King Lear* (c.1606).

The company was able to expand in 1608 and begin using the smaller indoor Blackfriars Theatre in the winter, keeping the Globe for summer performances. After it burned down in 1613, it was rebuilt the following year more splendidly than before. The Globe was finally pulled down in 1644, two years after the Puritans closed all London theatres. Three-and-a-half centuries later, American actor Sam Wanamaker financed a modern reconstruction of the playhouse, which opened 230m from the original site in 1997.

THE ROMANOV DYNASTY BEGINS IN RUSSIA

The Romanov dynasty officially began when sixteen-year-old Mikhail Romanov was elected the Tsar of Russia in 1613. When he learned that he was about to become the new ruler, he burst into tears, terrified at the responsibility. He faced many challenges, since there had been fifteen years of chaos and disorder after the death of the previous ruler, Fyodor I, the last tsar of the Rurik dynasty. However, his mother persuaded him to accept the throne, and he was crowned on 22 July.

Mikhail devoted his reign to making reforms and getting rid of invaders from Sweden and Poland. He was a popular ruler who improved links with other countries, increased Russian prosperity, raised living standards for ordinary people, and made Moscow a beautiful and powerful city.

He died in July 1645, and was succeeded by his son Aleksey, a religious and gentle ruler who managed to reunite Russia and Ukraine in 1645. After him came his son Fyodor, and then Peter the Great in 1725, a man who is often remembered as the country's most iconic ruler. Peter introduced many modernising reforms, and created a new city on the banks of the River Neva – Saint Petersburg, which became a centre of art, culture and trade. Russia was proclaimed an Empire in 1721, so Peter died as an Emperor. His wife then became ruler, followed by his grandson and a chain of less successful rulers.

In 1726, a new Empress called Catherine the Great came to the throne. She was highly educated and tried to decrease the power of the nobles in Russia, while expanding the borders of the country to include Crimea, Belarus and Lithuania. Her son Pavel became the next Tsar until he was assassinated, followed by Pavel's liberal and popular son Alexander I. The last ruler of the Romanov dynasty was Tsar Nicholas II, who came to the throne in 1894, and was executed along with his family in 1917, during the Russian Revolution.

POCAHONTAS CHANGES HER NAME TO REBECCA

Pocahontas was born around 1596, the daughter of the Powhatan Chief in what is now Virginia, USA. At the time Powhatan Native Americans numbered around 25,000 and included more than 30 Algonquian speaking tribes.

The English arrived and settled Jamestown in May 1607 when Pocahontas was about 11-years-old. Later in 1607 Captain John Smith was captured by Chief Powhatan's brother. Smith's account states that he was brought in front of Chief Powhatan, where his head was placed on two large stones and a warrior raised a club to smash in his brains. Before this could happen, Pocahontas rushed in and placed her head upon his, stopping the execution.

Whether this event actually happened or not is uncertain, but afterwards Smith was allowed to return to Jamestown and gifts of food were sent from the Powhatan to the starving English.

By the winter of 1608–9, the English visited various Powhatan tribes to trade for more corn, only to find a severe drought had drastically reduced the tribes' harvests and Chief Powhatan had decided to stop trading with the settlers who were demanding more food than his people had to spare.

In 1609 Chief Powhatan, tired of the constant English demand for food, moved his capital further inland and in the autumn Smith left Virginia due to a severe gunpowder wound.

In 1613 Captain Argyle discovered Pocahontas was living with the Patawomeck tribe and on 4 June he kidnapped Pocahontas in order to trade her for the return of English weapons and prisoners from the Powhatan.

During her captivity she was converted to Christianity and later in 1613 Pocahontas was baptised 'Rebecca'. In April 1614 she married John Rolfe becoming Lady Rebecca Rolfe. She gave birth to a son, Thomas. This marriage created the 'Peace of Pocahontas'; six years of peace between the Jamestown colonists and Powhatan's tribes.

The Virginia Company of London, who had funded the settling of Jamestown, paid for the Rolfe family to tour England to raise interest in their company. The Rolfes arrived in England on 3 June 1616 and visited many important people, including King James and Queen Anne.

In March 1617 the family began their return journey home to Virginia, but Pocahontas was taken seriously ill as the ship sailed down the Thames. She was taken ashore at Gravesend where she died at the age of 21 and was buried at St George's Church on 21 March 1617.

1620

CORNELIS DREBBEL BUILDS THE FIRST SUBMARINE

Submarines are considered a modern means of transportation, but in 1620 Cornelis Drebbel designed the first acknowledged 'submarine'. Drebbel was born in 1572 in the city of Alkmaar in the Netherlands and was apprenticed to an engraver, painter and alchemist named Hendrick Goltzius. While working for Goltzius, he not only became fascinated by inventions but he also married his master's younger sister, Sophia, with whom he had six children. As Drebbel's fame grew through his inventions, King James I of England – who was assembling a collection of inventors, explorers and thinkers to his royal court – invited Drebbel to England.

At King James I's court, Drebbel demonstrated a perpetual motion machine which was able to tell the time, date and the season. The invention enhanced the Dutchman's fame further and the Holy Roman Emperor, Rudolf II, invited him to Prague in 1610 but when the ruler was overthrown by his brother Matthias, Drebbel was arrested. Although he was freed and returned to England, he was once again imprisoned in Prague in 1619 before heading back to England once more.

Around this time, Drebbel began work on his most famous invention – the submarine. Drebbel's design was of a rowing boat with raised sides meeting at the top and was covered in greased leather. In the middle of the boat was a watertight cavity, a rudder and four oars. The submarine was sunk by filling pig bladders stored under the seat with water which was drawn in from pipes connected to the outside. To surface the vessel, the pig bladders were squashed flat to release the water and the skins were then tied with rope. Drebbel built two further designs which were both bigger than his first prototype with the final submarine having six oars and the capacity to transport 16 people.

This submarine was demonstrated on the Thames in front of King James and thousands of spectators. It was even alleged that the king was a passenger in the vessel, making him the first monarch to travel underwater. History has claimed that the submarine had the ability to stay submerged for up to three hours and could sink to four metres deep. However, it is now believed that the submarine was only partially submerged and it mostly relied on the current for its journey from Westminster to Greenwich.

After Charles I became king, Drebbel found employment in the Office of Ordnance, designing secret weapons for use by the royal household, including a floating bomb, which proved unsuccessful. He died on 7 November 1633, after falling into poverty and managing an ale house in London.

THE *MAYFLOWER* ARRIVES AT CAPE COD

In September 1620, 102 passengers on board a merchant ship called the *Mayflower*, departed Plymouth, England to begin a new life in North America. Originally, the ship was destined for Virginia but after storms forced the *Mayflower* off course, it landed at Cape Cod in Massachusetts and the first permanent European community in New England was founded.

The new colonists, who had been authorised to establish the new settlement by the King James I, were comprised of religious dissidents and entrepreneurs and were collectively known as the Pilgrims. Thirty-five of the Pilgrims had travelled to America to escape the dominion of the Church of England. As members of the English Separatist Church, they had previously absconded to the Netherlands where they hoped to freely practice their religion but having found little economic prospects and having heard of an English colony being established at Jamestown, Virginia, they were persuaded by their leader William Bradford to sail there.

Alongside 70 entrepreneurs, known to the Separatists as 'Strangers', recruited to ensure the new colony's success, the Separatists left Plymouth but the Atlantic crossing proved a struggle and the 180 ton, steered by its captain Christopher Jones, was taken 500 miles off course. When they saw land, the settlers composed and signed the 'Mayflower Compact' which fundamentally established a constitutional law with the rule of democracy, which is often cited as a pioneer of American democracy. On 21 November 1620, the *Mayflower* landed at Cape Cod.

The ship anchored and while a band of men embarked to find a suitable area to establish the new colony, a woman named Susanna White gave birth on board the *Mayflower* to a son, Peregrine, who became the first Englishman born in New England. When a suitable location was found, the settlers went ashore and named the new site Plymouth.

Within the first year, half the Pilgrims perished from disease but as the health of the survivors improved, William Bradford, who had taken the role of governor, invited the indigenous Indians to celebrate the harvest, which became the first thanksgiving and soon peace was agreed with many local tribes as the community began to flourish in the New World.

1629

THE SHIPWRECK AND MUTINY OF THE *BATAVIA*

On her maiden voyage, the 650-ton ship of the Dutch East India Company, *Batavia*, was shipwrecked when it struck Morning Reef off the coast of Western Australia. Although 40 people drowned, the majority of the 341 crew and passengers who had departed from Texel in the Netherlands, survived the shipwreck. The mutiny and subsequent murders made it one of the most infamous shipwrecks in history.

The *Batavia* had set sail for the Dutch East Indies on 27 October 1628 to collect spices from the region. On board were skipper Ariaen Jacobsz and a bankrupt pharmacist named Jeronimus Cornelisz who was fleeing from the Netherlands. The commander of the voyage was Francisco Pelsaert who had served with Jacobsz before and the pair were believed to dislike each other. During the maiden voyage, the skipper and the merchant, Cornelisz, planned to take over the ship and steer it to a new destination. After recruiting some crew for their cause, Jacobsz steered the ship off course after leaving Cape Town and an act took place to turn the crew against Pelsaert. However, before the mutiny was completed, the ship sank on 4 June 1629.

When no food or water was found on the islands, Pelsaert led a group which included his skipper, some officers and passengers who departed from the wreck to search for help and resources. The crew reached the city of Batavia, now known as Jakarta, after a 33 day voyage in a 9m longboat. Upon their arrival, the boatswain Jan Evertsz, was arrested and executed for negligence, for the sinking of the *Batavia*, and Jacobsz was arrested. When Pelsaert was sent by the governor to rescue the survivors and collect the treasure from the wreck he arrived to discover a devastating mutiny had occurred.

At the wreck site, the merchant Cornelisz had been left in charge of the survivors but fearing that Pelsaert would report his role in the attempted mutiny, he devised a plan to hijack a passing ship and escape to a new country, financed by the gold and silver salvaged from the wreck. After sending a group of soldiers to an island to signal ships, where he hoped they would die, he began to arrange the deaths of other survivors, and at least 110 were killed by his followers who began murdering out of boredom. However, the abanoned soldiers on the island had survived and when Pelsaert's rescue ship arrived, they reached him first to inform him of the atrocities of Cornelisz.

Trials took place on the islands, and the mutineers were executed. Cornelisz had his hands chopped off and was hanged. Jacobsz was tortured but due to a lack of evidence surrounding his role in the mutiny he was spared his life and he died in prison in Batavia. Within the year, Pelsaert, who was found partially responsible for the disaster, died in poverty. Only 68 of the 341 people who had departed from the Netherlands ever made it to Batavia.

CHRISTIAAN HUYGENS AND THE PENDULUM CLOCK

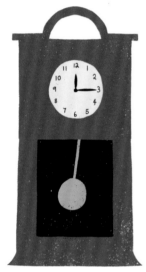

Born in The Hague on 14 April 1629, Christiaan Huygens was a Dutch mathematician, scientist and astronomer who discovered Titan – the largest moon of Saturn, developed the understanding of Saturn's rings and invented the pendulum clock.

Huygens was a keen mathematician and studied the subject along with law at Leiden University. In 1656 he invented the pendulum clock, which he patented the following year. He had developed his idea from the designs of Galileo Galilei, who had conceived the idea of a pendulum clock by the method of isochronism, whereby the swing of each pendulum would be the same for various swing sizes. Huygens built the pendulum but employed a clockmaker named Salomon Coster to design the clock itself.

As an astronomer, Huygens was the first person to propose that Saturn was encircled by a thin, flat ring. He was able to make the observation using a telescope which he had designed himself. Galileo had observed the rings of Saturn at the beginning of the 17th century but his telescope had been too weak to correctly understand what the rings were. On 25 March 1655, Huygens additionally discovered Titan, which is the biggest moon of Saturn. Again, Huygens had been inspired to search for the planet's satellites by Galileo's discovery of the four largest moons of Jupiter in 1610.

Huygens had proposed his own theory of gravity and on a visit to London in 1689 he presented his ideas before the Royal Society and met Isaac Newton. He died on 8 July 1695 after suffering ill health and loneliness.

1630

KING CHARLES II

Charles II was born on 29 May, 1630, in St. James's Palace, London. The English Civil War broke out between Parliament and the monarchy in 1642, ending with the execution of Charles I in January 1649. While England became a Commonwealth led by Oliver Cromwell, the younger Charles had already fled into exile in France, and then The Hague.

After a failed invasion of Scotland authorised by Charles and led by General Montrose, Charles agreed to a treaty with the Scots Parliament approving Presbyterian Church governance, which he formally agreed to upon arrival in Scotland in June 1650. He led a force into England but was quickly defeated by Cromwell's army at the Battle of Worcester in 1651. Forced to flee a second time, he narrowly escaped by hiding in an oak tree at Boscobel House, and spent almost a decade in exile on the continent.

When the English republican government collapsed after Cromwell's death in 1658, Charles was invited back to England, where he arrived in May 1660 to reclaim the throne. Although the men who had signed Charles I's death warrant were punished with execution or imprisonment, many others were pardoned. Charles's reign saw the Great Plague of 1665, the Great Fire of London in 1666, and the second Anglo-Dutch war, which ended with negotiations in 1667. In 1670, Charles signed a secret treaty with France, declaring himself Catholic and allying himself with the French against Dutch forces, in return for financial aid. Although Charles attempted to suspend laws that punished Catholics, he was forced to back down by Parliament in 1673.

Charles had numerous children with several mistresses, including Lady Castlemain and Nell Gwyn, but none with his wife, Catherine of Braganza. This left his Catholic brother James as heir to the Throne, a cause of much opposition in Parliament. Due to ongoing conflict, Charles dissolved Parliament in 1681, and ruled without it until his death in 1685.

DUTCH BRAZIL IS ESTABLISHED

In 1566, the Spanish Empire ruled the Low Countries, consisting mainly of the Netherlands and Belgium but a revolt, led by William of Orange and supported by Elizabeth I of England, which became known as the Eighty Years' War, resulted in the creation of a Dutch Republic in 1581 with the Netherlands freed from Spanish rule. By the end of the century, the Dutch colonisation of the Americas had begun, and by 1630 Dutch Brazil, also known as New Holland, was established.

The Spanish and Portuguese empires had already begun colonising the new world and the Dutch, who would become a prominent seafaring nation, wished to take advantage of the opportunities in the Americas. The Dutch Republic was given permission by the Spanish king to sail to Brazil in a fleet of 20 ships once a year. In 1609 a truce between the two countries was agreed, allowing the Dutch to trade with the Portuguese who occupied Brazil. The Dutch created the West India Company in 1621 to trade in the area, including control over the Atlantic slave trade and by 1624, at war with Portugal, the Dutch invaded Brazil.

By 16 February 1630, Dutch Brazil was established, with the Dutch obtaining Pernambuco, famed for its sugarcane. It established its capital at Mauritsstad, which is in modern-day Recife and created a major city at Natal, which was known as New Amsterdam before it was later established in New York. The Dutch West India Company established its headquarters in Recife and by 1634 the new explorers controlled much of the Brazilian coastline.

The Second Battle of Guararapes took place in 1649 with the Portuguese defeating the Dutch and ending the Dutch occupation of Brazil. Five years later, the Dutch surrendered the territory but it wasn't until 6 August 1661 that New Holland was conceded to Portugal in the Treaty of The Hague. Although Dutch Brazil only effectively lasted for 24 years, it was an important part of Brazil's struggle against further occupation.

1642

GALILEO GALILEI, THE 'FATHER OF SCIENCE'

Celebrated as the 'Father of Modern Science' and 'Father of Physics' Galileo Galilei was an astronomer and philosopher whose astronomical discoveries and support of Nicolaus Copernicus' theory of a heliocentric universe – that the Sun and not the Earth was at the centre of the Solar System – saw him declared a heretic. Considered a hero for his dedication to the research and teaching of science, Galileo has become one of the most distinguished individuals in world history.

Galileo was born on 15 February 1564 near Pisa, Italy. He began to study medicine at the University of Pisa but after realising his strengths and interests lay in other fields, he commenced the study of mathematics and philosophy. He moved to Padua where he was employed as the university's professor of mathematics until 1610. During this period, Galileo began experimenting with laws of motion and mechanics, conducting tests on pendulums and the speed of falling objects. His work with pendulums and astronomy would inspire the Dutch inventor Christiaan Huygens.

In 1609, Galileo heard of a new invention, the telescope, devised by Hans Lippershey. Galileo was fascinated by the idea and designed his own model, having never seen an existing creation. His telescope was much better than any in existence and Galileo turned his attention to the night sky. He began to make several amazing astronomical discoveries including mountains and valleys on the Moon, Sun spots, the phases of Venus and the four largest moons of Jupiter, which were named the Galilean moons in his honour. One of the moons, Ganymede, was discovered to be the largest moon in the Solar System.

However, the Catholic Church was unhappy at his support and public teachings of Copernicus, which disagreed with their beliefs. In 1616, the Church banned Galileo from teaching the Copernican theory. In 1632 he was accused of heresy when his book *Dialogue Concerning the Two Chief World Systems*, which recreated a debate about the Copernican theory between two men, was published. He was summoned before the Inquisition in Rome and was sentenced to life imprisonment.

This punishment was reduced to house arrest and Galileo was forced to spend the last years of his life at his home in Arcetri, in addition, he was commanded to retract his support of Copernicus. Although he began to lose his sight, he wrote another book, *Discourses Concerning Two New Sciences*, regarding the laws of motion and mechanics. On 8 January 1642, he died at his home.

THE FIRST ENGLISH CIVIL WAR BEGINS

The First English Civil War, which began on 22 August 1642, arguably stemmed from the death of Queen Elizabeth I in 1603 and the ascension of her cousin, King James VI of Scotland to the English and Irish thrones as James I. The first time a monarch had ruled over all three kingdoms. Although he reigned over a vast kingdom, his position was dangerous as each land favoured a different religion, with different histories and cultures. The Gunpowder Plot of 1605 by Catholic conspirators against the king and parliament was a precursor to the religious anxiety that would erupt during the rule of King Charles I and eventually lead to the civil war and his execution.

Charles was 24 when he succeeded his father James as king and continued the country's fight in the Thirty Years' War against Catholic powers, but withdrew from the war in 1630. To begin with, the new king was perhaps a meticulous monarch who had principles but soon there were rumblings that Charles was politically inept and also stubborn. On 10 March 1629, the king made himself unpopular with his subjects when he dissolved parliament to begin an era known as the 'Personal Rule'. Eight days earlier, members of parliament (MP) had passed three resolutions criticising the king's financial and religious policies. In the 17th century, England was mostly a Protestant country while the Scots were predominantly Calvinists and the Irish followers of Catholicism. When Charles ordered a new prayer book to be introduced in Scotland in July 1637, the Scots protested against the book, suspicious of a royal plot to reintroduce Catholicism. The Scots refused to accept the new prayer book and Charles summoned a new parliament, suddenly in need of finances to prepare an army to quash the Scots rebellion. The new 'Short Parliament' marked the end of 11 years of his 'Personal Rule' but it was ineffectual and was dissolved.

Following a clash with the Scottish army, Charles was humbled into agreeing a truce and summoned a 'Long Parliament'. However, the MPs used this opportunity to attack the king over his policies and as many of the parliamentarians were Protestants, or 'Puritans', they voiced anger at his religious reforms. After a rebellion in Ireland broke out whereby thousands of English and Scottish Protestants were murdered, Charles attempted to arrest five MPs who he thought were attempting to overthrow him, but they escaped.

On 22 August 1642, the First English Civil War effectively began when the king's Royalist army established themselves at Castle Hill in Nottingham. His 'Cavalier' army controlled the north and west of Britain against the Parliamentarian 'Roundhead' army who were based in the south and east. Although the king enjoyed the support of the Welsh and Cornish people, the Parliamentarian territory included London.

By mid-1643, the Royalist forces were dominant and it appeared they would soon win the war but the Parliamentarians formed an alliance with the Scots and in 1644 at the battle of Marston Moor, Charles lost stronghold of the north of Britain when his forces were defeated. Soon after, the Roundheads formed the New Model Army, a restructured force with Sir Thomas Fairfax and Oliver Cromwell as its leaders. The New Model Army defeated the Royalists at the Naseby in 1645 as Charles began to lose hope. The king surrendered to the Scots but they returned to Scotland and handed the monarch to the Parliamentarians. Although a captive, the king instigated a Second Civil War and drastic measures were conceived to have the king killed in the hope of ending the war. Charles was tried with high treason and after being found guilty, was beheaded on 30 January 1649. The Third Civil War would last until 1651, fought between the king's son, Charles II and the Parliamentarians, and it would not be until 1660 that a monarch would be restored to the throne.

1666

ISAAC NEWTON SEES AN APPLE FALL FROM A TREE

In 1665 Isaac Newton had just obtained his BA degree from Trinity College, Cambridge when the university was closed as a precaution against the Great Plague which lasted for a year – becoming the final major outbreak of the bubonic plague in England. Newton, who would become one of the greatest mathematicians and scientists in history, returned to his family home at Woolsthorpe Manor in Lincolnshire.

The famous episode in which Isaac Newton was sitting in the garden when an apple fell from a tree causing him to realise the laws of gravity was believed to have occurred in 1666. However, the legendary image of an apple actually hitting the scientist on the head is fictitious and instead Newton saw the apple land on the ground, which led him to understand that it was the Earth which drew objects towards it.

In 1726, the year before his death, Isaac Newton dined with his fellow Royal Society member, William Stukeley. In his biography of Newton, which was the first ever written of the celebrated scholar of the scientific revolution, Stukeley stated that on 15 April he and Newton had gone to the garden to drink tea under the shade of an apple tree. This setting reminded the elderly Newton of the apple incident and he informed Stukeley of the story. Newton questioned why the apple had dropped perpendicular to the Earth and not sideways or upwards? Stukeley, who would become famous for conducting some of the earliest archaeological investigation of Stonehenge, listened intently to Newton's story and his 'eureka moment' of discovering gravity.

Newton also described the story to John Conduitt, his assistant when serving as Master of the Royal Mint. Newton estimated that the same gravitational force which acted on the Moon additionally acted on other cosmological objects which he named 'universal gravitation'. His book, the *Principia*, developed the ideas of universal gravitation as well as the laws of motion.

Woolsthorpe Manor, which is now owned by the National Trust, is still said to be the home of the very same apple tree, which stands outside Newton's former bedroom window.

THE GREAT FIRE OF LONDON

The Great Fire of London started at the bakery of Thomas Farrinor on Pudding Lane near London Bridge, just after midnight on Sunday 2 September 1666. It spread to Thames Street, reaching riverfront warehouses filled with flammable materials and developing into an inferno. By the time the fire was extinguished on Wednesday 5 September, it had destroyed 13,200 houses and 87 churches, wiping out the homes of over 80 per cent of London's inhabitants inside the old Roman city walls.

In 1666, London was a sprawling medieval city with narrow streets, crowded with thatched oak houses. After a hot, dry summer, the wooden buildings burned easily, and strong winds encouraged the flames. The situation was worsened by the indecisiveness of Sir Thomas Bloodworth, the Lord Mayor of London, who failed to create firebreaks by demolishing buildings around the source of the flames, until it was too late. Firefighters were blocked by the narrow, jammed streets, as inhabitants abandoned attempts to put out the flames and rushed to save their possessions.

By dawn on Sunday, the houses on London Bridge were burning, and on Monday, many fashionable districts including the Royal Exchange were in flames. Thousands fled through the city gates, while others escaped onto the river in barges and boats. By Tuesday, the fire had spread across most of the old City, crossing the River Fleet and destroying St Paul's Cathedral. Fresh outbreaks were blamed on foreigners, prompting mob violence in the streets. The king's brother James, Duke of York, was put in charge of fighting the fire, which was contained as strong east winds died down. Finally, the Tower of London garrison used gunpowder to create firebreaks, halting the fire's spread eastward.

The diarist Samuel Pepys called the destroyed city 'the saddest sight of desolation I ever saw'. With as many as 100,000 people left homeless, and huge numbers of refugees camped outside the city, King Charles feared a full-scale rebellion. Although only a few deaths were officially documented, many more were probably trapped by the flames and died unrecorded. After the fire, the city was rebuilt along the old street plan, but with brick and stone houses and wider streets. Sir Christopher Wren built a new St Paul's Cathedral, as well as 50 new churches, and in the 1670s, a 62m column was erected near Pudding Lane to commemorate the fire's destruction.

1675

THE CONSTRUCTION OF THE ROYAL OBSERVATORY, GREENWICH

When King Charles II became King of England, Scotland and Ireland in 1660, following the restoration of the monarchy, European exploration of the world was well under way. It became clear that sailors required more accurate help with navigation, timekeeping and astronomical detail to assist them in travelling the world. In 1674 Sir Jonas Moore, who was the Surveyor-General at the Ordnance Office, convinced the king to build a new observatory in London, which would become the Royal Observatory, Greenwich.

Charles II was in favour of the idea and commissioned the new observatory to be built by Christopher Wren in 1675. Just nine years earlier, the Great Fire of London had rampaged through much of the city and the architect Christopher Wren had been tasked with rebuilding much of the city, most famously St Paul's Cathedral. Wren chose a hill in Greenwich as the site of the new observatory. The area chosen by Wren, himself former professor of astronomy at Oxford University, had experienced an illustrious history as the home of Greenwich Palace, where King Henry VIII and his daughter Queen Elizabeth I were both born. The palace was demolished in 1660 by Charles II but he agreed the area as suitable for the observatory. Charles appointed John Flamsteed as the first English Astronomer Royal on 4 March 1675. The king tasked the astronomer with 'rectifying the tables of the motions of the Heavens, and the places of the fixed stars, so as to find out the so much desired Longitude of places for Perfecting the Art of Navigation.' Flamsteed had written his first paper on astronomy by the age of 19 and by the end of his life he had classified over 3,000 stars. It was Flamsteed who laid the foundation stone of the Royal Observatory on 10 August 1675 and by 10 July 1676 the building, which became known as Flamsteed House, was completed.

Flamsteed House had been constructed at a cost of £520.45 and was the first purpose-built research facility in Britain. Sir Jonas Moore, who had persuaded the king to construct the observatory, personally provided the instruments and scientific equipment to be used by the astronomers.

On the roof of Flamsteed House, the first public time signal in Britain was installed in 1833. The time ball, which has been in operation every day since its installation, is hosted half way up a mast at 12.55 before being lifted to the top of the mast two minutes before the hour. At 13.00 the ball drops, this originally helped ship captains to check the rate of their marine clocks.

At the International Meridian Conference on 22 October 1884, Royal Observatory, Greenwich was selected as the world's Prime Meridian. The Prime Meridian is the line of longitude, defined as 0 degrees, which alongside the 180th meridian, forms a circle around the Earth. After it was chosen, countries across the world began using the Greenwich Prime Meridian as the basis for mapping and timekeeping. The Prime Meridian was marked by a brass strip in the courtyard of the observatory, which has now been replaced by a steel strip and since 1999 a green laser has been projected across London's night sky to mark the line of longitude.

On 15 February 1894, a French anarchist named Martial Bourdin detonated a chemical explosive he was carrying outside the observatory. Bourdin died 30 minutes after the explosion without explaining his motives. Police believed Bourdin had planned to flee back to France and that the bomb had gone off accidentally; the explosion is cited as the first 'international terrorist attack' in Britain.

When the Second World War broke out, the scientific functions of the observatory were moved across the country to Abinger, Bath and Bradford and since then, the observatory has been relocated several times. Royal Greenwich Observatory is now maintained as a museum only and forms part of the National Maritime Museum.

1703

THE MAN IN THE IRON MASK

The mystery of 'The Man in the Iron Mask' has sparked numerous debates for centuries, with many theories put forward leading to books, television programmes and films. Although it is still unknown who exactly the man was or why he was imprisoned for much of his life, it is a fascinating subject allowing for many intriguing stories.

It is known that the man died on 19 November 1703 and was buried under the name of Marchioly. Why he was a prisoner and who he was is uncertain but some of what is known may help in understanding the circumstances of the prisoner. He was known at the time of his arrest as Eustache Dauger and he was arrested around the year 1670 under orders of the French King Louis XIV, known as the Sun King. Dauger was in the custody of one man, Bénigne Dauvergne de Saint-Mars for the next 34 years, until the prisoner's death. It is important to understand that the 'iron mask' the prisoner wore was in fact not made of iron at all but rather a mask of black velvet cloth – no-one ever saw Dauger's face after his arrest.

In 1669 the War Secretary of the king, the Marquis de Louvois, wrote to the governor of the prison of Pignerol, Saint-Mars, to inform him that a new prisoner would be arriving. This prisoner was to be hidden away behind numerous doors and was not permitted to meet any other prisoners or speak of anything more than necessary, otherwise he would be executed. Saint Mars described Dauger as quiet and no trouble and the new prisoner did not meet any fellow prisoners who had a hope of being freed, for fear they would reveal his existence to the outside world.

On 18 September 1698, Saint-Mars became the governor of the Bastille fortress in Paris. Having taken Dauger to other prisons before this, he also transported Dauger here and placed him in a solitary cell. While there, an officer named Lieutenant du Junca recorded that the prisoner wore a mask of velvet and his face was concealed. When Dauger died on 19 November 1703 his furniture and clothes were burnt, metal from his cell was melted down and the cell itself whitewashed so as to remove all evidence of his existence.

His identity is still not known but the French historian and philosopher Voltaire, who was imprisoned in the Bastille in 1717 heard about the prisoner from other prisoners who had allegedly met the Man in the Iron Mask. Voltaire wrote that the prisoner was the older illegitimate brother of King Louis XIV while the French author Alexandre Dumas popularised the theory with his story in *The Three Musketeers*, but claimed that Dauger was in fact the identical twin of the king. That theory was made popular by a 1998 film starring Leonardo DiCaprio as Louis XIV and the prisoner.

Another theory is that the prisoner was the king's real father, which may explain why he was fond of the king despite his imprisonment. In 1890 French historian Louis Gendron discovered a message written by Louvois which refered to a prisoner identified as General Vivien de Bulonde who as a general at the Siege of Cuneo in 1691, retreated from the Austrians, leaving the king angered. Louis XIV ordered Bulonde to be imprisoned at Pignerol and locked in a cell and made to wear a mask. However, some historians claim the punishment was published in newspapers at the time and the prisoner was released shortly after.

THE GREAT STORM OF 1703

On 26 November 1603, a catastrophic week-long hurricane struck central and southern England. It was the worst storm in living memory, and English writer John Evelyn described it as 'not to be parallelled with anything happening in our age or in any history'.

In London, an estimated 2,000 chimney stacks collapsed, the lead roofing was blown off Westminster Abbey, 700 ships were driven down the Thames and Queen Anne had to shelter from disintegrating roofs in the palace cellar. Winds of up to 80mph killed 123 people and destroyed over 400 windmills, while men and animals were lifted into the air. It was reported that 4,000 oak trees were destroyed in the New Forest alone, and at Wells Palace, Bishop Richard Kidder and his wife were killed when two chimneystacks fell on them in their bed. Hundreds of people drowned in flooding at Somerset and Bristol, and at least 8,000 sailors were killed at sea. Numerous British vessels were wrecked, including 13 Royal Navy ships.

Many saw the storm as a divine punishment for the sins of the nation, and the government declared a day of fasting and repentance on 19 January 1704. The storm, unprecedented in scale and duration, was the first weather event to become a national news story, and news bulletins of casualties and damage were sold across the country.

1715

THE SUN KING DIES

When Louis XIV died at Versailles on 1 September 1715, he had ruled France for 72 years and 110 days, the longest reign of any monarch in Europe's history.

Louis, also known as the 'Sun King', was born in Saint-Germain-en-Laye on 5 September 1638. He became king at the age of four, after the death of his father Louis XIII. During his childhood, Louis's mother Queen Anne ruled as Regent of France, with Cardinal Mazarin as Chief Minister. Although Louis was declared of age in 1654, Mazarin continued to control France after helping to defeat a series of uprisings by French noblemen. In 1660, Louis married Maria Theresa, daughter of Philip IV of Spain, to secure peace between their two countries. When Mazarin died the following year, the 23-year-old king declared that he would rule without a chief minister, claiming a God-given right to rule as an absolute monarch – a king with total, dictatorial power.

Louis introduced new taxes, decreased France's debts, expanded its army and navy and secured control over its dangerous nobles. He also began building a magnificent palace at Versailles, which hosted dazzling entertainments and became the seat of government from 1682. As well as increasing trade and overseeing the building of roads, canals, ports and ships, Louis was a great patron of the arts, supporting painters, musicians and writers like Molière and Racine. During his reign, the aristocracy of Europe adopted the language of France as well as its fashions and customs. However, Louis was also a staunch Catholic, and ended religious toleration of French Protestants (Huguenots) in 1685, forcing around 200,000 to flee to England and Holland.

Louis also oversaw a period of aggressive French foreign policy, and in 1667 launched the War of Dutch Devolution, claiming a share of the Spanish Netherlands as part of his wife's inheritance. Although he was forced to retreat by William of Orange, he went on to invade the Netherlands in 1672. With the support of his cousin, English King Charles II, he took on the Dutch and their Spanish allies, emerging victorious in 1678 after the first treaty of Nijmegan. By the 1680s, France had become the most powerful country in Europe. However, the long War of the Spanish Succession (1701–14) cost Louis dearly, with defeats at the Battles of Blenheim (1704) and Ramilles (1706). Peace was eventually settled with the Treaty of Utrecht in 1713, and although France retained its territory, it was forced to give up some of its control.

The Sun King lived extravagantly and had a series of mistresses, including Louise de La Vallière and Françoise-Athénaïs, Marquise de Montespan. Although he had many illegitimate children, only one of his six children with his wife Maria Theresa (the crown prince or *dauphin*) lived to adulthood. After her death, he secretly married his new mistress Françoise d'Aubigné, in around 1683. He suffered a series of personal losses towards the end of his life, including the deaths of his son the *dauphin* and two of his grandsons. When Louis died at the age of 77, it was his five-year-old great-grandson who inherited the throne as Louis XV.

Despite his tyranny and intolerance, Louis continually pursued power and prosperity, and remains a symbol of the splendour of France.

THE FIRST JACOBITE REBELLION

In September 1715, John Erskine, the Earl of Mar raised the Jacobite standard in an attempt to restore the Catholic monarchy. The Catholic King James II had been forced into exile in 1688, and replaced by the Protestant William of Orange. James's son, James Frances Edward Stuart (later known as the 'Old Pretender') was raised Catholic in France. His supporters, known as Jacobites (from 'Jacobus', the Latin for 'James') hoped to restore him to the Throne as James III of England and VIII of Scotland.

James had tried to invade Scotland with a French fleet in 1708, but was driven away by English warships. In 1714, the German Protestant George I ascended the British throne, and James appealed to Pope Clement XI for help in a new Jacobite rising. In 1715 however, the Earl of Mar launched the rising, also known as 'the Fifteen', without James' permission. By October, he had taken control of large areas of northern Scotland, including Inverness and Aberdeen. However, he was indecisive and slow, allowing the Duke of Argyll's English army to gather its strength. After advancing towards Perth, their forces met at the Battle of Sheriffmuir in November. Here, Argyll halted the Jacobite advance, and went on to defeat Mar's army at the Battle of Preston.

James finally arrived in Scotland on 22 December, too late to save the rebellion. He was delayed by illness, and by the time he reached Perth on 9 January 1715, Argyll's men were advancing with heavy artillery and the Jacobite army had been reduced to less than 5,000 men. On 30 January, Mar retreated with his forces from Perth. James, hearing of the English advance, sailed from Monrose on 5 February and returned to France. This abandonment caused bitterness among the Scottish rebels, and many Jacobites were taken prisoner and sentenced for treason. After the death of Louis XIV, James was no longer welcome in France, and eventually moved to Rome. He set up a court in exile and lived in splendour under the protection of the Pope until his death in January 1766.

1727

GEORGE II BECOMES KING OF ENGLAND

George Augustus was born in Hanover, Germany on 10 November 1683 and grew up as heir to the electorate of Hanover. In 1705 he married Caroline of Ansbach and the pair went on to have nine children, one of whom was Frederick, Prince of Wales. Known as the 'king who wasn't there', George's reign held highs and lows.

When his father was crowned George I, King of Great Britain and Ireland in 1714, George Augustus was designated Prince of Wales. George I did not enjoy a close relationship with his son. This was to such an extent that when the king died, the young George did not travel back to Germany for his father's funeral and at this time, rather than face criticism from the public, he was praised for his dedication to England.

At the age of 43, he became King George II and was crowned at Westminster Abbey on 22 October 1727. He was the last British monarch to be born outside Great Britain and also went on to become the last British monarch to lead his army in battle, at the Battle of Dettingen in 1743. During George I's reign the control of the monarchy had gradually transferred to a more modern government, with a cabinet and this evolution continued during George II's reign. The first acknowledged prime minister, Robert Walpole, led the government during both kings' reigns and settled many matters at home and abroad in place of the royals.

During his reign, British expansion across the world increased with successful conquests in India and North America, and George II defended the monarchy from being toppled in the final Jacobite rebellion of 1746. However, he was not always a popular figure and frequent trips back to Hanover, leaving his wife to rule as regent, resulted in newspapers labelling him the 'absent king'. When his son Frederick died, George made his grandson his successor.

On 25 October 1760, George II died and George III inherited the throne.

HANDEL COMPOSES 'ZADOK THE PRIEST'

At 6am on 7 September 1992, the radio station Classic FM launched with the composition 'Zadok the Priest'. The first time the anthem had ever been heard in public was at the coronation of King George II on 11 October 1727 and it has been sung at every British coronation since. One of the most recognisable pieces of classical music, it was the first composition by George Frideric Handel as a British citizen, after King George I had naturalised the German composer.

The Organist and Composer to the Chapel Royal in 1727 was Maurice Greene but the new king overlooked him in favour of Handel, who was more famous for his opera compositions. Handel wrote four new anthems for the coronation, including 'The King Shall Rejoice', 'My Heart is Inditing' and 'Let thy Hand be Strengthened' but only 'Zadok the Priest' has endured. The text used in the anthem, which is only five lines long, describes the anointing of Solomon, used in a passage from the Kind James Bible. The words have been used in every coronation since that of King Edgar in 973 AD at Bath Abbey.

When the choir first performed 'Zadok the Priest' at George II's coronation, it was sung during the wrong part of the service, after they had forgotten to sing one of the other anthems entirely. It is believed that 47 singers and 92 instrumentalists were employed to perform the anthem.

The piece is referenced in the 'UEFA Champions League Anthem' which is played before every match in the prestigious European football tournament. It was written by the English composer Tony Britten in 1992 for the new competition and is influenced by Handel's composition.

SIR ISAAC NEWTON DIES

One of the greatest scientists in world history, Sir Isaac Newton was born on 25 December 1642 in Woolsthorpe, Lincolnshire. His father was a farmer who died just three months before Newton was born and although he was meant to follow in his father's footsteps, he instead studied at Trinity College at Cambridge University from 1661. It was during a forced hiatus from university that Newton began developing some of the most groundbreaking scientific theories in history.

When the Great Plague required Newton to return to his home of Woolsthorpe in 1665, he started to formulate his concepts of calculus, light and of course gravity, having famously witnessed an apple fall from a tree. In 1667, Newton returned to university where he was elected as a fellow and in the following year he assembled the first reflecting telescope. In London, the Royal Society requested Newton to present a demonstration of the telescope and he was subsequently elected to the Royal Society.

Newton conducted experiments which concluded that white light was a combination of all the colours in the spectrum and was composed of particles, not waves. Newton's work was criticised, especially by the Royal Society member Robert Hooke and Newton suffered a breakdown and disappeared from public life. When the astronomer Edmund Halley visited Newton, he convinced the scientist to organise his scattered notes on the paths of celestial bodies which was published as *Principia*. The book established the law of gravity and three laws of motion. Not just a scientist, Newton served as Master of the Royal Mint in 1699 and changed the pound coin from silver to gold.

Building on the work of Copernicus and Galileo, Newton established the heliocentric model of the Solar System. In 1703, Newton became president of the Royal Society, after which he published his second major book, *Opticks*, which detailed his experiments with the colour spectrum and ideas of electricity. Queen Anne knighted the scientist in 1705. Having never married, Newton lived with his niece in his later life, at Cranbury Park. He died on 20 March 1727 and was buried at Westminster Abbey.

1743

A BRITISH MONARCH LEADS THEIR TROOPS INTO BATTLE FOR THE LAST TIME

Although Britain has been at war many times since the middle of the 18th century, 27 June 1743 marked the last occasion whereby a British monarch led their troops into battle. On that day, King George II fought with his army at the Battle of Dettingen, an encounter against the French during the War of the Austrian Succession, which lasted between 1740 and 1748. George II survived the battle and so King James IV of Scotland remained as the last Great British monarch to die in battle, having been killed in the Battle of Flodden in 1513.

George II was born in Hanover and from a young age had been educated in military tactics, which encouraged him to personally engage in the 1743 battle. Dettingen, in modern-day Bavaria, Germany, was the site of the conflict where British forces fought alongside Hanoverian and Austrian forces against a French army of around 23,000 men. The war surrounded the Pragmatic Sanction of 1713 which supported Maria Theresa, the daughter of the Holy Roman Emperor, Charles VI, to become sovereign of the Habsburg monarchy. The army which Great Britain allied itself to was around 35,000-men strong and known as the Pragmatic Army, in support of Maria Theresa.

During the battle, the king's horse bolted and a British ensign at the battle, Cyrus Trapaud, stopped the horse and saved the king's life, for which he received a promotion. The battle was fought near the Main river and resulted in a victory for the Pragmatic Army after the French line collapsed. Handel composed *Dettingen Te Deum* to honour the triumph and it was performed on 27 November 1743 in London before the king whose popularity increased after leading his troops to victory.

THOMAS JEFFERSON

Regularly nominated as one of the greatest American presidents, Thomas Jefferson was the principal author of the *Declaration of Independence*, one of the Founding Fathers of the United States and the first US Secretary of State. His decree that 'all men are created equal' has been cited as perhaps the most important phrase in American history.

Born on 13 April 1743 in Shadwell, Virginia as the third of ten children, Thomas Jefferson grew up to be a rather tall and apparently 'awkward' figure but an intellectual and thoughtful gentleman. His first major political position was as the second governor of Virginia for two years before preceding Benjamin Franklin as the US Minister to France by which time he was a supporter of the French Revolution. Jefferson became the inaugural US Secretary of State in 1790. When he was encouraged to run for the presidency in 1796 he reluctantly announced his candidacy and came close to winning the election but was beaten by John Adams, and although he opposed Adams he served as his vice president from 1797 to 1801.

In 1776, Jefferson had been the key author of the *Declaration of Independence* which was adopted by the Second Continental Congress in Philadelphia. The declaration proclaimed that the 13 American colonies at war with Great Britain had independently formed the United States of America. It was signed by the 56 delegates to the congress and contained Jefferson's most famous passage 'that all men are created equal'. Although a foundation of American history and society, it attracted controversy as many of the Founding Fathers, including Jefferson, owned slaves. In fact, Jefferson owned hundreds of slaves and was alleged to have had a relationship with his slave Sally Hemmings following his wife's death and fathered six children with her. In 1807 however, during his second term as president, Jefferson signed in the Act Prohibiting Importation of Slaves which stated that no new slaves could be imported into the country from 1808. This was a big step towards illegalising the international slave trade and a turning point to banning slavery in America.

Jefferson became the third President of the United States of America in 1801 defeating John Adams and won a re-election in 1804 against Charles C. Pinckney. One of his major achievements during his presidency was the Louisiana Purchase of 1803 when the US acquired 828,000 square miles known as the Louisiana Territory from France. Jefferson organised the payment of £11,250,000 to pay for the land which included the territory of 15 modern-day states and two Canadian provinces, including Arkansas, Iowa, Oklahoma and Kansas, parts of New Mexico and Texas, and Louisiana. Napoleon had decided to sell the land as his hopes of a new empire began to fade but the purchase was originally met with disapproval as some people believed the purchase of new land to be unconstitutional.

After retiring to Monticello following his retirement and with James Madison serving as the new president, Jefferson died aged 83 on 4 July 1826. He is one of the four presidents featured on Mount Rushmore and the Jefferson Memorial in Washington, D.C. features a 5.7m statue of the former president which was built in 1943 on the 200th anniversary of his birth.

1746

BONNIE PRINCE CHARLIE AND THE JACOBITE RISING

In April 1746, Charles Edward Stuart, known as the 'Young Pretender', fled from the defeat of the Highland army by English forces at the Battle of Culloden.

The rebellion was the attempt of Charles, the grandson of the exiled Catholic King James II of England, to regain the English throne from George I. Taking advantage of the absence of English government troops, which were fighting the War of the Austrian Succession on the Continent, he sailed from France to Scotland in June 1745 and raised the Jacobite standard Glenfidden in August. Supported by members of several Highland clans, including the MacDonalds and the Camerons, Charles led an army of 3,000 men and rapidly took control of Scottish territory. They entered Perth and Edinburgh in September, and on the 21st, defeated English forces led by Lieutenant General Sir John Cope at the Battle of Prestonpans.

Charles decided to attempt an invasion of England, banking on French support. The rebels marched south, taking Carlisle and Preston in November, before entering Derby on 4 December. However, as French forces failed to appear, and Lowland Scotland failed to rise, Charles' officers voted to retreat to Scotland. They lost control of Carlisle, and after a series of smaller defeats, were outnumbered and crushed by the Duke of Cumberland's English army at the Battle of Culloden on 16 April.

The battle was over in less than an hour and between 1,500 and 2,000 Jacobites were killed, many of them slaughtered by English artillery as they waited for the command to charge. Although many Highlanders escaped the battle, they were mercilessly hunted down by government troops in the following weeks; thousands were executed or transported to the British colonies. Bonnie Prince Charlie, meanwhile, escaped back to France. Culloden was the last battle fought on British soil, and marked the failure of the last great Jacobite rising, as well as the destruction of the Highland clans and the end of an era for Scotland.

FRANCISCO GOYA

Francisco José de Goya y Lucientes was born in the village of Fuendetodos in Aragon on 30 March 1746. He later moved with his parents to Saragossa and aged 14 began studying with the painter José Luzán Martínez. Today he is regarded as the most important Spanish artist of the age. In 1763, Goya joined the Madrid studio of the painter brothers Francisco and Ramón Bayeu and married their sister Josepha in 1773.

In 1774, the German painter Anton Raphael Mengs asked Goya to work on preliminary paintings for the Royal Tapestry Factory at Santa Bárbara. Goya painted designs for 63 of the tapestries for two royal palaces, including nine hunting scenes for the dining room at one.

Following this Goya received many more commissions from the aristocracy. Aged 40 Goya was appointed painter to the Bourbon king, Charles III, and in 1789 he was promoted to court painter under the newly crowned Charles IV.

A serious illness in 1792 left Goya permanently deaf. In 1799, he completed and published a series of eighty etchings called *Los Caprichos,* which introduce a nightmarish world of witches, ghosts, and fantastic creatures. That same year, Goya was promoted to first court painter and spent the next two years working on a large-scale portrait of the family of Charles IV. Goya painted the royal family in the foreground and, in the background, himself at an easel. The style of the painting was particularly natural for the time.

The enlightened monarchy of Charles IV came to an end when Napoleon's armies invaded Spain in 1808. The Bourbon monarchy was restored with Napoleon's fall in 1814, but the new king, Ferdinand VII, son of Charles IV, did not share the enlightened views of his predecessor. At this time Goya painted two paintings commemorating Spain's uprising against the French occupation *The Second of May 1808* and *The Third of May 1808,* which both depict brutal scenes of war.

Between 1810 and 1820 Goya continued his account of the atrocities of war in a series of 85 prints called *The Disasters of War.* The series depicts the horrors witnessed during Spain's struggle for independence from France. Unlike *Los Caprichos*, this series was never published during Goya's lifetime.

During the reign of Ferdinand VII Goya received no royal commissions and became isolated from political and intellectual life in Madrid. Between 1820 and 1823, he completed a series of sinister and horrifying private works 'The Black Paintings' in fresco at his country home, Quinta del Sordo (Deaf Man's House).

Unhappy with the political situation in Spain, Goya retired to Bordeaux in 1824 where he died on 16 April 1828.

WEARING OF THE KILT IS BANNED

On 1 August 1746 the Dress Act 1746 came into force making 'the Highland Dress', including tartan or a kilt, illegal in Scotland. The only exception was for soldiers of the Black Watch regiment, whose uniform was the kilt.

Nowadays it would be easy to consider such an act laughable, but at the time it was the very serious result of a 30-year attempt by the British government to end the military threat of the Jacobite Highland clans. The Jacobite Risings between 1689 and 1746 were strongly supported by clan regiments, loyal only to their clan chiefs. At the time it was only in the Scottish Highlands that these 'private armies' or clan regiments remained. The Highland clans were regarded as ungovernable and a military threat. The different Highland clan regiments were identifiable by the tartan on their kilt and the kilt became a symbol of resistance to the British government.

The law was repealed in 1782, by which time years of enforcement of the law had ensured that kilts and tartans were no longer ordinary Highland wear, but within two years the Highland Society of Edinburgh was founded with the aim of promoting the general use of the Highland dress.

1755

MARIE ANTOINETTE IS BORN

Born in Vienna, Austria on 2 November 1755, Marie Antoinette married the future French King Louis XVI when she was just 15 years old. She came to symbolise all the evils of the monarchy, and has often been blamed for helping to provoke the French Revolution.

Marie Antoinette was the youngest daughter of Emperor Frances I, and her marriage to Louis was designed to ensure peace between the Austrian Empire and France. She arrived in France in 1770, and became Queen at the age of 19, after the death of Louis XV in 1774. She was not close to her husband, and instead enjoyed parties, gambling and fashion. She gained a reputation for extravagance, and spent much of her time at *Petit Trianon*, her own private palace in Versailles. She finally became pregnant after eight years of marriage, and a daughter was born in December 1778, followed by a son in October 1781.

Meanwhile, there were rumours of her adultery with a Swedish ambassador, and the Affair of the Diamond Necklace in 1785 – in which she was wrongly accused of selling off a valuable French jewel – damaged her reputation even further. France was suffering poor harvests and financial chaos, and her lavish spending made her unpopular with the people. This contributed to the legend – almost certainly untrue – that when she was told the people had no bread, she replied, 'Let them eat cake!'

In July 1789, a group of French workers and peasants stormed the Bastille prison, and that October, a crowd of an estimated 10,000 people gathered at Versailles, demanding the royal couple's return to Paris. The Queen sent letters to other European monarchs, begging for support, and hatched a failed plot to flee France in June 1791. The royal family was placed under arrest in August 1792, and the monarchy was abolished in September. Louis was executed that December by the new revolutionary government, and the Queen was sent to the guillotine on 16 October 1793.

A DICTIONARY OF THE ENGLISH LANGUAGE IS COMPLETED BY SAMUEL JOHNSON

Published in London in 1755, Samuel Johnson's famous dictionary took over eight years to complete and listed 40,000 words.

Although there had been previous English dictionaries, there were none which were as large, complex or impressively precise in the definition of each word. It was elegantly divided and ordered, as well as extremely thorough; the word 'turn', for example, had 16 different definitions, while 'take' was given 134. The dictionary was also the first to illustrate definitions with quotations, which were taken from the whole span of English literature. There are over 114,000 quotations in the dictionary, often from great writers including Chaucer, Milton, Shakespeare and Dryden.

The dictionary had been commissioned by a group of London booksellers, who hoped that it might help control the rapidly changing rules of the English language. Johnson was paid 1,500 guineas for his efforts, and he compiled the dictionary single-handedly – with just six helpers copying down lists of quotations. Many of his definitions revealed his own prejudices and sense of humour. One of his most famous reveals his opinion of the Scots, defining the word 'oats' as 'a grain which in England is generally given to horses, but in Scotland supports the people'.

Johnson's dictionary was recognised as a great achievement as soon as it was published. Critics were amazed that such a vast work could have been produced by a single man. Although the original dictionary was an enormous two-volume publication, a shorter single-volume version produced in 1756 was widely used all the way into the 20th century. It remained the standard dictionary until Noah Webster's in 1828, and has had a lasting influence not just on how dictionaries are written but on how English is spoken.

THE LISBON EARTHQUAKE

On the morning of 1 November 1755, a devastating earthquake hit the Portuguese capital of Lisbon, killing up to 50,000 people. Lisbon was Portugal's largest city, a wealthy port and trading hub with a population of around 300,000.

Eyewitnesses reported a series of shocks over a period of less than ten minutes, which demolished large public buildings as well as around 12,000 homes, and opened giant 5m cracks in the town centre. The disaster occurred on All Saints Day, so many of the city's population were attending religious services, and were trapped and killed as churches across the city collapsed. Eighty-five per cent of the city's buildings were destroyed, including libraries, the Opera House and the Royal Palace; centuries of art, literature and architecture were wiped out as fires spread and burned for six days following the shock. The earthquake also created a tsunami which hit the city's coastal areas around 40 minutes later, with waves that reached 6m in height. The waves also hit Cadiz in Spain at heights of 20m and travelled across the Caribbean Sea to reach Martinique.

The earthquake caused significant damage across the region, including in the Algarve and Madeira, and shocks were felt as far as Finland and North Africa. Modern seismologists agree that the quake's epicentre was located in the Atlantic, to the West of the Iberian Peninsula, and estimate that it had a magnitude in the range of 8.5 to 9.0 on the moment magnitude scale.

In the aftermath of the disaster, which many saw as a divine punishment, thousands were buried at sea, and the army pressed survivors into reconstruction work. The city was rapidly rebuilt with widened streets and large squares, to form the Lisbon we recognise today.

1759

THE GUINNESS BREWERY IS FOUNDED

On 31 December 1759 Arthur Guinness signed a 9,000-year lease on a small and dilapidated property at St James's Gate, Dublin and began to brew ale.

Born in Celbridge, County Kildare in 1725, Arthur Guinness had previously established an ale brewery in Leixlip, County Kildare in 1752 after inheriting £100 from his godfather Archbishop Price. But, at the age of 34, Arthur was looking to expand and headed to the capital.

Ten years after establishment, in May 1769, Arthur exported his beer for the first time when he shipped six-and-a-half barrels to England. By 1799 a dark beer from London called 'porter' – due to its popularity with the city's street and river porters – was also becoming increasingly popular in Dublin. Arthur decided to stop brewing ales and to concentrate on this black beer.

In 1803 Arthur died and his son, also Arthur, took over the brewery. In 1821, instructions for brewing Guinness Superior Porter were recorded – the historic beginnings of today's Guinness Original. Sea-crossings were perilous at this time, but the business expanded rapidly and by the 1860s Guinness beer was being shipped as far as New Zealand. On the death of Arthur's grandson, Sir Benjamin Guinness, in 1868, the business was worth over £1 million and the original site at St James's Gate had grown from about 1 acre to over 64 acres. In 1886, Arthur's great-grandson, Edward, sold 65 per cent of the business by public offering on the London Stock Exchange for £6 million.

THE BRITISH MUSEUM OPENS

The British Museum in London was first opened to the public on 15 January 1759, in Montagu House in Bloomsbury. It was largely based on the collection of Sir Hans Sloane, who had gathered around 71,000 objects and curiosities, including manuscripts, printed books, plant specimens, prints and drawings. When he died in 1753, he left his collection to King George II, for the nation. That year, the king agreed to an act of Parliament which established the museum, and added the libraries of Sir Robert Cotton and Sir Robert Harley, Earl of Oxford.

The British Museum was the first of its kind – a 'universal' museum which aimed to collect everything, as well as a national institution which was open to the public for free. In 1757, the king contributed the Royal Library, and from 1778 onwards, the museum gained many objects brought back from the voyages of Captain Cook and other explorers.

When Montagu House became too small, the museum's present building, designed by Sir Robert Smirke, was constructed on the same site between 1823 and 1852. In 1881, the natural history collections were transferred to the new Natural History Museum in South Kensington, and in 1973, the Museum's enormous book collection became the basis of the new British Library. The British Museum still houses some of the most famous objects in the world, including the Rosetta Stone, the Elgin Marbles from the Parthenon in Athens, Greek sculptures from the Mausoleum of Halicarnassus and the Temple of Artemis, and the treasure hoard from Sutton Hoo in Suffolk. The collection, which contains around 8 million works, tells the story of human culture and history through the ages. It is one of the largest and most popular in the world, and is still free to the public.

WILLIAM WILBERFORCE, LEADER OF THE MOVEMENT TO ABOLISH SLAVERY

William Wilberforce was an English politician and philanthropist who devoted his life to the abolition of the slave trade.

Born in Hull on 24 August 1759, he was the son of a wealthy merchant and attended St. John's College, Cambridge, where he formed a lifelong friendship with the future British Prime Minister William Pitt. He began a political career and became an MP, enjoying a lively social life including drinking and gambling. This changed in 1784, when his conversion to evangelical Christianity prompted an interest in social reform. He was strongly influenced by the abolitionist Thomas Clarkson, who was campaigning to end Britain's trading of African slaves in the West Indies.

In 1787, Wilberforce became involved in the new Society for Effecting the Abolition of the Slave Trade, and in 1789 he introduced 12 resolutions against the slave trade in the House of Commons. Despite his powerful speeches and the support of Pitt, these were not passed. Later attempts in 1791 and 1792 also failed, and the war against Napoleon slowed the campaign even further. It was not until 1807 that Wilberforce finally succeeded in passing a bill to abolish the slave trade in the British West Indies.

However, this did nothing to free people who were already enslaved, and in 1821 he began campaigning for all slaves to be freed. He became vice president of the Anti-Slavery Society, which aimed to abolish slavery throughout the British Empire, and continued to represent the cause in parliament until he retired in 1825. He was motivated by a desire to put Christian values into practice, and also worked on social reform in Britain, aiming to improve education and hygiene, as well as to prevent cruelty to animals. The Slavery Abolition Act was finally passed on 26 July 1833, and Wilberforce died three days later.

1770

CAPTAIN COOK REACHES AUSTRALIA

In 1766, the Royal Society revealed that a Transit of Venus would occur in three years' time, whereby the planet would pass in front of the Sun. However, they stated that the phenomenon would only be observable in the Southern Hemisphere and so the Royal Navy ship HMS *Endeavour* was commissioned to sail south in order that the astronomer Charles Green could watch the event, in the hope of determining longitude. This wasn't the only reason for the mission, as the British government hoped to discover the fabled south continent known as Terra Australis and James Cook was promoted to lieutenant to command the ship. It was an appointment which secured Cook's fame and shaped the course of history.

Cook was born in a village close to Middlesbrough on 27 October 1728. He enlisted in the Royal Navy in 1755 and served in North America, where he was trained in surveying and charting coastlines. At the age of 39, Cook was considered to be the perfect commander of the voyage to the Southern Hemisphere as he would be able to chart the coastline of the new territories. *Endeavour* set sail on 26 August 1768 and rounded Cape Horn before arriving at Tahiti on 13 April 1769 having sailed across the Pacific. There, Charles Green was able to observe the Transit of Venus but the surveillance was not very accurate. However, Cook continued the mission as *Endeavour* travelled to New Zealand, claiming the North and South Islands for the British Empire.

On 19 April 1770, Cook reached the east coastline of Australia, becoming the first European to view it. The west coast of Australia had previously been discovered by the Dutch explorer Willem Janszoon in 1606 but had not been colonised. Four days later, Cook saw indigenous Australians at Brush Island and on 29 April the crew landed at the Kurnell Peninsula which he named Botany Bay, after deciding against his original name of Stingray Bay. As Cook claimed the land for the British Empire, specimens were collected by the botanist Joseph Banks who later convinced the British government that Botany Bay would be an ideal location to establish a new penal colony.

Endeavour departed for home but on 11 June the ship was damaged when it hit the Great Barrier Reef, causing a delay to the journey. When he returned to England, Cook was acclaimed as a hero and would sail on two more voyages before meeting his end in Hawaii in 1779.

THE COMPOSER LUDWIG VAN BEETHOVEN IS BORN

Beethoven, one of history's most famous and influential classical music composers, was born in December 1770. Growing up in the town of Bonn, in the Holy Roman Empire (now in modern-day Germany), Beethoven was one of seven children, and his first music teacher was his father – who wanted him to be a child prodigy like Mozart. He became the town's assistant organist and wrote his first piano compositions at the age of twelve, supporting the family after his father's death by playing the viola in the court orchestra.

In 1792, Beethoven left Bonn for Vienna, where he studied with the great composer Joseph Haydn and became a well-known pianist. In 1795, he published several hugely successful piano concertos, and as the new century began, he composed piece after piece of music that proved his genius as a composer – including his famous Piano Sonata No. 14 (the 'Moonlight Sonata') in 1802, and his Symphony No. 3 (the 'Eroica Symphony') in 1804, his grandest and most original piece so far.

However, at the same time, Beethoven was gradually losing his hearing, and by the age of 44 was almost totally deaf. Despite this, he continued to compose at a furious pace, producing an opera called *Fidelio*, six symphonies, five string quartets and seven piano sonatas, amongst many other works, in the years between 1803 and 1812. He composed some of his greatest pieces at the end of his life when he was completely deaf, including his ninth and final symphony, completed in 1824. There was much that was new and revolutionary about his music, and the work's finale, the famous 'Ode to Joy', marked the first time that choral voices had been used in a major symphony.

Beethoven died on 26 March 1827. He never married or had children, but he lives on in his music, and is widely thought of as one of the greatest composers of all time.

LEXELL'S COMET BECOMES THE CLOSEST TO PASS EARTH

On 1 July 1770 a comet passed Earth at a distance of 0.015 astronomical units, the equivalent to 1.4 million miles, which became the closest comet to pass Earth in history. Known as Lexell's Comet, it still holds the record but has not been seen since 1770.

The French astronomer Charles Messier had just observed the planet Jupiter on the night of 14 June 1770 when he noticed a new comet in the constellation of Sagittarius. Messier – who discovered 13 comets over his lifetime and is regarded as a 'comet hunter' – continued to follow the course of the comet over the next few nights, although at first the path of the comet was quite faint. However, as it grew in size it was spotted by other astronomers, including in Japan.

As it became the closest comet to ever pass Earth, its tail appeared to be the length of four diameters of the Moon and the nucleus of the comet itself seemed as big as Jupiter. Messier saw Lexell's Comet, which was recorded with the name D/1770 L1, on 3 October 1770 as it moved past the Sun but it has never been seen again and is believed to be a 'lost comet'.

Interestingly, the comet wasn't named after its French discoverer but rather the Swedish astronomer Anders Johan Lexell, who computed the orbit of the comet. Lexell realised that the comet had a different orbit before it passed Jupiter in 1767 and calculated that once it passed the planet again in 1779 it would be ejected from the Inner Solar System. In addition to calculating comet's orbits for the following ten years, Lexell also computed the orbit of Uranus, proving that it was a planet and not a comet. A lunar crater on the southern part of the Moon is named in his honour.

1773

THE BOSTON TEA PARTY

On the night of 16 December 1773, a gathering of Patriots loyal to the American colonies, known as the Sons of Liberty led by Samuel Adams, boarded three ships at Griffin's Wharf in Boston: the *Beaver*, *Dartmouth* and *Eleanor*. Although it is unknown, it is estimated that around 116 men from colonial society, who wished to protest against tax levied against colonists by the British Parliament, dumped 46 tons of tea into Boston Harbour. But why did they do it and what were the consequences?

The colonies of British America were waging a war against French-held territories of North America during the Seven Years' War. American colonists of areas such as Boston, Massachusetts were angered by a new 1773 Tea Act passed by the British Parliament, which dishonoured their civil rights of 'no taxation without representation' and which they believed was using taxes to fund the war. The East India Company, which transported tea to the colonies was taxed less by the new Tea Act and so was able to sell tea for less. This affected smugglers such as Samuel Adams, who may well have used their personal interests to stir a revolt against the British.

The Sons of Liberty boarded the boats dressed as Mohawk Indians, to identify themselves as Americans and not British, and also to disguise themselves in the hope of avoiding being identified and punished. They went aboard the ships, which were actually American built and owned but carrying cargo belonging to the British East India Company and began throwing over 46 tons of tea, stored in 342 crates. The event wasn't actually known as the Boston Tea Party until around 1826 and only some of the Patriots identities are known now. George Washington, the first President of the United States, had actually condemned the conduct of the Patriots but recognised their cause and saw the event as a catalyst for revolution.

A second Boston Tea Party was carried out in 1774 and similar events were undertaken in other colonies. The British government, left furious by the destruction, responded sternly and eventually in 1775 the American War of Independence began.

CAPTAIN COOK BECOMES THE FIRST EUROPEAN TO CROSS THE ANTARCTIC CIRCLE

Although Captain James Cook had become the first European to discover the east coast of Australia in 1770, he embarked on a second voyage to circumnavigate the world and ascertain whether a great landmass existed below Australia. On Cook's first voyage aboard *Endeavour*, he had traced the coast of New Zealand and understood that it did not join onto a larger southern mass but a land called Terra Australis was still believed to exist. Cook was commissioned by the British government and Royal Society to look for the continent, circumnavigating the globe as southerly as possible. Following a delay, when the botanist Joseph Banks withdrew from the voyage after unsuccessfully demanding an extra deck be added to the ship, Cook's second voyage set sail from Plymouth on 13 July 1772.

For the voyage, Cook took two cargo ships built in Whitby: *Resolution* and *Adventure*. During the historic voyage, a sea clock designed by John Harrison was tested and proved to be a successful model for measuring longitude. The ships, which were stocked with beef, beer, biscuits and livestock including sheep, goats, hogs and poultry, passed the Cape of Good Hope at the southern point of Africa and continued to sail south but by the end of the year began to experience increasingly cold and hostile temperatures. In December 1772, the crew had been issued with heavy winter clothing and beheld ice islands through the heavy fog in which they were sailing. Then on 17 January, Cook sailed his ships through the Antarctic Circle, the most southerly of the five primary circles of latitude. However, as ice began to impede their journey, Cook ordered the voyage change direction to the north-east and out of the Antarctic Circle. At one stage, Cook was only 75 miles from the Earth's southernmost continent, Antarctica.

The voyage returned to England in 1775 but Cook, eager to discover a fabled North-West Passage linking the Atlantic and Pacific oceans, set out on a third and final voyage soon after. However, he was unable to discover the passage and instead travelled south to Hawaii. When Cook took the island's king hostage following the theft of a boat, a fight broke out and Cook was stabbed to death on 14 February 1779.

1775

THE AMERICAN WAR OF INDEPENDENCE BEGINS

Also known as the Revolutionary War, the American War of Independence, saw the thirteen North American colonies win their independence from Great Britain. The war was part of the American Revolution which would end in 1783 with the Treaty of Paris and the official acknowledgement by Britain of the independence of the United States. The war would not be limited to North America however, as France, Spain and the Netherlands supported the colonists fight for independence, while conflicts also began in India.

Tensions had arisen between the colonies and British government as early as 1765 as the colonies believed they were being taxed without fair representation. The grievances, most audibly voiced by those with commercial interests, led to violence in 1770 when British soldiers killed five men during a protest which became known as the Boston Massacre. Soon after in 1773, the Boston Tea Party occurred and in response to the escalating animosity, colonial delegates gathered in Philadelphia to discuss their objections to the British crown. This was the First Continental Congress of September 1774, attended by George Washington, Samuel Adams, John Adams and others. Although the congress did not demand independence, the delegates criticised the policy of taxation without representation and issued a declaration of rights to each citizen. By the time a second congress was scheduled to meet in May 1775, the war had already started.

On 19 April 1775, local militia of the colonies clashed with British forces at Lexington and Concord in Massachusetts, which became the first official encounters of the war. At the Second Continental Congress, new delegates including Benjamin Franklin and Thomas Jefferson voted in favour of a Continental Army to be established with Washington as the Commander in Chief. The first major battle of the war was at Breed's Hill in Boston, commonly known as the Battle of Bunker Hill. Although the British army suffered casualties, the Continental Army was defeated but nevertheless encouraged. The Continental Congress then signed the Declaration of Independence on 4 July 1776 and in New York, the Continental Army met with success against the British, who were subsequently forced to flee Boston in March 1776 and retreated to Canada. By this point, the majority of colonists supported the cause and Washington's army featured women, African-American soldiers and even Native Americans.

Washington was soon forced out of New York but escaped across the Delaware River and his army recovered to win a vital victory at Princeton. During the war, Britain had been attempting to separate New England from the other colonies but in 1777 the Continental Army defeated the British at the Battle of Saratoga, which proved to be a turning point of the war. France, which was covertly supporting the struggle for independence, openly declared war against Britain. 1778 saw both sides attack and retreat but the Continental Army suffered a setback when General Benedict Arnold defected to the British and soldiers began to mutiny. However, in 1781, the Continental Army secured a major triumph at Yorktown as Washington moved against the British with 14,000 soldiers and 36 French warships blocked any soldiers escaping or reinforcements arriving. The British officer Charles Cornwallis was forced to surrender on 19 October and the war was effectively over, although the war against France and Spain continued. On 3 September 1783, the Treaty of Paris was signed as Britain finally recognised the independence of the United States of America.

JAMES WATT REVEALS HIS STEAM ENGINE

It is often easy to celebrate the inventions of men such as James Watt without considering their personal stories. While the Scottish engineer made key modifications to steam engines during his life and invented the Watt steam engine, which would transform manufacturing during the Industrial Revolution, his life was riddled with misfortune. James Watt was born in Greenock, Scotland on 18 January 1736, the son of a shipbuilder. A Watt family story is that the young James had a fascination with a steaming kettle at the family home and was obsessed with taking his toys apart and then reconstructing them, which seemed to foreshadow his life as an engineer and inventor. When his mother died and his father became ill, he travelled to London by horseback, journeying for 12 days in the hope of finding employment. He began making mathematical instruments such as parallel rulers but soon returned to Scotland.

He began working at the University of Glasgow, where he met Professor John Robinson who introduced Watt to the knowledge of steam and in 1763 the university asked Watt to repair one of their Newcomen steam engines. The patent for the first working steam engine had been granted in 1698 and the Newcomen engines were the most widely-used across Britain. However, Watt found them to be ridiculously inefficient and so began designing a modified version. At the same time, he married his cousin Margaret and they had five children but only two survived to adulthood.

Watt realised that a separate chamber in the engine would allow the steam to condense, which meant it didn't require cooling and reheating, which would speed up the process and be more fuel efficient. When a mine owner named John Roebuck invested in his design, Watt began to produce a workable model but suffered from insomnia and depression. However, his wife supported him and ensured he continued his work.

Bad news struck when Roebuck announced he was broke as his mines were flooded, which he had hoped Watt's new engine would fix and in 1772 Watt's wife died in childbirth and he was left in debt. However, he met Matthew Boulton who financially backed Watt and provided with him with the necessary apparatus to complete his design. In 1775 the duo manufactured the Watt steam engine and it was a success, with Cornish miners becoming their first customers. With alterations, giving the engine a new rotary movement, the engines began to be used in flour, paper, cotton and iron mills across Britain and by 1790 both men were fabulously wealthy.

In 1800, Watt and Boulton retired, passing the business to their sons. More tragedy struck Watt when his son Gregory died four years after and Watt himself died in 1819 and was buried next to his business partner Boulton. In 2011 new £50 bank notes began circulation with Watt and Boulton on the reverse, becoming the first note to feature two Britons. The unit of measurement, the watt, was named in his honour and his name now appears on many lightbulbs around the world.

J. M. W. TURNER, THE PAINTER OF LIGHT

Joseph Mallord William (J. M. W.) Turner was born in London in April 1775, although he never knew the exact date of his birth. He was a talented artist from an early age, and sold his drawings from his father's barber shop. In 1789, he was admitted to the school of The Royal Academy of Art at the age of 14, and was accepted into the academy a year later.

He travelled through Scotland, Wales and the Lake District, drawing inspiration from British landscapes for his early watercolours. He also toured Europe, travelling through France and Switzerland in 1802, followed by several visits to Italy. He was recognised as a master of painting nature, and often focused on the dramatic effects of light and weather, painting storms and seascapes, including works like *Fishermen at Sea* (1796) and *Dutch Boats in a Gale* (1801).

He became known as the 'Painter of Light', creating luminous scenes in oil paint and watercolour. As he grew older, his work became more atmospheric in quality. Paintings like *Frosty Morning* (1813) and *Snowstorm: Hannibal Crossing the Alps* (1812) replaced detail with pearly washes of colour and light effects. He was an eccentric and secretive man who never married, although he had long-lasting relationships with two widows, Sarah Danby and Sophia Caroline Booth. Some of his best-known paintings, including *The Fighting Temeraire* (1839) were made during his last years, and he produced thousands of works in his lifetime. He died in 1851 and was buried in St Pauls Cathedral. His love of light and colour paved the way for Impressionism, and he is recognised as perhaps the greatest landscape artist of the nineteenth century.

1783

THE FIRST HOT AIR BALLOON ASCENT

Air travel history was made on 21 November 1783 when the first manned
hot air balloon was successfully completed. The remarkable balloon
was designed and constructed by the French Montgolfier brothers,
Joseph-Michel and Jacques-Etienne. Etienne had actually made the first
tethered hot air balloon ascent in history just a month earlier on 15
October, when he soared to an altitude of 24m, which was the length
of the tether. Another man then made the tethered ascent, namely
Jean-Francois Pilatre de Rozier, a French chemistry teacher.

It was Rozier and Marquis François Laurent d'Arlandes who volunteered
to make history by flying in the first untethered human-carrying vessel.
Originally, the French King Louis XVI ordered that condemned criminals should
be used as test pilots for the balloon flights but Rozier and d'Arlandes persuaded
the king to let them embark on the momentous task.

Rozier and d'Arlandes took off from the Chateau de la Muette in Paris, watched by
the king, as well as the American Founding Father Benjamin Franklin. The balloon rose
to just over 900m into the air and lasted 25 minutes, during which Rozier and d'Arlandes
travelled over five miles. In fact, the balloon had the potential to go about four times as
far but the men grew worried about burning embers engulfing the balloon in flames.

In 1785, during an attempt to cross the English Channel in a hot air balloon, Rozier
became the first person in history to die in an air crash when his balloon suddenly
deflated.

THE FIRST PARACHUTE DESCENT IS ATTEMPTED

There had been attempts to create parachutes since the Renaissance, and Leonardo da
Vinci had sketched a design for one in his notebooks. However, it was not until 1783 that
the first publically recorded and witnessed parachute jump took place.

Louis-Sébastien Lenormand was a French physicist and inventor, who became
interested in how to slow down a falling object. He first tested his ideas by jumping from
a tree with the help of two large umbrellas. Finally, on 26 December 1783, watched by

a large crowd, he jumped from the tower of the Montpellier observatory using a 4m parachute with a rigid wooden frame. He designed it in the hope that it would help people trapped in burning buildings to escape the flames.

Two years later, in 1785, Lenormand coined the term 'parachute', from the Latin word *para* (meaning 'against') and the French *chute* ('fall') – a contraption 'against falling'. Soon others were attempting to design and test parachutes, and in 1789, the French aeronaut André Garnerin made the first descent in a silk parachute.

JOHN MICHELL PROPOSES THE THEORY OF BLACK HOLES

A black hole is an area of space that has such a strong gravitational pull that nothing – including light – can escape from inside it.

The idea of black holes was first proposed by John Michell in the late 18th century. Born in Nottinghamshire in 1724, Michell was an English clergyman and natural philosopher. One of the greatest unrecognised scientists in history, he also made many important discoveries about gravity, magnetism and geology. He was educated at Cambridge, where he later also taught maths, geometry and philosophy. On 27 November 1783, he read out his theory of black holes at the Royal Society, based on the idea that if a star was massive and dense enough, not even light would be able to escape from its gravity – making it invisible to us. He called these huge objects 'dark stars'.

Michell's ideas were so ahead of his time that they were dismissed, and he died without gaining recognition for his theory. However, in the twentieth century, astronomers began to find evidence for Michell's 'dark stars', and thanks to Einstein's theory of general relativity, now believe that black holes may exist in the centres of many galaxies.

1787

THE FIRST FLEET DEPARTS FROM ENGLAND

By the middle of the 18th century, Britain's prisons began to swell with inmates and when the 13 former-British colonies in North America stopped accepting new convicts following the American War of Independence in 1783, the British government began to plan for a new land to send the country's unwanted criminals. Fortunately, Captain James Cook had discovered New South Wales on Australia's east coast in 1770 and had claimed the land for Great Britain, reporting that the land would be ideal for a settlement. On 6 December 1785 the Orders in Council were issued in London, calling for the establishment of a new penal colony in New South Wales and the British government hired nine transportation ships and alongside two Royal Navy vessels, the First Fleet was established. Although some of the 775 convicts who began the voyage would only be transported for seven or 14 years, many were sentenced to life in the new land founded by Cook.

On 13 May 1787, eleven ships left Portsmouth to establish the new penal colony. By the time the fleet had left the harbour, some of the prisoners had been on board the six convict ships for almost seven months. The fleet, which was commanded by Captain Arthur Phillip sailed southwest to Rio de Janeiro before travelling to Cape Town and then on to Botany Bay in Australia, where the new penal colony was originally scheduled to be established. On the three store ships was equipment for building a new community on the other side of the world, including ropes, crockery, seeds and agricultural equipment, medical supplies and surgical instruments, prison equipment including handcuffs and a wooden frame intended for use as the first governor's house. Until the new settlers could make use of Australia's supplies and food, they would be reliant on the fleet's stocks. Between 18 to 20 January 1788, the fleet arrived at Botany Bay, beginning with HMS *Supply*, but in contrast to the recommendations, Captain Phillip found the land to be unsuitable, with a lack of fresh water being a key predicament.

On 26 January the fleet docked at Sydney Cove in Port Jackson which Captain Phillip – who would become the first governor of New South Wales – believed to be far more suitable, with fresh water and shelter. Before the transportation began, around 300,000 Aboriginal Australians populated the land but European dominance grew rapidly from 1788 to 1850 as over 162,000 convicts were transported to Australia in 806 ships.

DELAWARE BECOMES THE FIRST STATE OF AMERICA

Before the naval exploration of the 16th century began, the east coast of America, including the state now known as Delaware, was occupied by Native Americans. In 1631, Dutch seafarers landed at Zwaanendael and began to colonise the area and by the time the US Declaration of Independence was ratified in 1776 during the American War of Independence against Great Britain, the state of Delaware was one of the thirteen colonies along the east coast of the land which became the United States.

The other twelve states were Connecticut, Georgia, Maryland, Massachusetts Bay, New Hampshire, New Jersey, New York, North Carolina, Pennsylvania, Rhode Island and Providence Plantations, South Carolina and Virginia. However, Delaware was the first of these to sign the United States Constitution on 7 December 1787 by a vote of 30 to 0. Four days later Pennsylvania ratified the Constitution and by May 1790 the thirteen states had all endorsed it. Because it was the first state to ratify the Constitution, Delaware is simply nicknamed 'the First State'.

Also known as the 'Blue Hen State' as its state bird is the blue hen, and the 'Diamond State' after the Founding Father Thomas Jefferson referred to it as a 'jewel among the states', its name originates from Thomas West, 3rd Baron De La Warr, who was born in Hampshire, England but who encouraged settlers to stay in North America in 1610. After killing many Native Americans and destroying their homes, he created an area for the settlers and was appointed as Virginia's first colonial governor. Having returned to England, he set sail once more for Virginia, after learning of his deputy-governor's cruelty to the new settlers, but he died on the voyage in 1618. A river, bay and even tribe of Native American's called the Delaware Indians, are named after him.

MARYLEBONE CRICKET CLUB (MCC) IS FOUNDED

Before Thomas Lord leased a new cricket ground on Dorset Fields in Marylebone, aristocrats and noblemen had played cricket in White Conduit Fields in Islington. The new site became known as Marylebone Cricket Club (MCC) but it had actually emerged from an older club which existed earlier in the 18th century, fundamentally a social and gambling club named the 'Noblemen and Gentlemen's Club'. Wishing for a more secluded spot, they asked bowler Thomas Lord to establish a new ground.

On 31 May 1787, Lord staged the first match at the ground – Middlesex v Essex – and MCC was formed. The following year, the Laws of Cricket were revised by MCC and the club remains the custodian of the laws. One of the first laws created by MCC was that the wickets should be set 22 yards apart. Starting from the 20th century, the England cricket team was organised by MCC and until 1977, outside of Test matches England was officially recognised as 'MCC'.

After moving to Marylebone Bank in Regents Park between 1811 and 1813, Lord's moved to St John's Wood, previously a duck pond and Lord's Cricket Ground, which can now hold 28,000 spectators, became the home to MCC. In 2014 the two hundredth anniversary of the move to St John's Wood was celebrated with a MCC XI against a Rest of the World XI.

In 1825, Thomas Lord sold the ground to William Ward, a director at the Bank of England, for £5,000. Lord then retired and despite many changes of ownership of the ground since his death in 1832, the venue has continued to be named Lord's.

1789

GEORGE WASHINGTON IS ELECTED AS THE FIRST PRESIDENT OF AMERICA

Born on 22 February 1732 at Pope's Creek in Virginia, British America, George Washington would become the Commander in Chief of the Continental Army during the American War of Independence, a Founding Father of the United States and most famously the first President of the United States in 1789.

Washington became the first President of the United States in 1789 after being unanimously elected by the Electoral College of the ten eligible states able to vote. He was similarly unanimously elected in 1792 for his second term as president when he received all 132 electoral votes of the now 15 states. His inauguration was held in Manhattan in New York City, on the portico of Federal Hall on 30 April 1789. The United States Constitution had been ratified in June 1788, allowing for the role of president and Washington delivered the first inaugural address, wearing a dark brown suit, white stockings, a red coat and a steel-hilted sword. To move from his home of Mount Vernon to the presidential mansion in New York, he had actually needed to borrow $600 as his money was tied up in other matters but when he was honoured with the first presidency, he actually refused a salary as he believed he was performing a public service and it should be carried out for free. However, when he was paid a salary of $25,000 he claimed, in fact, that it didn't cover his household expenses.

During his term as president he signed the first Copyright law into legislation on 31 May 1790, protecting the authors of maps, charts and books. Additionally, he declared the first Thanksgiving holiday in America on 26 November 1789.

He also created the United States Mint and the Dollar as the states' official currency and first appeared on a one-dollar bill in 1869. The Washington Monument is named after him and on completion in 1888 was the tallest structure in the world, standing in Washington, D.C., the capital of the United States, also named after the first president. He is furthermore one of the four celebrated presidents of Mount Rushmore. Although he owned slaves from a young age and purchased his last slave in 1772, he believed the tradition to be morally wrong and was one of the few Founding Fathers to request his slaves be freed in his will. He died on 14 December 1799 at his home in Mount Vernon, Virginia.

THE MUTINY ON THE *BOUNTY*

The Royal Navy vessel HMS *Bounty* departed England for the island of Tahiti in the South Pacific in December 1787. The crew's mission was to collect a cargo of breadfruit sapling to transport to British colonies of the West Indies to use as food for slaves. It was a journey which would go down in history to become the notorious 'Mutiny on the Bounty'.

The *Bounty* arrived in Tahiti in October 1788 and stayed on the island for five months where the crew enjoyed a delightful sojourn full of pleasures, perfect weather and wonderful hospitality of the natives. When the *Bounty* set sail for the West Indies the crew began to grow infuriated and feelings of discontentment regarding the leadership of the captain Lieutenant William Bligh resulted in a 25-man collective of the petty officers and seamen, led by the master's mate, Fletcher Christian, seizing the ship. Whether this was due to Bligh's harsh control of the crew and his oppressive nature towards his men, or the sailor's desire to return to the lavish lifestyle enjoyed on Tahiti, what is known for certain is that on 28 April 1789, Bligh and 18 of his loyal crew were cast off in a 7m long boat and left to die in the Pacific. The rebellion of Christian is surprising as he knew Bligh before the journey and had a good relationship with him on land but when Bligh appealed to the mutiny leader for mercy, Christian was indifferent.

The remaining crew on the *Bounty* set sail for Tubuai, south of Tahiti but failed to establish a colony there so returned to Tahiti where 16 of the original crew remained, despite the risk of encountering the angered Royal Navy. Fletcher Christian, eight of his shipmates, six Tahitian men, eleven women and one child then sailed the South Pacific for a safe area to settle. In January 1790 they reached the Pitcairn Islands, 1,000 miles east of Tahiti, and decided to establish a home there. The mutineers who stayed on Tahiti, however, were captured and returned to England were three of the men were hanged for their role in the mutiny against Bligh.

As for Bligh and his stranded men, they miraculously survived and reached Timor in the East Indies on 14 June 1789, following a journey of 3,600 miles. Bligh would later become the governor of New South Wales in Australia (where he would again face a mutiny) and died in London in 1817.

In 1808, an American vessel, *Topaz*, was lured to Pitcairn after seeing smoke on the island and there discovered a colony of women and children led by John Adams, the sole survivor of the mutineers. Following the arrival of the British at Pitcairn, the sailors stripped and burned the *Bounty* but sickness and unsuitable conditions led to the death of all the men but Adams. The ending to Christian's story became uncertain, with Adams citing numerous versions of his death, including insanity, murder and suicide.

In 1838, the Pitcairn Islands were incorporated into the British Empire and today 55 people, mostly *Bounty* descendants, live there.

THE STORMING OF THE BASTILLE

Commemorated today as Bastille Day – a French public holiday on 14 July – the Storming of the Bastille in 1789 was one of the major instigators of the French Revolution which lasted from 1789 to 1799 and saw the downfall of the monarchy, the establishment of a republic and the rise of Napoleon Bonaparte and his visions of a French Empire.

Originally constructed in 1370 as a fortification protecting Paris from attacks by English forces during the Hundred Years' War, the Bastille was first used as a prison in the 17th century with its cells becoming home to spies, criminals and political enemies of France. It stood 30m tall with eight towers of a similar height, surrounded by a moat 24m wide.

With food shortages in France and anger growing towards King Louis XVI, an organisation called The Third Estate, which represented the needs of the common man, declared itself the National Assembly and demanded a new Constitution. Although the king primarily agreed to the National Assembly, he dismissed his finance minister Jacques Necker and surrounded the city with his army. The people of France were furious and took arms.

Shortly before the fortress was stormed, one of the remaining prisoners shouted to the mobs from his window that the captives within were being massacred and needed help, but realising the dangers of the man's cries, the prison governor had him transferred to an insane asylum. On 13 July, the day before it was stormed, revolutionary fighters started firing at guards on the fortress towers and a day later, a crowd armed with muskets, swords and homemade weaponry began to congregate at the Bastille's gate. The following day, they successfully stormed the Bastille with around 100 revolutionaries losing their lives.

As an icon of the authoritarian rule of Louis XVI, the mob seized the Bastille as a sign of their anger against the crown. Although the fortress which dominated the skyline of Paris was only home to seven prisoners when it was stormed, the mob was more intent on obtaining the large ammunition stores it held. Bernard-René de Launay, the governor of the Bastille refused to hand the supplies over and was seized and killed following a violent struggle. His head was chopped off by a butcher and carried around the city on a spike. Almost all of the 114 soldiers who were defending the Bastille at the time were eventually released after being overwhelmed by the mob.

After four-fifths of the French Army had joined the revolution, the king was forced to accept a new government and by 1792 the monarchy had been abolished, with Louis XVI and his wife Marie Antoinette sent to the notorious guillotine in 1793. As a symbol of the monarchy's oppression, the Bastille was torn down by the National Assembly in 1790.

1791

THE BRANDENBURG GATE IS COMPLETED

One of the most famous landmarks in Europe, the Brandenburg Gate, which stands in the centre of Berlin, the capital of Germany, has a fascinating history as a symbol of peace, division, power and war but is now a monument of unity.

The construction of the Brandenburg Gate began in 1788, designed by the architect Carl Gotthard Langhans by order of the Prussian King Frederick William II, at a time before the unification of Germany. The king's intention was to build a structure to represent peace and to act as an entrance to the city of Berlin. The neoclassical triumphal arch, originally known as the Peace Gate, was topped by a 'Quadriga' – a chariot, ridden by the goddess of peace and drawn by four horses – and only the royal family were initially allowed to walk through the central arch of the gate.

In 1806, Napoleon Bonaparte led his French army in a ceremonial procession through the Brandenburg Gate after his victory over Prussia at the Battle of Jena-Auerstedt. He ordered the Quadriga to be dismantled and taken to Paris where it remained until Emperor Bonaparte's demise in 1814. The Quadriga was restored, the goddess became Victoria, goddess of victory and the square in which the gate stood was renamed Pariser Platz, in honour of the Prussian and allied occupation of the French capital.

When Adolf Hitler and his Nazi Party came to power, they used the gate in a procession and as a propaganda symbol of German might. Following the Second World War, in which the monument was badly damaged (but not destroyed), Berlin was divided up when the Berlin Wall was erected.

In 1961, the Berlin Wall separated East and West Berlin and the Brandenburg Gate stood in the East, with the Wall built around the historic site. Access to the gate by East Berliners was also restricted by a smaller wall. When the Berlin Wall came down to end the Cold War in November 1989, the gate once again became the symbol of the city's unity.

THE HAITIAN REVOLUTION

Before its independence, Haiti was a French colony called St. Domingue which used African slaves to harvest sugar and coffee beans. However, during the French revolution, the Caribbean island's mixed-race population began to campaign for civil rights, and thousands of slaves in the north of the colony organised and planned a massive rebellion which began on 22 August 1791.

Mistreated slaves rose up across the island, and with the help of mixed-race supporters, they fought to end slavery within the colony. Hearing news of the revolt, American leaders rushed to provide support for St. Domingue's white slave-owners. The next American government, however, shifted tactics and began to provide aid to the rebels. Over the following years, the country was torn apart by rival factions, including Spanish colonists and British forces from Jamaica, sparking a civil war. Eventually, the French Revolutionary Government convinced one of the rebel leaders, Toussaint L'Ouverture, that they were committed to ending slavery, and in 1793 offered freedom to slaves who joined a French army. Slavery was officially abolished by the government in 1794, and in 1825, they finally recognised the new Haiti as an independent state ruled by non-whites and former slaves.

The Haitian revolution was the greatest slave uprising since Spartacus's rebellion against the Romans almost 1,900 years before. Unlike Spartacus's attempt, it was successful, making it one of the most significant events in racial history.

THE DEATH OF WOLFGANG MOZART

Born in Salzburg, in modern-day Austria, Wolfgang Amadeus Mozart was taught music from a young age by his father, a composer. Mozart composed his first piece of music around the age of four, gave his first public concert at six, wrote his first symphony aged eight and his first opera aged eleven. His father took him on several tours of Europe, where he was recognised as a child prodigy.

He became the organist and concertmaster at the court of Salzburg, where he composed a huge variety of works, including five violin concertos and a series of acclaimed piano concertos. He moved to Vienna in 1781, where he married Constanze

Weber. Often inspired by the work of composers Bach and Handel, he now produced some of his best work, and between 1784 and 1787, he composed nine piano concertos, five string quartets, two successful operas (*The Marriage of Figaro* and *Don Giovanni*) and the famous chamber music masterpiece, *Eine Kleine Nachtmusik*. He was at the centre of the musical world in Vienna, living in style and loving to be well dressed. He enjoyed dancing, singing and billiards, and kept several pets including a dog, a canary and a starling.

However, Mozart's circumstances worsened towards the end of the decade, due to a mixture of illness and lavish spending. Despite this, his final year was one of his most productive, and he produced iconic works including the opera *The Magic Flute* and the unfinished Requim K. 626. He fell ill in late 1791 and died of a fever before his 36th birthday. Despite his short life, his reputation continued to grow after his death and he recognised among the most talented and influential composers in musical history.

1794

MAXIMILIEN ROBESPIERRE GOES TO THE GUILLOTINE

Maximilien Robespierre was born in Arras, France in 1758. He studied law and in 1789 was elected to be a representative of the Arras commoners in the Estates General – a general assembly representing the French estates of the realm: the clergy (First Estate), the nobles (Second Estate) and the common people (Third Estate).

In June 1789 the Third Estate declared itself the National Assembly and Robespierre became a prominent member. In December 1792, Robespierre successfully argued in favour of King Louis XVI's execution, and in May 1793 he encouraged an uprising over military defeats and food shortages.

On 27 July 1793, Robespierre was elected to the Committee of Public Safety, which was formed in April to protect France against its enemies, both foreign and domestic, and to oversee the government. Under his leadership, the committee totally controlled the French government. Faced with the threat of civil war and foreign invasion, the Revolutionary government inaugurated the 'Reign of Terror' in September. In less than a year, 300,000 suspected 'enemies of the Revolution' were arrested; at least 10,000 died in prison, and 17,000 were officially executed, many by guillotine in the Place de la Revolution.

On 4 June 1794, Robespierre was elected president of the National Assembly. Six days later, a law was passed that suspended a suspect's right to public trial and to legal assistance. In just one month, 1,400 enemies of the Revolution were guillotined. This escalation of 'the Terror', when there was no longer a real threat of foreign attack, was opposed by a coalition of National Assembly members and on 27 July 1794, Robespierre and his allies were placed under arrest. Robespierre was taken to prison in Paris, but the warden refused to imprison him, and he fled to the Hôtel de Ville – the city hall. On hearing that the National Convention had declared him an outlaw, he shot himself in the head but only succeeded in wounding his jaw.

Shortly after troops attacked the Hôtel de Ville and seized Robespierre and his allies. The next evening, on 28 July, Robespierre and 21 others were guillotined without a trial in the Place de la Revolution: the Reign of Terror was at an end.

VICE ADMIRAL HORATIO NELSON IS BLINDED IN CORSICA

Nelson was a British officer in the Royal Navy, who played a crucial role in the naval battles of the Napoleonic Wars against France. He was wounded several times in combat, and in 1794, he lost the sight of his right eye during a campaign in Corsica.

Nelson was born in Norfolk and joined the Navy at a young age, making his first voyage at the age of 12, to the Falkland Islands. Gaining a reputation for courage, he rose quickly through the ranks, and in 1778, he was given command of his own ship. The French Revolutionary Wars broke in 1793, and in January, Nelson was put in command of a 64-gun ship called the HMS *Agamemnon*.

He sailed into the Mediterranean, and was sent to capture Corsica, in the hope that it would provide a new British naval base near the coast of France. In January 1794, Nelson carried out a series of raids along the Corsican coast, and in April his squadron surrounded the town of Bastia and eventually forced it to surrender. It was soon after this, during a land attack on Calvi, a nearby town, that Nelson was hit in the right eye by debris caused by a bullet striking a sandbag. The eye was damaged beyond repair.

However, despite this, and despite the amputation of his right arm in 1797, he became one of Britain's most successful commanders. In 1797, he was knighted and made a rear admiral for his heroic actions at the Battle of Cape St. Vincent. He had a genius for military strategy, and led Britain to victory against Napoleon's fleet at the Battle of the Nile in August 1798, and at the Battle of Trafalgar in 1805. He was shot through the chest by a sniper during the battle, and died just half an hour before British victory was announced.

1796

EDWARD JENNER ADMINISTERS THE FIRST VACCINATION

In the 1700s smallpox was the most feared and greatest killer of the time. Among children, it accounted for one in three of all deaths.

In 1721 Lady Mary Wortley Montagu introduced the practice of inoculating smallpox with a milder strain of smallpox; a practice she had witnessed in Turkey where she had lived as the wife of the British Ambassador. This practice of deliberately giving people smallpox was called 'variolation' and many surgeons had businesses administering it. However, the identification of a suitable strain of the disease was not a precise science, and deaths from variolation itself were fairly common.

Edward Jenner, a doctor from Gloucestershire, had noticed that milkmaids, who contracted a disease called cowpox, did not catch smallpox. Unlike smallpox, which caused severe skin eruptions and dangerous fevers, the milkmaids who caught cowpox would feel off-colour for a few days and develop a small number of pocks, usually on the hands.

In 1796, a dairymaid, Sarah Nelmes, consulted Dr Jenner about a rash on her hand. He diagnosed cowpox rather than smallpox after Sarah confirmed that one of her cows had recently had cowpox. Jenner realised that this was his opportunity to test the protective properties of cowpox.

On 14 May 1796, Jenner took fluid from one of Sarah's cowpox blisters and scratched it into the skin of James Phipps, the eight-year-old son of his gardener. A few days later, James became mildly ill with cowpox, but was well again a week later. This confirmed that cowpox could pass from person to person as well as from cow to person. On 1 July, Jenner inoculated the boy again, this time with smallpox matter, and no disease developed. The vaccine was a success.

Doctors all over the world soon adopted Jenner's technique, leading to a rapid decline in cases of the devastating disease.

MUNGO PARK REACHES THE CENTRE OF THE NIGER RIVER

In the history of exploration and discovery, Mungo Park is often a forgotten figure but the Scottish surgeon's fascinating journey into Africa is an enthralling story. Born on 11 September 1771 in Selkirkshire, Park became a surgeon but when he was introduced to Joseph Banks, a botanist who had sailed to Australia in 1768 with Captain James Cook, Park offered Banks his exploration services.

Banks was treasurer of the Association for Promoting the Discovery of the Interior of Africa, an organisation which had two major objectives: firstly to discover the exact site of the semi-mythical city of Timbuktu; and secondly to track the course of the Niger River. Having already sent Major Daniel Houghton to discover the river's course in 1790, and with Houghton dying in the Sahara, the society required a new volunteer and Park was their candidate.

Park departed from Portsmouth and travelled 200 miles along the Gambia River beginning on 21 June 1795. At his side was Dr Laidley who provided a guide, equipment and who acted as a mobile postal service. The explorer had begun the expedition dressed in smart European clothing accessorised with an umbrella and tall hat, in which he stored his notes. Trouble began when Park encountered the local Bondou people who took his umbrella and best coat and quickly he was taken prisoner. With only one grammar book and Houghton's journal to assist him he found himself in a quandary.

However, he managed to escape with the assistance of his companion, a former slave called Johnson, and with just a few possessions, including a horse and compass, Park continued his journey and even pressed on when Johnson refused to persist. With the aid of local Africans, Park reached the Niger River at Segou on 21 July 1796 and became the first European to reach its centre. Not satisfied, he journeyed on another 80 miles before lack of provisions forced him to turn around.

Believing he was dead, his return to Britain was greatly celebrated and his account *Travels in the Interior Districts of Africa* made the Scottish explorer famous. Nevertheless, the fame was not enough for Park and in 1805 he went back to Africa to track the river to its end. The expedition was doomed and Park died in 1806 when he drowned. Today, the Royal Scottish Geographical Society annually awards the Mungo Park Medal for exploration and research.

ROBERT BURNS, THE BARD OF AYRSHIRE

The famous Scottish poet Robert Burns died in Dumfries on 21 July 1796. He is one of Scotland's best-known cultural figures, and his poems, including 'Auld Lang Syne', have made him famous around the world.

Burns was born on 25 January 1759 in Alloway, Scotland. The son of a tenant farmer, he grew up in poverty with little formal schooling, although his father encouraged him to read widely. He began to write songs and poems as a young man, often in praise of various young women. In 1786, he had an illegitimate daughter with his mother's servant girl, Elizabeth Paton. Soon after, he proposed to Jean Armour, whose father forbade them to marry, despite her pregnancy. He then fell in love with Mary Campbell, and considered emigrating with her to the West Indies. Her sudden death and the publication of his first verse collection, however, kept him in Scotland.

Published on 31 July 1786, *Poems, Chiefly in the Scottish Dialect* was a huge and unexpected success. Burns went up to Edinburgh, where he was celebrated by critics for poems including 'The Twa Dogs' and 'To a Mouse'. He finally married Jean Armour in 1788 and settled in Dumfries in 1791, where he worked as an Excise Officer. He continued to write many songs and poems, including the well-known 'A Man's a Man for A' That' and 'Tam o' Shanter', and worked on several projects to collect traditional Scottish songs. However, his early poverty and later dissolute lifestyle damaged his health, and he was only 37 when he died in 1796.

1804

THE POETRY OF WILLIAM BLAKE

During the First World War, the United Kingdom's Poet Laureate, Robert Bridges, was putting together an anthology to raise the nation's morale. In 1916, the fatalities suffered during the War were incredibly high and when Bridges discovered William Blake's poem 'And did those feet in ancient time', he asked the composer Sir Hubert Parry to set the poem to music, in a style which would allow a listening audience to join in. The anthem 'Jerusalem' was performed for the first time in March 1916 at a Fight for Right rally, whose aim was to increase support for the country and boost troops' morale.

Prior to the composition of 'Jerusalem', Blake's poem which had first appeared in 1804 as a preface to his epic *Milton: A Poem in Two Books*, had not been eminent for the next century. The poem was inspired by the story that during his 'unknown years' between childhood and the beginning of his ministry, Jesus travelled to England and journeyed to Glastonbury, while the theme of the poem depicts a Second Coming of Jesus to Earth and the establishment of a New Jerusalem.

William Blake was born in London on 28 November 1757 and although he wasn't renowned as a poet during his life, he is now considered one of the most inspirational Romantic poets. His 1794 'The Tyger' is one of his most celebrated works and often cited as the 'most anthologised poem in English.' Blake was respectful of the Bible but intolerant of the Church of England. 'And did those feet in ancient time' contains Blake's famous phrase 'dark Satanic mills' which is one of the most prominent images from the poem. Two main theories have arisen regarding the phrase, the first of which links it to the early Industrial Revolution. In particular, the Albion Flour Mills which were nearby to Blake's home and which burned down in 1791. The second theory of the phrase is that Blake is referring to the Church of England and its conformity.

The anthem itself has grown in popularity ever since 1916 and King George V was even alleged to have stated he preferred it to the British national anthem 'God Save the King'. While the Labour Party leader Clement Attlee promised to build 'a new Jerusalem' during the 1945 general election, the anthem was more recently used as the opening hymn for the London 2012 Olympic Games.

WILLIAM TELL IS PERFORMED FOR THE FIRST TIME

The poet and playwright Friedrich Schiller was born in Wurttemburg, Germany in 1759. Towards his later years, he became friends with Johann Wolfgang Goethe, a fellow German writer and statesman. When Goethe travelled to Switzerland in the late-18th century he heard of the legend of William Tell and returned to Germany to encourage Schiller to compose a play about the heroic figure. Schiller wrote the play and it was first performed on 17 March 1804 in Weimar, directed by Goethe. Since that performance, the play has been adapted many times and the opera *Guillaume Tell* by Gioachino Rossini, was based on Schiller's masterpiece.

The story of William Tell, which first arose in the *White Book of Sarnen*, was written in 1474 by a scribe named Hans Schreiber. William Tell was believed to be a tall, strong man and importantly a deadly shot with a crossbow. The story, set during the Old Swiss Confederacy in the early-14th century, saw Tell resist the Habsburg Empire's attempts to subjugate his homeland. The villain of the story is an overlord name Gessler who raised a pole in the village of Altdorf and hung his hat on it, insisting that the citizens bow before it. When Tell and his son, Robert, visited the village on 18 November 1307, they passed the hat without bowing, whereby the guards arrested the Swiss legend. The following scene is perhaps one of the most famous tales in history, as Gessler sought to test the marksman by having him shoot an apple from his son's head. If Tell missed, both he and his son would be executed. Tell pulled the trigger and split the apple in two. When Gessler asked why Tell had pulled two crossbows from his quiver, Tell informed him that if he had missed and killed Robert, he would have instantly killed Gessler. Tell was arrested but later killed Gessler with the second crossbow bolt.

Rossini's opera, adapted from Schiller's renowned play, includes the 'William Tell Overture', which is his most celebrated piece of music and has been used since as the theme tune for the fictional American Old West hero, the Lone Ranger.

NAPOLEON BONAPARTE IS CROWNED AS EMPEROR

On 2 December 1804, Napoleon Bonaparte became the 'Emperor of the French'. The coronation took place in Notre Dame Cathedral in Paris, and marked the establishment of a new French Empire.

Napoleon was born in Corsica in 1769, and served in the French army. He was a supporter of the French Revolution, and after the fall of the French monarchy, he was made a military commander. He quickly achieved a series of victories, including in Italy and Egypt, although he was defeated by English naval leader Lord Nelson in the Battle of the Nile. In 1799 he returned to France and overthrew the Directory, the government that was then in charge of the country. In February 1800, he set himself up as 'first consul', and confirmed his power with a new constitution. Although France was still called a republic, Napoleon had really established a dictatorship.

Later that year, Napoleon led his armies to victory after a series of battles in Austria, and began to reform the economy and religion of France, establishing Roman Catholicism as the official faith. In 1802, he established the Napoleonic Code, a new system of French law which forbade privileges based on family and birth. In 1804, at the age of 35, he became Emperor, and his wife became the Empress Josephine. During the coronation, he wore a golden laurel wreath that symbolised the power of the Roman emperors. Instead of waiting to be crowned, he took the crown from Pope Pius VII and placed it on his own head.

Napoleon was Emperor from 1804 until 1814, when he was defeated by English and Russian armies, and forced into exile on the island of Elba. He escaped the island in March 1815, and returned to power in Paris, before finally being defeated by the British in the Battle of Waterloo that June.

1805

TROOPING THE COLOUR BECOMES AN ANNUAL EVENT

Today Trooping the Colour is an annual display of pageantry held on the occasion of the Sovereign's Official Birthday and is carried out by the Household Division on Horse Guards Parade.

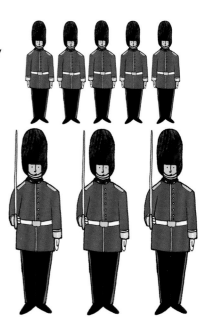

The flags of the different regiments of the British Army were historically described as 'colours' because they displayed the uniform colours and insignia worn by the soldiers of different units. The colours of a regiment were used as a rallying point on the battlefield. Without modern communications it was very easy for soldiers to become disorientated and separated from their regiments during battle.

In order that every soldier the colours of his own regiment they were 'trooped' in front of the soldiers every day and this custom dates back to the 17th century. In London, the Foot Guards used to do this as part of their daily Guard Mounting on Horse Guards and the modern parade ceremony is along similar lines.

The Grenadier Guards are amongst the oldest regiments of the British Army and have served as the personal bodyguards of the Sovereign since the monarchy was restored after the English Civil War in 1660.

The first traceable mention of the Sovereign's Birthday being 'marked' by the Grenadier Guards is in 1748 and again, after George III became king in 1760, it was ordered that parades should mark the king's Birthday.

From 1805, with some exceptions – notably the two World Wars – Trooping the Colour became an annual event to mark the Sovereign's birthday.

HANS CHRISTIAN ANDERSON

Hans Christian Anderson, a writer famous for his influential and timeless fairy tales, was born in the city of Odense, in Denmark on 2 April 1805. He was an only child, and grew up reading stories from the *Arabian Nights*. After writing a successful short story in 1829, he received a royal travelling grant which allowed him to travel through Europe. He authored several well-received autobiographies, travel narratives and novels, including 'Only a Fiddler'.

His original fairy tales for children were initially ignored by readers and critics. Between 1835 and 1837, Anderson published his first volume of *Fairy Tales* in instalments, a collection of nine stories which included 'The Tinderbox', 'Thumbelina', 'The Little Mermaid', 'The Princess and Pea', and 'The Emperor's New Clothes'. In 1845, he published a second collection, *Fairy Tales Told for Children*, which included 'The Steadfast Tin Soldier', and 'Wild Swans'. Finally, in 1845, English translations of his folktales and stories began to gain attention and acclaim abroad. He travelled to England two years later, where he met Charles Dickens, another author who cared deeply about children and their suffering in the Victorian period.

Anderson's stories gradually became recognised by audiences in Scandinavia, the United States and across the globe. He died near Copenhagen in 1875, by which time he was revered in Denmark as a 'national treasure'. His fairy tales have become loved classics, and have influenced many generations of British children's authors, from A. A. Milne to Beatrix Potter. Many have been adapted for stage and screen, including a Disney version of 'The Little Mermaid'.

THE BATTLE OF AUSTERLITZ

Europe had been at war since the start of the French Revolutionary Wars in 1792. In May 1803, after a year-long truce, Britain, supported by Russia and Austria, declared war on France.

Napoleon gathered a French army, known as the *Grande Armée*, and by 1805, it had grown to a force of 350,000 well-trained men. In August, Napoleon, who was now the Emperor of the French, began to focus on the threat from Austria and Russia. On 25 September, French troops began to cross the river Rhine, catching the Austrians by surprise and capturing Vienna in November. The allied Austrian and Russian forces decided to seek battle in order to regain the city.

Napoleon faced a difficult challenge, especially since his army of 68,000 men would have to fight the much larger Russian and Austrian forces, which numbered 90,000. However, he was able to pull off a great victory by setting a trap for the allies. He deliberately left a large gap in his forces on the Pratzen Plateau, where the allies then launched their main attack with 40,000 men. However, Napoleon had hidden reinforcements under the command of Marshal Nicholas Soult, which then appeared and took the Austrians and Russians by surprise, splitting their forces in half. The French were now able to attack their enemies, forcing them to retreat and pursuing them across the plain. The allied armies lost 15,000 men, with another 11,000 captured by the French. Napoleon's troops, in contrast, lost 9,000.

The battle was one of Napoleon's greatest victories, and forced Austria to make peace with France under the Treaty of Pressburg. Just two days after the battle, Francis I of Austria agreed to end hostilities, and arranged for Alexander I to take his army back to Russia.

1812

CHARLES DICKENS

Born in Landport, Portsmouth on 7 February 1812, Charles John Huffam Dickens is considered the greatest ever Victorian writer, the author of bestselling novels such as *Great Expectations* and *Nicholas Nickleby*, and creator of renowned characters including Miss Havisham, the Artful Dodger and Ebenezer Scrooge. A celebrity in his own time, Dickens remains consistently popular and was even the featured person on the £10 note from 1992 to 2003.

Life wasn't always easy for Dickens and much of what happened in his life influenced his stories, with his 1849 novel *David Copperfield* being his most autobiographical work, while descriptions of the world of the workhouses in *Oliver Twist* stemmed from Dickens' own childhood. Aged 12, he was removed from school and sent to work in a boot polishing 'blacking' factory when his father John was imprisoned for debt. Here he beheld many hardships which would influence his writing and life as a campaigner for social reforms, children's rights and education. In the middle of the 19th century, the average lifetime of a Londoner was only 27.

In 1833, Dickens became a parliamentary reporter for the *Morning Chronicle* newspaper and began producing sketches under his alias Boz. Three years later, his first novel *The Pickwick Papers*, published under his alias, was released to acclaim and in the same year he married Catherine Hogarth, who was the daughter of one of Dickens' editors. They would together have ten children.

Over his life, Dickens wrote 15 novels, many short stories, letters and plays, while also lecturing in England and America and editing two journals. He began a relationship with the actress Ellen Ternan and separated from his wife in 1858. In June 1865, he and Ellen survived the infamous Staplehurst Rail Crash when their train plunged off a bridge. Their first class carriage remained on the track and Dickens tended to the wounded and dying, offering round a flask of brandy. He managed to return to his carriage to collect his uncompleted draft of *Our Mutual Friend* but his health suffered after the incident.

An early member of the paranormal organisation The Ghost Club, alongside Arthur Conan Doyle, his fascination with spirits possibly influenced one of his most influential novels, *A Christmas Carol*. The story of miserly Scrooge being visited by three ghosts has been retold for years and has influenced the modern idea of Christmas more than any other story. The first Christmas card was actually sent in 1843, the same year as the world first read about Tiny Tim.

On 8 June 1870, after finishing a day's writing of his latest novel *The Mystery of Edwin Drood*, Dickens had a stroke and died the following day, leaving the book unfinished. He is buried in Poet's Corner in Westminster Abbey.

JOHANN LUDWIG BURCKHARDT REDISCOVERS PETRA

The ancient city of Petra, now in southern Jordan, was established by the Nabataean people of northern Arabia around 300 BC. Known as the Rose City because of the colour of the stone from which the rock-cut architecture is carved, it has been a UNESCO World Heritage Site since 1985 and is famed as one of the New7Wonders of the World. Each year it welcomes half-a-million visitors and has appeared in films such as *Indiana Jones and the Last Crusade*, but for hundreds of years it was a 'lost city' until it was revealed by the explorer Johann Ludwig Burckhardt.

Burckhardt, also known as Jean Louis, was born to a family of wealthy silk merchants in Switzerland on 24 November 1784. He travelled to England in the hope of working for the Civil Service but when he failed to gain employment there, he was hired by the African Association who led the exploration of the African continent. He was sent on an expedition from Cairo to Timbuktu, hoping to trace the route of the Niger River but first he studied Arabic, medicine and science at Cambridge University. During this time he also began to dress in typical Arabic clothing.

In 1809 he departed England for Aleppo in Syria to practise Arabic language and customs and adopted an Arabic name. During his journey he sojourned at Malta and heard of a man named Doctor Seetzen who had left Cairo to seek a lost city named Petra but had been murdered along the way. Having lived in Syria for two years and realising his identity as a European son of silk merchants had been disguised, he headed for Cairo. Unfortunately, on his journey a local governor and his tour guide took his valuables and left him for dead in the desert. Luckily, he encountered a nearby Bedouin camp who helped guide him.

On the way to Cairo, he began to hear rumours of ruins through a narrow valley in the former Roman province of Arabia Petraea near the tomb of Aaron, brother of Moses. Realising this was Doctor Seetzen's lost city, Burckhardt informed his guide he wished to sacrifice a goat at the tomb. On 22 August 1812, the Swiss explorer beheld Petra, becoming the first European to discover the Rose City cut into the mountains.

Of Petra, he said: 'great must have been the opulence of a city, which could dedicate such monuments to the memory of its rulers' but he did not stay long for fear he would be unveiled as a European and a treasure hunter. He spent a further three years travelling in North Africa and Arabia but never reached the Niger River, dying of dysentery in Cairo on 15 October 1817. His tombstone was inscribed with his Arabic name, Sheikh Ibrahim Ibn Abdallah.

THE ASSASSINATION OF THE PRIME MINISTER

Spencer Perceval has the unfortunate record as the only British prime minister to ever be assassinated. Born in London on 1 November 1762, Perceval also holds the honour of being the only attorney general to become prime minister, but his assassination at the hands of disgruntled Englishman John Bellingham means his achievements in politics are not often remembered.

John Bellingham had been falsely imprisoned while in Russia and had requested support from the British Embassy but they failed to provide assistance. When Bellingham eventually returned to England in 1809, the same year which Perceval became prime minister, the Tory government refused his request for compensation and Bellingham's grievances turned his mind to murder. He purchased two .50 calibre pistols and had a tailor sew an extra pocket inside his coat, in which to store the weapons.

On 11 May 1812, while on his way into the House of Commons, Perceval entered into the lobby where John Bellingham was waiting, having told acquaintants he had some business to attend to. Bellingham sat waiting by the fireplace and seeing the prime minister approach, shot him in the chest. Perceval is said to have exclaimed 'I am murdered!' and collapsed at the feet of the MP William Smith, who was the grandfather of Florence Nightingale. John Bellingham sat back down by the fireplace and waited to be arrested. Meanwhile, Perceval succumbed to his wound and died, leaving 12 children.

Bellingham was tried and shortly after executed, stating that he originally wished to murder the British Ambassador to Russia but had settled on the prime minister as the head of the government responsible for his struggles. A memorial was granted to Perceval in Westminster Abbey and in July 2014 a plaque was unveiled in St Stephen's Hall, nearby to where the murder was committed.

1815

THE BIGGEST VOLCANIC ERUPTION IN HISTORY

Mount Tambora stood over 4,300m high at the beginning of 1815. At the end of the year it was reduced to 2,851m following the largest volcanic eruption in recorded history, which caused death, destruction and the 'Year Without a Summer'.

Mount Tambora sits on the island of Sumbawa, part of Indonesia, in the Java Sea. On 5 April 1815 a small volcanic eruption took place and ash began to fall. But five days later on 10 April, an explosion was heard over 1,200 miles away as Mount Tambora experienced an Ultraplinian eruption – a super colossal eruption and the biggest in known history. The ground was recorded to have shaken as columns of flames flew up into the air and formed plumes of gas and smoke miles high. Boulders and debris from the mountain were thrown around the air by force, causing chaos to the inhabitants of Sumbawa.

As ash rained down for weeks on the village of Tambora, homes were destroyed, crops ruined and water contaminated. In the instant devastation of the eruption, 10,000 people were killed but with the starvation and disease that followed, the death toll extended to possibly 70,000 people. When the British governor of Java, Stamford Raffles, visited the island following the destruction, he found many dead and few survivors. The eruption had left a crater four miles wide and 600m deep.

The effects of the eruption were felt around the world. The following year was known as 'The Year Without a Summer', as a critical drop in climate caused by the eruption led to crop shortages in North America, Europe and Asia. Meanwhile, remarkable sunsets caused by excessive levels of ash known as tephra in the atmosphere, were painted by J. M. W. Turner in England and Mary Shelley began to write *Frankenstein* after ceaseless rainfall, caused by the eruption, forced her to stay indoors when friends challenged each other to write a scary story during a holiday in Switzerland.

The mountain is still active and the most recent eruption occurred in 1967.

THE BATTLE OF WATERLOO

The Battle of Waterloo marked the end of the Napoleonic Wars and ushered in almost a century of relative peace in Europe. The battle did not actually take place in the village of Waterloo, which is in present-day Belgium, but rather in nearby villages. However, the commander of the allied forces, the Duke of Wellington, established his headquarters in the village of Waterloo, south of Brussels, and it is doubtful that Napoleon Bonaparte ever set foot in Waterloo. The ferocious battle would conclude with the permanent exile of Napoleon and the fall of the French Empire.

Napoleon had been crowned Emperor of the French in 1804 and had conquered much of Europe during the early-19th century. However, his army had lost the Peninsula War of 1808 to 1814 when his forces were forced from the Iberian Peninsula by Spanish, Portuguese and British troops and had been humiliated after an initially successful but ultimately failed invasion of Russia. Following another loss at the Battle of Nations, Napoleon was forced to abdicate and was exiled to Elba in the Mediterranean after Paris was marched on by the allied troops. Although the powers of Europe hoped this would signal the end of war in Europe, Napoleon returned to France on 26 February 1815 with the support of 1,500 supporters and when crowds enthusiastically welcomed the exiled hero home, the restored King Louis XVIII was forced to flee. Napoleon then embarked on a final attempt to dominate Europe, which became known as the Hundred Days.

Hearing of Napoleon's return, the allies, who were formed as the Seventh Coalition, and included the United Kingdom, Prussia, Netherlands, Austria, Spain, Portugal, Russia, the Ottoman Empire and many other kingdoms, began to prepare for another war, while Napoleon hurriedly prepared his army to surprise his enemies. Napoleon marched into Belgium and on 16 June 1815 he defeated Prussian forces at the Battle of Ligny, but the Prussian forces were not completely destroyed. At the same time, Arthur Wellesley, the 1st Duke of Wellington established the large army of around 70,000 men near Waterloo. The Duke of Wellington had risen to prominence during the Peninsula War and was seen as the finest military tactician in Europe, having not lost a battle in 12 years of warfare. Napoleon himself had a large army, numbering around 72,000 men and on 18 June 1815 the two armies collided.

Unusually, Napoleon made several tactical errors and was hesitant in his decisions, one of which was to wait until midday before giving the order to attack. Napoleon had wanted the ground to dry following heavy rainfall overnight but the delay allowed the surviving Prussian forces, numbering 50,000 and under the leadership of Marshal Gebhard Leberecht von Blucher, to arrive at the battle and outnumber the French, who were defeated. Casualties on both sides were heavy as the battle was fought at close-quarters, with the musket being the major weapon of the era. French casualties, including the dead, wounded and captured numbered 33,000 while the Seventh Coalition suffered 22,000 casualties. After the battle ended, Napoleon was believed to have rode away in tears.

On 22 June, the Emperor of the French abdicated once more and attempted to escape to the United States, but the ports were blocked and he surrendered. Napoleon was exiled to the British island of Saint Helena, where he died six years later. The British Empire would grow in dominance during the 19th century and the Duke of Wellington became prime minister in 1828. For his service in the conflict, he was awarded the equivalent of £15 million.

THE ELGIN MARBLES ARE DISPLAYED IN THE BRITISH MUSEUM

Perhaps the most controversial museum display in the world, the Elgin Marbles have been on display at the British Museum since 1817. But how did the marble sculptures from Athens come to be housed in the most popular visitor attraction in the United Kingdom and why do some people think they should be returned to Greece?

The Parthenon stands on the Acropolis of Athens, built between 447 and 432 BC and dedicated to the goddess Athena while the Athenian Empire was at its most dominant. The decoration of the Parthenon temple with classical marble sculptures was completed by the Greek architect Phidias, whose statue of Zeus at Olympia was one of the Seven Wonders of the Ancient World. In 1687 the Parthenon was almost completely destroyed when it was used as a gunpowder store during a war between the Venetians and Ottoman Empire, who at the time occupied Athens. An explosion blew the roof off the temple and destroyed many of the sculptures within.

Two centuries later, with the Ottoman Empire still a dominant world force, the 7th earl of Elgin Thomas Bruce was the British ambassador to the Ottoman Empire and after assisting the empire in their aim to push the French out of Egypt (which was in Ottoman hands), he was given permission to remove the remaining pieces of the Parthenon sculptures as recognition of his help.

Lord Elgin assembled his collection between 1801 and 1805 as the ancient articles became known as the Elgin Marbles. They consist of around half of the surviving Parthenon sculptures including 75m of the original 159m of friezes, 15 of the 92 metopes (marble panels), 17 figures from the Parthenon's pediments and various other pieces. The collection also includes objects from other monuments of the Acropolis such as the Erechtheion, Propylaia and Temple of Athena Nike.

Originally, Elgin intended to donate the collection to Great Britain but when he returned home he suffered financial difficulties and sought a buyer for the marbles. In 1810 he began negotiations with the British government, expecting to sell the collection for £73,600 but the government eventually bought the marbles for £35,000 and granted them to the British Museum in 1816.

In 1817, the Elgin Marbles were first displayed to the public with the display completed in 1832, and have been one of the most popular spectacles ever since. Mainly housed in Room 18 are the sculptures which decorated the outside of the Parthenon, while Rooms 18a and 18b display fragments of the Parthenon sculpture and other architectural objects. Remnants of the Parthenon are also located in the Acropolis Museum in Athens in addition to in the Louvre in Paris, Vatican Museums, Copenhagen and Munich.

Since the 1980s the Greek government has argued for the restoration of all the Parthenon marbles to Athens and claimed that Lord Elgin removed the sculptures illegally. Debates about the rightful resting place of the marbles are ongoing but archaeologists are agreed that the surviving sculptures would not be able to be restored to the Parthenon in the original design.

KARL DRAIS INVENTS THE FIRST FORM OF BICYCLE

Karl Drais, a German inventor who was born on 29 April 1785 is not one of the most famed inventors in history but his 'Laufmaschine' was potentially one of the major transportation discoveries of the 19th century and paved the way for the modern bicycle. Drais was born into an influential, if not wealthy family and his father was the most powerful judge in Baden, the inventor's place of birth, but Drais' tale was not to be met with a happy end.

Karl Friedrich Christian Ludwig Freiherr Drais Von Sauerbronn, as he was baptised, also invented an early form of typewriter and a meat grinder but it was his 'Laufmaschine', or 'Dandy Horse', which was his great achievement. It was the earliest form of mechanised public transportation and the first to use the principle of fixing two wheels in line, such as the modern bicycle or motorbike. Unlike the bicycle, it was not propelled by pedals, rather the rider pushed themselves along the ground with their feet while the handlebars and front wheel were hinged to allow for steering. Drais first publicly rode the 'Laufmaschine' on 12 June 1817 in Mannheim, Germany using the area's best road. He travelled for less than five miles, which took him over an hour but it was evident that his machine was a success.

Mount Tambora's eruption halfway around the world in 1815 had resulted in Europe having two poor harvests and Drais had designed the Dandy Horse as a replacement for a real horse, which he lacked the assistance of due to a dearth of crops. Just as Tambora's deadly eruption somehow influenced literature, it also could be argued to have helped discover today's public transport.

In 1822, Drais' father, the judge, played a part in a case which resulted in students attacking his son, due to their anger at the judge. Drais was himself a liberal but moved to Brazil for five years where he worked as a surveyor. When he returned home, the judge died but Drais was attacked once more. He retreated to a remote village where he invented a railroad handcar. He later dropped his title of Baron as he wished to show his solidarity with the liberals but his powerful enemies attempted to have him locked up for insanity and on 10 December 1851 he died without a penny.

JANE AUSTEN DIES

One of the most celebrated English authors of all time, Jane Austen was born in the village of Steventon, Hampshire on 16 December 1775. During her lifetime, she would become a successful writer, although each of her novels was published anonymously. From 1811 to 1816 she had four novels published and after her death, aged 41 in 1817, two more of her novels were posthumously published. The six novels, which are still in print, have inspired many adaptations for film and television.

As one of eight children to a clergyman, Jane Austen began to write as a teenager. Her father died in 1805, shortly after the Austen family had moved to Bath and Jane, her sister Cassandra and their mother moved several times before settling in Chawton, near to her birth place of Steventon. With the help of her brother Henry, her first novel *Sense and Sensibility* was published in 1811 which she had originally penned in epistolary form in 1795, but had later rewritten as a narrative. In 1813, *Pride and Prejudice* was published, which had originally been called *First Impressions*. Featuring possibly Austen's most famous character, Mr Fitzwilliam Darcy, the novel's themes of morality, education and marriage has made it an enduringly popular novel and it is believed to have sold over 20 million copies. The novel was described by its author as her 'own, darling child' and is one of the most famous examples of the genres of romance and satire.

During her short life, her novels *Mansfield Park* and *Emma* were also published, with the latter dedicated to the Prince Regent, who later became King George IV. In 1816, she began to suffer from ill health and moved to Winchester but she died on 18 July 1817. Following her death, two more novels, *Persuasion* and *Northanger Abbey* were published and a final novel by the Romantic author was left unfinished. In 2013, the Bank of England revealed that Jane Austen would appear on the £10 note, which was an indication of the legacy of the distinguished author.

THE LADY WITH THE LAMP

Florence Nightingale was born in Florence, Italy on 12 May 1820 and named after the city of her birth. A celebrated English reformer and nurse, she became a Victorian cultural icon; she was known as the 'Lady with the Lamp', making her rounds to check on wounded soldiers at night.

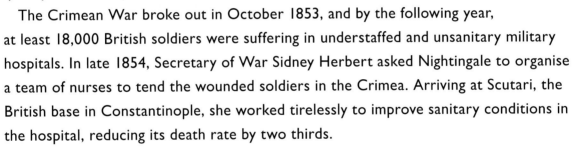

The daughter of a wealthy British landowner, Nightingale was educated by her father, but rebelled against the role expected of an upper class woman by deciding, in 1844, to become a nurse. She enrolled at a nursing school in Germany, and returned to London in the early 1850s, where she took a nursing job at a Middlesex hospital, and quickly became superintendent.

The Crimean War broke out in October 1853, and by the following year, at least 18,000 British soldiers were suffering in understaffed and unsanitary military hospitals. In late 1854, Secretary of War Sidney Herbert asked Nightingale to organise a team of nurses to tend the wounded soldiers in the Crimea. Arriving at Scutari, the British base in Constantinople, she worked tirelessly to improve sanitary conditions in the hospital, reducing its death rate by two thirds.

The Nightingale Fund was established to train nurses, and when Nightingale returned to England after the end of the Crimean conflict in 1856, she used the money to set up the Nightingale Training School at St. Thomas' Hospital in 1860. Although she was bedridden during her later years, she continued to advocate clean living conditions in hospitals, workhouses and working-class homes. She was awarded the Royal Red Cross by Queen Victoria in 1883 and died in her sleep on 13 August 1910, at the age of 90. Her book *Notes on Nursing* (1859) quickly became the basis for modern nursing and is still read today.

THE HMS *BEAGLE* IS LAUNCHED

HMS *Beagle* is one of the most illustrious ships of the Royal Navy, having carried the naturalist Charles Darwin as his discoveries led to his groundbreaking theory of evolution. It was launched on 11 May 1820 at a cost of £7,803, built at the Royal Navy dockyards on the Thames. The 28m-long vessel was the third of nine ships to actually be named *Beagle* and had been built as a 10-gun, two-mast boat intended for scouting and practicable duties. During a naval display for King George VI in 1820 it became the first ship to pass under the old London Bridge.

Beagle didn't begin her first voyage until 1826 under the command of Lieutenant Pringle Stokes with a mission of surveying the coast of South America alongside HMS *Adventure*. However, the mission was not completed as Stokes became depressed with the difficulty of the task amid the harsh winter conditions and remained in his cabin for four weeks. Driven to suicide in 1828, Stokes shot himself in the head but the bullet lodged in his skull and he only died 12 days afterwards from gangrene.

In 1831, *Beagle* set sail on her second voyage which was to become the vessel's most famous journey. With a duty to complete the survey of the first voyage and circumnavigate the globe, the ship had a refit and became one of the first vessels to have a lightning conductor installed.

Lieutenant Robert FitzRoy, the newly appointed captain of the *Beagle*, decided he needed a geologist on board and so it came to be that 22-year-old Charles Darwin, who was preparing for a life in the clergy, joined the voyage. During the expedition, the survey began by Stokes was completed and in 1833 the *Beagle* helped the British take control of the Falkland Islands. The settlement of Darwin was named after the naturalist after he carried out a zoological survey on the islands and stayed the night there. The scientific journal written by Darwin about the expedition is known as 'The Voyage of the *Beagle*'. It returned to England in 1836.

The third and final voyage lasted from 1837 to 1843 as the crew of the *Beagle* completed the first full survey of the Australian coasts. In 1845, the vessel was stripped of its masts and moored in Essex as a lookout against smugglers. It was eventually sold for scrap in 1870 and in 2012 a reconstruction of the *Beagle* was commenced by the Nao Victoria Museum in Chile.

THE BRITISH REGENCY PERIOD IS ENDED

When Prince George Augustus Frederick ascended to the throne as King George IV on 29 January 1820, aged 57, he had already been 'acting King' or 'Regent' since 1810 during George III's final period of insanity. Prince George's accession as George IV actually made very little difference to his existing powers as Regent.

As Prince of Wales, George had had several mistresses and in 1785 he secretly married Catholic widow Maria Fitzherbert in contravention of the Act of Settlement and the Royal Marriage Act. They had at least two illegitimate children. Unlike his father, George III, he was extravagant with money and became badly in debt. His father agreed to pay his debts, but in return the Prince of Wales was forced to deny his marriage to Maria and marry his cousin Princess Caroline of Brunswick instead. The prince agreed and they were married on 8 April 1795 at the Chapel Royal in St James's Palace. The marriage was a disaster and they were formally separated after the birth of their only child, Princess Charlotte, in 1796. The prince remained attached to Maria Fitzherbert for the rest of his life.

George IV loved the fine things in life and undertook both the rebuilding of Buckingham Palace and Windsor Castle. During the 'Regency Period' architect John Nash, among others, designed and built many fine buildings in London, Brighton, Bath and Cheltenham.

George's heavy drinking and indulgent lifestyle, including the consumption of huge amounts of food eventually made him obese and he suffered from gout. Towards the end of his life he also suffered periods of mental instability like his father before him. George IV died of a heart attack at Windsor Castle in 1830. His only legitimate daughter Charlotte had died in childbirth in 1817, so he was succeeded by his brother, William.

1821

SIMÓN BOLÍVAR WINS VENEZUELA'S INDEPENDENCE

Born on 24 July 1783 in Caracas, then part of the Spanish Empire, Simón Bolívar was a Venezuelan military leader who was a key figure in the revolutions against the Spanish which led to the establishments of Venezuela, Ecuador, Bolivia, Colombia and Panama. Not only was Bolívar a commander of the forces which defeated the Spanish rulers, he was an educated politician who served as president of several of the independent countries and ruled over much of the territory of South America.

Bolívar was born into a wealthy family, who owned copper and gold mines and was sent to Spain as a young man to receive his education. In Europe, he was introduced to the teachings of leading philosophical thinkers of the Enlightenment and his ideas of forcing the Spanish Empire from his home began to take shape. In 1802 he married Maria Teresa in Madrid but upon returning to Venezuela a year later as a newlywed couple, Maria died of yellow fever, leaving her husband distraught. He returned to Europe, believing that her death was his reason to launch a political career. In Rome, Bolívar swore to liberate his country from Spanish rule.

Having returned to Venezuela, it declared itself independent from Spain in 1810 and on 14 May 1813 Bolívar began his Campaña Admirable, or 'Admirable Campaign' to truly free the country from Spanish authority. He was proclaimed El Libertador (the Liberator), and he proclaimed the restoration of the Venezuelan republic. He served as the President of the Second Republic of Venezuela from 1813 to 1814 but following internal unrest, he was forced to flee to Jamaica where he wrote his 'Letters from Jamaica' setting out his dream for an independent South American republic. With support from Haiti, Bolívar returned to the continent and was involved in several military battles, claiming many territories.

El Libertador's greatest moment was arguably as commander in chief of the forces against Spanish Royalists at the Battle of Carabobo on 24 June 1821 which resulted in a clear victory for Bolívar. Following the battle, Gran Colombia was established, which incorporated much of Colombia, Panama, Ecuador, Peru and of course Venezuela. Four years later, the Republic of Bolivia was established and named after the military hero, who was also voted its president. Bolívar served as the first president of Gran Colombia until 1830 but following an assassination attempt and the collapse of Gran Colombia, he planned to move to Europe, but died of tuberculosis on 17 December 1830 in Santa Marta. Today he is remembered through statues, road names, plazas and airports.

NAPOLEON DIES IN EXILE ON SAINT HELENA

On 5 May 1821, Napoleon Bonaparte, the former Emperor of France, died as a prisoner on the remote island of Saint Helena in the southern Atlantic Ocean.

Napoleon had become Emperor in 1804, and by 1807 his Empire stretched across Europe, from Italy and Spain to Sweden and Holland. However, from about 1810, his fortunes began to change. He suffered a string of military defeats which included the disastrous failure of his invasion of Russia. France's enemies, including Sweden, Russia, Spain, Portugal and Britain, now banded together against him, and he was defeated at the Battle of Leipzig in October 1813. In 1814, he was forced to surrender and sent into exile on the Island of Elba.

However, he escaped from Elba early the following year, and marched towards Paris with an army. He resumed power and led France back into battle with a victory against the Prussians on 16 June 1815. However, just two days later, he was defeated by the Duke of Wellington's British army at the Battle of Waterloo.

Finally, on 22 June 1815, Napoleon gave up his powers, and was sent into exile by the British, this time to the island of Saint Helena. Although he was free to do as he wished on the island, his health began to suffer, and by early 1821 he was bedridden with what was probably stomach cancer. He finally died on 5 May as a man who shaped the history of Europe, and is still remembered as a formidable leader and military commander.

1829

ROBERT PEEL CREATES THE MODERN POLICE FORCE

At the beginning of the 19th century, London was growing in size and population and by 1815 it had become the largest city in the world, with around 1.3 million inhabitants. Yet there was no organised police force in operation, catching criminals and keeping crime to a minimum. When Robert Peel became home secretary in 1822 he decided that needed to change.

Peel, who was born in Bury, Lancashire in 1788, entered parliament as a Tory politician in 1809 and as home secretary he introduced new criminal law, prison reforms and furthermore established the Metropolitan Police, inspired by previously organised police forces such as the City of Glasgow Police which had existed since 1800.

Following the Metropolitan Police Act of 1829, one thousand permanently appointed policemen were employed to keep the peace in London. The approved force of 895 constables, 88 sergeants, 20 inspectors and 8 superintendents replaced the disorganised system of parish constables and watchmen and groups such as the Bow Street Runners. However, they did not operate in the square mile of the City of London, which is still an independent police force.

The 'Bobbies' or 'Peelers' as the police were known, in honour of Robert Peel, began to patrol on 29 September 1829, dressed in blue tail-coats and top hats, designed to look similar to ordinary residents and detached from red-coated soldiers. Each policeman was issued with a wooden truncheon, handcuffs and a wooden rattle to raise alarm, which was later replaced by a whistle.

The regulations to gain employment as a policeman were strict for the period with an age-range of 20 to 27-years-old, a minimum height of 5 foot 7 inches and physically fit while 'Bobbies' were expected to be literate and have no criminal history. Police worked seven days a week, only had five days of holiday a year and were paid £1 per week. They were required to wear their uniform even off duty and were not allowed to vote.

The Metropolitan Police became an example for regional forces across London boroughs and counties and towns around England, following the County Police Act of 1839. Amazingly, Peel's birthplace of Bury was the only major town not to have its own police force and remained a part of the Lancashire constabulary until 1974.

As for Peel himself, he became prime minister twice and was the first person to have his photograph taken in office. While he was one of the founders of the modern Conservative Party, it is believed that Queen Victoria disliked him. When riding on Constitution Hill in 1850, he was thrown from his horse and died on 2 July.

THE FIRST UNIVERSITY BOAT RACE

The Boat Race, also known as the University Boat Race or the Oxford and Cambridge Boat Race, is one of the great British sporting rivalries, stretching back to 1829. As of 2016, Cambridge have won the race 82 times while Oxford have triumphed on 79 occasions. The race is competed between eight rowers in each boat with a coxswain to steer and the crews are cheered on by around 250,000 spectators along the banks of the Thames in London while millions more watch on television.

The race originated on 10 June 1829 when Charles Merivale, a student at St John's College, Cambridge challenged his old friend Charles Wordsworth, who was studying at Christ Church, Oxford to a boat race at Henley-on-Thames. Wordsworth accepted and beat his Cambridge compatriot. In a second race of 1836, the venue was changed from Westminster to Putney and on this occasion, Cambridge won. The race has been held annually since 1856 along a 4.2 mile stretch of the Thames from Putney to Mortlake. It is claimed that each rower trains for two hours per every stroke.

One of the most remarkable finishes was in 1877 when a dead heat was called but the result has been questioned as the judge, 'Honest' John Phelps, was over 70 years old and blind in one eye. However, rumours he was drunk under a bush were quashed. Another memorable moment of the Boat Race was in 1978 when the Cambridge boat sank after filling up with water due to strong winds. Oxford rowed home easily to victory. At the end of the race, the tradition is that the losing team challenges the champions to a rematch next year.

The fastest ever finish time is 16 minutes 19 seconds by Cambridge in 1998 while their crew the following year is the tallest ever at an average height of 6 foot 7 inches. The rower with the most victories in the boat race is Boris Rankov with 6 wins for Oxford.

ROBERT STEPHENSON'S *ROCKET* IS BUILT

Along a railway track one mile long in Rainhill, Lancashire in October 1829, the Rainhill Trials took place to decide whether stationary steam engines or locomotives would be used to pull new trains along the new Liverpool and Manchester Railway. On the day the competition began, only five locomotives started the challenge, one of which was Stephenson's *Rocket*, which would become a template for steam engines over the next 150 years.

The Rainhill Trials were an open contest with a £500 reward for the winning design. The locomotives had to undergo several tests to win the competition as they were run up and down the track. The first locomotive to drop out of the competition was the *Cycloped* which used a horse on a treadmill, rather than steam, to power the locomotive. However, an accident resulted in the horse falling through the floor of the engine. *Perseverance* was the next locomotive to exit the competition after it failed to reach the necessary 10 miles per hour to advance in the trials. *Sans Pareil* was included in the competition even though it was 140kg overweight but after completing eight trips, a cylinder cracked and it was disqualified. Finally, the crowd favourite, *Novelty*, which was lightweight and fast, suffered a damaged boiler pipe and had to retire. Stephenson's *Rocket* remained as the only locomotive to complete the trials and won the prize money. In addition, the Stephenson's were awarded the contract to provide locomotives for the new railway. Their *Rocket* had achieved a top speed of 30 miles per hour while hauling 13 tons and was considered a great achievement of transportation.

Stephenson's *Rocket* was not the first steam locomotive in history but it was the most advanced, featuring a smokestack chimney at the front and a cylindrical boiler in the middle, with a firebox at the rear. The *Rocket* was the first locomotive to have a multi-tube boiler, incorporating 25 copper tubes instead of a single or twin flue, all of which allowed it to travel faster than its competitors. It had been built by the civil engineer George Stephenson (who had engineered the new railway itself), alongside his son Robert and Henry Booth. George Stephenson's other inventions included a cucumber straightener while he also designed a rather cruel method of fattening chickens.

At the opening of the Liverpool and Manchester Railway on 15 September 1830, the Duke of Wellington, Arthur Wellesley, who was the prime minister at the time and who had defeated Napoleon at the Battle of Waterloo, rode on one of the new trains but the day was not a complete success after the MP for Liverpool, William Huskisson, was knocked down by the *Rocket*, becoming the first known railway casualty, and upon reaching Liverpool Road railway station, the prime minister was pelted with vegetables by a hostile crowd. However, the news of Huskisson's death, which was reported around the world, opened up the concept of affordable long-distance transport. By 1850, over 6,200 miles of railway were in place across the country.

1846

NEPTUNE IS DISCOVERED BY JOHANN GOTTFRIED GALLE

Johann Gottfried Galle was a German astronomer, who discovered an inner dark ring of Saturn in 1838 and shortly after he discovered three new comets. A few years afterward, Galle, who worked at the Berlin Observatory, had written a thesis which he sent to the French mathematician Urbain Le Verrier but for a long time he did not get a reply. A year after Galle had posted his thesis to Le Verrier, he received a reply at the observatory and that night, one of the great scientific moments of the 19th century took place.

On the morning of 23 September 1846, Galle read Le Verrier's letter, suggesting the astronomer search the sky for an undiscovered planet which the mathematician had believed to have located during his research of Uranus. That night, with the assistance of Heinrich Louis d'Arrest, Galle discovered the planet Neptune, just one degree off the coordinates suggested by Le Verrier. For the next two nights Galle tracked the star, whose motion made clear to the astronomer that it was definitely a planet. Although he continued to work in the field of astronomy for many years, he never accepted to be recognised as Neptune's discoverer, stating that Le Verrier had calculated the planet's existence. One of the rings of Neptune, in addition to craters on the Moon and Mars were named after Galle.

Neptune, which is the furthest planet from the Sun in the Solar System – since Pluto was reclassified as a dwarf planet – takes around 60,190 days to orbit the Sun. Named after the Roman god of the sea, Neptune is fifteen times the mass of the Earth and has 14 known moons, the largest of which is Triton, which was discovered by English astronomer William Lassell just over a fortnight after Neptune's discovery. In 1989, NASA's *Voyager 2* became the first spacecraft to observe Neptune, passing about 3,000 miles from the planet's north pole, having left Earth in 1977.

THE SAXOPHONE IS PATENTED BY ADOLPHE SAX

Antoine-Joseph 'Adolphe' Sax was born on 6 November 1814 in Dinant, a city in present-day Belgium but at the time a part of the French Empire. He is famed for being the inventor of the saxophone although he also invented three less familiar 'sax' instruments – the saxotromba, saxhorn and saxtuba. It was incredible that he managed to invent anything, given the several near-death experiences Sax encountered during his childhood.

Sax's mother and father were both instrument designers and made adjustments to the horn which inspired Sax to begin making his own instruments as a young boy. At the Royal Conservatory of Brussels, he studied the flute, clarinet and the voice. The young inventor's childhood was mired by near-misses with death which included the following incidents: Sax was hit on the head by a cobblestone; he fell into a river and was saved from drowning; he was burnt in a gunpowder explosion; fell from a three storey height and hit his head; and he fell onto a hot frying pan. Even his mother said that Sax wouldn't live, such was his misfortune.

After moving to Paris in 1841 he began working on new instruments called saxhorns which were early models of the more recognised flugelhorn. On 28 June 1846 a patent was obtained by Sax for the saxophone, a brass instrument of the woodwind family, played through a single-reed mouthpiece, which he created for use in orchestras and concert bands. He became renowned for his new instrument and was invited to teach the saxophone class at the music school the Paris Conservatory in 1857.

Many rivals claimed the authenticity of Sax's patents of his instruments and he was involved in several proceedings which cause him to twice go bankrupt. When he died in February 1894 he was penniless.

THE LIBERTY BELL IS CRACKED

In 1751, the city of Philadelphia ordered a new bell from the Whitechapel Bell Foundry, which is now the oldest manufacturing company in Britain. The foundry, which would also cast Big Ben, delivered the bell the following year but it was believed to have sustained damage while being shipped across the Atlantic Ocean. When it was tested for sound, the clapper broke the bell's rim and so two local founders, John Pass and John Stow, recast the bell by breaking it down, melting it and recast it. When a celebration was held to mark the first sounding of the new bell, many witnesses were dissatisfied with the flat noise, so Pass and Stow recast it quickly once again and their names were inscribed on the bell.

The bell, made of copper and tin, was hung in the steeple of the Pennsylvania State House, where the United States Constitution and Declaration of Independence were both adopted and was inscribed with the Biblical passage 'PROCLAIM LIBERTY throughout all the land unto all the inhabitants thereof'. In its early years, the 900kg bell was rung to summon lawmakers to legislative meetings and to notify civilians of announcements and public assemblies. It was believed to have been rung to mark the first reading of the Declaration of Independence on 8 July 1776 as one of many bells sounded to celebrate the event.

There are separate accounts of how the recast bell was cracked but it was believed to have happened between 1817 and 1846. One of the most popular stories is that the bell cracked when it was struck to announce the death of the Chief Justice of the United States, John Marshall, in 1835. However, another version by the daily newspaper Public Ledger, wrote that the bell was rung on 23 February 1846 to mark George Washington's birthday, when around midday a crack was discovered. The paper actually revealed that the bell had already been cracked for a while but was greatly extended on that day.

The symbol of American independence was not known as the Liberty Bell until the 1830s when abolitionists who were opposed to the Atlantic slave trade, used the bell as an icon of anti-slavery. As the bell grew in prominence, the city of Philadelphia, who owned the bell, allowed it to be exhibited across the country but over time it broke further and parts of it were chipped off for souvenirs. By 1915 it had been stopped from travelling and is now housed in Philadelphia's Independence National Historic Park.

1847

BRAM STOKER, AUTHOR OF *DRACULA*

Bram Stoker was born on 8 November 1847 in Dublin, Ireland and was the third of seven children. Although Stoker is famous as a writer of horror novels, his first book, published in 1879, was a handbook in legal administration called *The Duties of a Petty Clerk*. After attending Trinity College, Dublin, he worked as a civil servant at Dublin Castle. However, he also wrote theatre reviews for the *Dublin Evening Mail*, and in 1876, he became friends with famous actor Henry Irving after writing a positive review of his performance in *Hamlet*. Irving invited him to become the manager of his Lyceum Theatre in London, a role Stoker performed for 27 years. He wrote as many as 50 letters a day for the actor, and accompanied him on his tours to America.

Stoker published his first novel, a thriller called *The Snake's Pass*, in 1890. He produced his masterpiece, *Dracula*, in 1897 – a classic of horror fiction which is written mainly in the form of letters and diary entries. Drawing on European folklore and mythology, it tells the story of Jonathan Harker, who encounters the vampire Count Dracula in his Transylvanian castle. The novel's supernatural adventures were an immediate success, and its popularity has continued to grow ever since. It has inspired a host of adaptations, including the film *Nosferatu* in 1922, and the film *Dracula*, starring actor Bela Lugosi, in 1931.

After the success of *Dracula*, Stoker published a further 19 novels in his lifetime, including *Miss Betty* (1898), *The Jewel of Seven Stars* (1904) and *The Lair of the White Worm* (1911). He continued to work as the Lyceum's manager until Irving's death in 1905. He remained part of London's high society and the arts until his death in April 1912.

THE BRONTË SISTERS PUBLISH ENGLISH CLASSICS

Charlotte, Emily and Anne Brontë were sisters and writers whose novels have become classics of English literature. In 1847, Charlotte's famous novel *Jane Eyre* was published, as was Emily's *Wuthering Heights*, and Anne's *Agnes Grey*. The books appeared under the pen names Currer (Charlotte), Ellis (Emily) and Acton (Anne) Bell.

The daughters of Patrick Brontë, an Anglican clergyman, the three girls were all born in Thornton, Yorkshire: Charlotte in 1816, Emily in 1818, and Anne in 1820. They had one other surviving sibling, a brother called Branwell, and after their mother's death in 1821, their Aunt Elizabeth came to live with them. Often left alone in their isolated home on the moors, the sisters began to write stories at an early age. They all also worked as teachers and governesses at different times, experiences which are reflected in their writing.

Jane Eyre follows the story of an orphan who becomes a governess at the grand house Thornfield Hall and falls in love with her brooding master, Mr. Rochester. It caused a popular sensation when it was published and is now recognised as an iconic work of gothic and feminist fiction. Emily's novel *Wuthering Heights*, her only work, focuses on the destructive love between Heathcliff and Catherine Earnshaw. At the time, critics were impressed by its originality and imagination, but saw it as unpolished and 'disagreeable'. It is now viewed as one of the greatest novels in English literature. Both books have been adapted many times, including a 1939 film version of *Wuthering Heights*, starring Laurence Olivier as Heathcliff. Three of the four siblings died of tuberculosis: Branwell and Emily in 1848, Anne in 1849. After her marriage and the publication of two more novels (*Shirley* and *Villette*), Charlotte died during pregnancy in 1855.

THOMAS EDISON, INVENTOR WHO HELD 1,093 PATENTS

Thomas Edison was an American inventor and businessman who created many new devices which changed lives around the world, including the electric lightbulb and the phonograph.

Born in Ohio on 11 February 1847, Edison grew up in Michigan, and only attended school for three months. Although a childhood illness left him with hearing difficulties, he was continually experimenting and inventing from an early age. He started selling newspapers aged 12, and became a telegraph operator in Kentucky at 19. In 1870, after a series of small successes, he set up his first small laboratory in New Jersey. After inventing a telegraph that could send two signals on the same wire, he moved in 1876 to Menlo Park, where he built a new research facility – now recognised as the world's first real industrial laboratory. He became known as 'the wizard of Menlo Park' and invented the phonograph, a device for recording sound which made him famous across the world.

Edison now began to work on a system of electric lighting, and in 1880, he patented an electric lamp which used a carbon filament. It was the first practical lightbulb, and became the basis of the Edison Electric Light Company which he founded with the help of J. P. Morgan. Edison produced hundreds of further inventions, including the 'kinetograph', the first motion picture camera. He opened an even larger laboratory in West Orange, New Jersey, and developed the first battery for an electric car. As he grew older, he spent less time inventing and more on his roles as a business manager and industrialist. When he died in 1931, aged 84, he was one of the most famous and respected men in the world. He led American's technological revolution, and his many inventions helped to create the modern electric world.

1851

HERMAN MELVILLE'S *MOBY-DICK* IS PUBLISHED

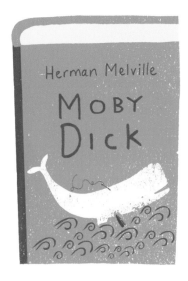

Moby Dick; or, The Whale, a novel by American author Herman Melville, was published in London in October 1851, and in America the following month. It was dedicated to Nathaniel Hawthorne, Melville's friend and fellow author.

Melville was born in New York in 1819, and spent time as a young man in the U.S. Navy and on a whaling ship in the South Seas. He drew on these experiences in writing *Moby Dick*, which tells the story of Captain Ahab, who is on a quest for revenge against the giant white whale who destroyed his ship and severed his leg. Narrated by a character called Ishmael, the novel is set on the ship *Pequod*, and gives a detailed and realistic account of life on a whaling expedition.

Melville had published several earlier novels, including the romantic adventure *Typee* (1846), which was a success. *Moby Dick*, in contrast, was a tragic and epic tale, which explores everything from class and social status to the existence of god. It was not successful, and English reviewers gave it particularly poor reviews. By the time Melville died in 1891, mostly forgotten as a writer, the novel had sold only approximately 3,200 copies. However, it was rediscovered after his death, and from the 1920s, it began to be recognised as a great American novel with deep symbolic power. The author D. H. Lawrence called it 'one of the strangest and most wonderful books in the world'. The story has been adapted into a huge range of formats, from film and television to comic books. Now seen as one of the most famous works of American fiction, the book's opening line – 'Call me Ishmael' – is one of the best-known in literature.

THE GREAT EXHIBITION AT CRYSTAL PALACE

The Great Exhibition took place in London's Hyde Park between 1 May and 11 October 1851. Organised by Prince Albert, the husband of English Queen Victoria, it was the first in a series of World's Fair exhibitions that became popular during the second half of the 19th century.

An enormous glasshouse, called The Crystal Palace, was designed by Joseph Paxton to house the show. Constructed in just nine months from cast iron and British-made glass, it was 564m long and 138m wide. Inside, the space was filled with magnificent statues and fountains, and enclosed some of Hyde Park's towering full-grown trees.

The exhibition displayed everything from technological wonders and moving machinery to arts and textiles, as well as raw materials like iron and steel. Over 10,000 exhibitors set up eight miles of tables. There were scientific instruments, intricate clocks and surgical tools, all designed to show off the latest advances and best craftsmanship in every field. Although it was an international exhibition, and countries from around the world were invited to display their goods, the event was designed to showcase Great Britain's superiority as a leader of culture and industry.

The exhibition was hugely popular, with around six million visitors. Queen Victoria and her family visited three times, and many famous Victorians, including Charles Dickens, Lewis Caroll and Charlotte Brontë also attended. It also made a huge profit, which was used to set up London's Victoria & Albert, Natural History and Science Museums.

After the exhibition, the structure was moved and rebuilt in South London as Crystal Palace, where it remained until it burned down in November 1936. The Great Exhibition increased British pride at home and prestige abroad, inspired dozens of later international fairs, and is still seen as a symbol of the achievements of the Victorian age.

THE DEATH OF *FRANKENSTEIN* AUTHOR, MARY SHELLEY

When Mary Shelley died on 1 February 1851, she was most famous for writing the Gothic novel *Frankenstein*, which is considered one of the earliest works of science fiction.

The only daughter of the philosopher William Godwin and well-known feminist writer Mary Wollstonecraft, she was born in London in August 1797. Her mother died soon after her birth, and although she had little formal education, she spent much of her childhood reading and writing. In 1814, aged 17, she met the married poet Percy Bysshe Shelley, and eloped with him to France and Switzerland before returning to England that September. In February 1815, she gave birth to a premature baby girl, who died soon afterwards.

In May 1816, Mary and Percy Shelley spent the summer in Geneva with the poet Lord Byron and his doctor John William Polodori. One evening during a storm, Byron suggested they should entertain themselves by each writing a horror story. Mary began working on the tale of a young science student, Victor Frankenstein, who creates a grotesque monster in a laboratory experiment. The novel *Frankenstein: or, the Modern Promethius*, was published in 1818 with a preface by Shelley. The couple eventually married in December 1816, after the suicide of Shelley's first wife Harriet, which closely followed the suicide of Mary's half-sister Fanny Imlay.

More tragedy followed after the Shelleys left England for Italy in March 1818, with the death of their daughter Clara in September, and of their son William in June 1819. Mary's depression was only eased by the birth of her fourth child, Percy Florence, in November 1819. She returned to writing, producing the historical novel *Valperga* as well as several plays. However, while spending the summer of 1822 in the Bay of Lerici, Shelley was drowned on a sailing trip, leaving Mary a poor widow. She returned to England the following year, and supported her son through her writing, editing her husband's poems and producing several more novels, including *The Last Man* (1826).

1856

THE GREAT TRAIN WRECK

In 1856, two trains collided between Camp Hill Station and Fort Washington Station in the state of Pennsylvania, USA. It was at the time the deadliest railroad disaster in the world and was described as the first big transportation catastrophe. It became known as The Great Train Wreck of 1856 but has also been described as the Camp Hill Disaster and the Picnic Train Tragedy.

The accident occurred on the morning of 17 July 1856 when an excursion train, hired for specific journeys, left Master Street station in Philadelphia carrying a group of 1,500 passengers from St Michael's Roman Catholic Church. The special, pulled by the locomotive *Shakamaxon*, was running late and ran slowly, often having to stop, due to the large number of passengers on board, who sat in 12 overloaded cars.

Meanwhile, at Wissahickon station, a train named *Aramingo* waited for the special to pass by on a single track lane, which had only opened the previous year. Although the special was late, the conductor at Wissahickon did not contact the depot by telegraph to ask of the *Shakamaxon's* whereabouts, at which point *Aramingo* pulled out of the station and began its journey.

As both trains approached a blind curve just past Camp Hill station, with the Picnic Special travelling downhill, the trains neared and it was too late when they saw each other rounding the curve. The collision occurred at 6.18 am and the explosion of the train's boilers colliding was heard up to five miles away. The three first cars of the Picnic Special were decimated in the crash and the blaze of the fire was seen for several miles.

A crowd from nearby towns gathered but due to the intense heat and smoke, people were unable to rescue the victims. A Quaker woman named Mary Johnson Ambler gathered first-aid equipment and walked two miles to the wreck where she provided medical assistance. Such was the important work shown by her, the town and train station were renamed Ambler in 1868 following her death.

The engineer of the Picnic Special died in the crash as did 66 passengers, while over 100 were injured. *Aramingo's* conductor survived the collision uninjured but after admitting the blame for the incident, committed suicide. He was absolved by a jury for any blame posthumously.

NIKOLA TESLA, INVENTOR OF THE ALTERNATING CURRENT SYSTEM

The alternating current (AC) system is one of the most important inventions of the 19th century, allowing for the transfer of electricity over great distances, but the genius behind the discovery, Nikola Tesla, has often been overshadowed by the other great inventor of the era, Thomas Edison. Tesla was not appreciated in his lifetime but his contribution towards everyday life included the fluorescent lightbulb, the first working radio and the remote control.

Tesla was born on 10 July 1856 into a Serbian family in Smiljan which was part of the Austro-Hungarian Empire. At university, Tesla studied maths, physics and philosophy before moving to Paris where he worked repairing direct current (DC) power plants at the Continental Edison Company. With a letter of recommendation, he travelled to the United States, arriving in New York in 1884 and gaining employment at Thomas Edison's main laboratory. He discovered the rotating magnetic field which was the source of his idea for the AC system, which would be used in generators and motors. The AC system challenged Edison's DC system in what became known as the Battle of the Currents. Edison was worried about the new AC system gaining dominance so attempted to prove the new electricity's danger. To do this, Edison demonstrated AC on animals and endorsed it as a new method to electrocute criminals who were facing capital punishment. In 1890, William Kemmler, a convicted murderer, became the first person to die via the electric chair.

In the 1890s, Tesla invented the high-voltage Tesla coil, which helped create futuristic tools such as the radar. At the 1893 World Exposition in Chicago, Tesla demonstrated his AC system and it was favoured to Edison's electric system and began to be used the world over and is still used as the main system to this day. In addition to designing the first hydroelectric generating plant at Niagara Falls, Tesla displayed the first use of electricity being transmitted wirelessly. However, despite all this groundbreaking work, Tesla was not nearly as appreciated as Edison and he died penniless in New York in 1943, aged 86.

1859

BIG BEN RINGS FOR THE FIRST TIME

Often confused as the name of the tower or the clock, Big Ben is actually the nickname of the Great Bell which chimes from the top of the Elizabeth Tower, which is at the north end of the Houses of Parliament. The bell was made near Stockton-on-Tees by John Warner & Sons. It weighed 16.3 tonnes and was transported to London by rail and sea. Upon reaching the capital, it was loaded on board a carriage and pulled across Westminster Bridge by 16 white horses. As the tower was not yet completed, Big Ben was hung in New Palace Yard and tested each day. Unfortunately, in October 1857 a crack appeared in the bell and when no-one accepted responsibility, a new bell was cast at the Whitechapel Foundry in April 1858, weighing 2.5 tonnes lighter.

There are two common theories where the name 'Big Ben' originated – however, there is no absolutely certain answer. The first theory is that it was named after Sir Benjamin Hall, who was the First Commissioner for Works from 1855 to 1858. He actually oversaw the installation of the bell and the rebuilding of the Houses of Parliament and his name is inscribed on the bell. Another notion, although less probable, is that it was named after a champion heavyweight boxer of the time called Ben Caunt, whose boxing nickname was 'Big Ben'.

The new bell, made of tin and copper, was too large to fit vertically up the shaft of the tower so was winched up on its side and this process took 30 hours. Big Ben's first strike was on 11 July 1859 but in September that year it cracked and stayed silent for four years. In 1863, the Royal Astronomer Sir George Airy discovered a solution by turning the bell by a quarter so that the hammer struck a different point. He also replaced the hammer with a lighter version and by cutting a square in the side of the bell, he prevented the crack spreading. The final cost of making and installing the 2.28m tall bell was £22,000. Besides a few occasions, Big Ben has continued to ring ever since. However, in April 2016, Parliament announced that repairs would take place on the Elizabeth Tower which would see the clock and chimes of Big Ben temporarily stop.

CHARLES DICKENS' *A TALE OF TWO CITIES* – THE BESTSELLING NOVEL IN HISTORY – IS PUBLISHED

Frequently claimed to be the bestselling novel in history with over 200 million copies sold, *A Tale of Two Cities* is one of only two historical novels by the Victorian author Charles Dickens - the other being *Barnaby Rudge*.

Set in London and Paris in the years before and during the French Revolution and Reign of Terror it begins with one of the most renowned opening lines in literature: 'It was the best of times, it was the worst of times' which begins a famous sentence of 120 words.

Due to the subject matter of the French Revolution, Dickens' 12th novel contains less humour than most of his novels but was a phenomenally well-received story. It first appeared on 30 April 1859 featuring in the first edition of the periodical *All the Year Round*, edited by Dickens himself after he retired as editor of the magazine *Household Words* having fallen out with its publisher. *A Tale of Two Cities* was released in 31 weekly instalments, ending on 26 November. Another of Dickens' popular titles, *Great Expectations* would also be serialised in *All the Year Round* the following year. Many other celebrated works of fiction such as *Pride and Prejudice* and *The Three Musketeers* are also regarded as some of the bestselling novels in history, but along with *A Tale of Two Cities*, the data does not exist to know exactly how many copies these books have sold.

ON THE ORIGIN OF SPECIES

Charles Darwin was born in Shrewsbury on 12 February 1809 into an enlightened family who would provide his education for his groundbreaking theory of evolution by natural selection. One of his grandfathers was the pottery manufacturer Josiah Wedgewood while the other was Erasmus Darwin, whose book *Zoonomia* discussed the evolution theory for one of the first times. Both men were staunch abolitionists of the slave trade and inspired Charles Darwin to be a progressive and liberal thinker.

Although he began to study medicine at Edinburgh University, Darwin did not enjoy the surgery aspect of his studies but heard many lecturers speak of theories on evolution, or 'transmutation' as the concept was known in the 1820s. Darwin left

Edinburgh and started to study Divinity at Cambridge but after graduating he was chosen to sail around the world on board the HMS *Beagle* where he collected specimens and examined fossils and local geology. In 1835 he arrived at the Galapagos Islands where he studied finches, mockingbirds and tortoises. By 1838 the *Beagle* had returned and as Darwin began to write about his travels around the world, the idea of evolution by natural selection – where animals who were better suited to their habitats survived longer and reproduced more – began to develop. The concept was a controversial one as it disagreed with English science of the era which was organised by the church, whose views were that species did not evolve and that humans were entirely separate from all other animals. Worried about the public reaction to his theory, Darwin continued to gather evidence but in 1851 his daughter Anne died aged 10 and Darwin himself grew ill.

However, in 1858, an enthusiast of Darwin's work, named Alfred Russel Wallace wrote to Darwin to ask his advice regarding publishing his own theory of natural selection. Not wishing for Wallace to take credit for the theory first but also not wishing to sadden his admirer, Darwin presented his theory, alongside Wallace's to the Linnean Society, which was the primary Natural History organisation in Britain. Tragedy struck once more when his son died as a baby shortly after, but the following year Darwin, who was still unsure whether to reveal his theory to a mass audience, published the radical *On the Origin of Species* on 24 November. The book, written for a general audience, was incredibly popular and introduced the idea that species evolved over generations by natural selection.

By 1869 the book was a worldwide hit and new editions were published regularly. In the fifth edition, Darwin pioneered the expression 'survival of the fittest' which has become synonymous to his life's work. Two years later, he published *The Descent of Man*, which proved to be another popular philosophy, as Darwin detailed the account of human evolution. Upon his death on 19 April 1882, he was buried at Westminster Abbey. Since 2000, Darwin has appeared on the reverse of the Bank of England ten pound note, alongside the *Beagle* and a hummingbird.

1863

THE FIRST UNDERGROUND RAILWAY

In the 19th century, the population of London was steadily increasing and a mass of people began commuting in to work in the city from nearby areas. As the streets became busier, new ideas of transport infrastructure were discussed. One of the leading advocates for a new underground railway system was Charles Pearson, the Solicitor to the City of London and briefly a member of parliament. He first published a pamphlet promoting the new mode of transport in 1845 but it was rejected. In 1852 Pearson established the City Terminus Company in order to construct a railway from Farringdon to King's Cross, at which point the plans started to gather support.

The Metropolitan Railway, which would become the world's first underground railway, would run between Paddington and Farringdon and serve six intermediate stations. Construction of the 'Met' was estimated to cost approximately £1 million, but with the outbreak of the Crimean War, it became difficult to raise finances and resources. The construction dates were delayed but eventually, at a final cost of £1.3 million and a few accidents along the way, the world's first underground railway was established.

The 3.75-mile railway, was constructed under the planning of chief engineer John Fowler, who was additionally responsible for the Forth Railway Bridge in Scotland. The first complete trip actually took place in May 1862 with amongst others, the future prime minister William Gladstone on board. The first trains were steam locomotives which hauled gas-lit wooden carriages. Unfortunately, Charles Pearson died in 1862, not living to see the Metropolitan Railway open to the public for the first time on 10 January 1863 when 38,000 civilians took a trip on the underground and history was made.

The Metropolitan Railway continued to operate until 1933 during which time the London Underground network had rapidly expanded. The 'Tube' now consists of 270 stations and 11 lines, with a total length of 250 miles but only 45 per cent of the network is in fact underground. It is the 11th busiest metro system in the world, carrying around 1.3 billion passengers a year – the busiest metro system is the Beijing Subway in China. In 2013, London Underground celebrated its 150th anniversary.

ABRAHAM LINCOLN'S EMANCIPATION PROCLAMATION

The victory of Abraham Lincoln in the Presidential race of November 1860 prompted the state of South Carolina to secede (formally withdraw) from the United States (known as 'the Union'). Six more of the southern states seceded from the United States in January and February 1861 and established the Confederate States of America (known as the 'Confederacy') on 9 February 1861. A further four states seceded in April and May 1861. Despite attempts to reach a compromise, hostilities between the Union and Confederacy began on 12 April 1861, when Confederate artillery fired on Fort Sumter, a sea fort off the coast of South Carolina. Thus began the start of the American Civil War.

The Emancipation Proclamation was a historic executive order issued by President Abraham Lincoln on 22 September 1863, five days after the Union victory at the Battle of Antietam. It proclaimed the freedom of approximately 3 million enslaved people living in 10 of the rebellious southern states (the state of Tennessee was excluded). The proclamation broadened Lincoln's war aims to abolish slavery as well as reunite the nation. It also discouraged England and France from aiding the Confederacy. Thousands of slaves freed by the proclamation escaped to Union-controlled lands and many of them joined the Union army. The increase in manpower available to the Union army and the damage inflicted to southern industry by depleting their source of labour had a significant impact on the outcome of the war. Seven months after the end of the American Civil War, on 6 December 1865, the Thirteenth Amendment to the US Constitution was ratified, formally abolishing slavery.

THE FOOTBALL ASSOCIATION IS FOUNDED

When Ebenezer Morley of Hull moved south to Barnes, London in 1858 he formed Barnes Football Club. In 1862, many players signed for the club but there was turmoil when the players started to disagree about the rules. Morley recognised that with different laws for the game being implemented across the country, with Cambridge and Sheffield Rules being the major two guidelines, it was necessary to formulate universal laws of the game.

Morley wrote to *Bell's Life* newspaper, proposing a single set of rules for football and organised a meeting at the Freemasons' Tavern in Covent Garden, London to establish an organisation to govern the popular sport. The first meeting was held on 26 October 1863 and the Football Association (FA) was formed, becoming the first football association in the world.

Representatives from eleven London clubs and schools met at six meetings to decide the laws of the game. In fact, the only original representative which is still active and hasn't become a rugby club is Civil Service FC, which was represented at the meetings by Mr Warne of the War Office. The annual subscription to the FA was one guinea.

Morley was the FA's first secretary and he drafted the *Laws of the Game* at his home. Those laws were very different to modern football rules, including no forward passes allowed, no penalties and no substitutions. The first official rule book stated 'no player shall carry the ball' as the game attempted to move away from the laws of rugby. Some clubs actually decided not to join the FA when the laws against handling the ball, and hacking, tripping and holding opponents were applied. Instead, those clubs formed the Rugby Football Union in 1871. As it was played under 'association rules' football became known as 'soccer', which was an abbreviation for 'association'.

The first match played under the new laws took place on 19 December 1863 between Barnes and Richmond following much enthusiasm. Of course, it ended 0–0.

1864

WISDEN CRICKETERS' ALMANACK IS PUBLISHED

Referred to as the 'Bible of Cricket', *Wisden Cricketers' Almanack* was founded by John Wisden, a cricketer who retired from playing the game just one year before starting the book as a rival to *The Guide to Cricketers* by Fred Lillywhite. Since that year, it has been published annually with no interruptions which makes it the longest-running sporting annual in the world.

The first edition of the almanack was 112 pages and cost one shilling. As an almanack it included several topics not fixed on its key theme of cricket, including the dates of battles in the English Civil War and an account of the trial of King Charles I. If found in good condition, a copy of the edition could be worth as much as £25,000.

Until its sixth edition it was simply known as *The Cricketer's Almanack* and it has been owned by several publishing houses since its creation. It wasn't until 1938, Wisden's 75th year, that the celebrated yellow cover was used, with various browns and pinks used before this date. To celebrate its 100th edition in 1963, John Wisden & Co, who owned the almanack at the time, presented the Wisden Trophy to the winners of a Test match between England and the West Indies. With the approval of the Marylebone Cricket Club and the West Indies Cricket Board, it has been awarded to the winner of each Test series between the two teams since, in a similar manner to the Ashes, which is competed for between England and Australia.

In 2000, a panel of 100 cricketers worldwide were asked by Wisden to pick their five cricketers of the century. The winners were Don Bradman, Garry Sobers, Jack Hobbs, Viv Richards and Shane Warne. In 2003, England's Michael Vaughan became the first player to feature on the front cover while in 2009 England batsman Claire Taylor became the first woman to be named one of the Wisden Cricketers of the Year.

THE CLIFTON SUSPENSION BRIDGE IS OPENED

The Clifton Suspension Bridge was opened on the 8 December 1864 in front of a crowd of 150,000 people. The bridge was designed by Isambard Kingdom Brunel, arguably the greatest engineer of the Victorian era, after he won a competition to design a new bridge linking Clifton in Bristol to Leigh Woods in Somerset, in 1829. Brunel was only 23-years-old when he submitted his design for the wrought iron bridge.

Originally in 1754, a Bristolian wine merchant named William Vick, left £1,000 in his will for a bridge to span the Avon Gorge and River Avon but it was not until Brunel's design that the bridge construction began. However, the Bristol Riots of 1831, during which Brunel was made a special constable, halted production to the project.

Isambard Kingdom Brunel died in 1859, aged 53 and work resumed on the completion of the bridge in 1862 under the design and guidance of Sir John Hawkshaw and William Henry Barlow, who increased the suspension chains from two to three on either side. It had taken 33 years to complete but it is considered a British icon, a wonder of engineering and one of Brunel's greatest legacies.

The bridge was designed for horse-drawn traffic but has always operated as a toll bridge, with vehicles crossing the bridge now paying £1. Over 4 million vehicles cross the 214m span bridge each year but no planes fly under the bridge anymore, with its 75m clearance, unlike the early days of aviation when daredevil pilots would fly beneath Brunel's creation.

The Grade I-listed building was described by Brunel as 'My darling . . . my first child' but it's almost certain he never envisioned it as the site of the first modern bungee jump, which it became in April 1979.

1873

AMERICAN OUTLAW JESSE JAMES AND THE FIRST TRAIN ROBBERY IN THE OLD WEST

The American frontier, also known as the Old or Wild West was a period of North American history beginning with English colonialism in the 17th century and ending in 1912 as the land to the west was incorporated into USA. The era is legendary for its cowboys and outlaws such as Butch Cassidy, Billy the Kid and the Dalton Gang but it was Jesse James and his James-Younger gang who made infamous history when they committed the first train robbery in the Old West in 1873.

Jesse James is one of the most notorious outlaws of the era, infamous for being a robber, murderer and bank robber. During the American Civil War of 1861 to 1865, Jesse James and his brother Frank James were guerrilla soldiers for the Confederate Army and fought against Union soldiers. After the war, alongside fellow guerrilla soldiers, they formed the James-Younger gang of which Bob, Cole, Jim and John Younger were members. As a gang they became well-known for robberies in Missouri and on 21 July 1873, they carried out the first major train robbery in the Old West, although a gang called the Reno brothers had supposedly carried out a train robbery on the Mississippi Railroad in 1866. James and his gang used stolen tools to wrench one of the rail tracks free and tied a rope to the rail in order to pull it loose. When the train approached it derailed and wrecked at a curve, killing the engineer John Rafferty. They boarded the train and forced the guard John Burgess to open the safe, hoping to discover a large haul but the money inside was relatively low, just $2,000. So James and the gang went through the carriages, robbing the passengers and obtaining another $1,000 which overall equated to $50,000 in today's money.

After the Younger brothers were captured during the attempted robbery of the Northfield First National Bank in Minnesota in 1876, the James-Younger gang separated. On 3 April 1882 Jesse James was shot by a member of his gang, Robert Ford, who wanted to receive a monetary reward for bringing James to the authorities.

LEVI STRAUSS PATENTS JEANS

Levi Strauss was born in Buttenheim, in the Kingdom of Bavaria, now part of Germany, on 26 February 1829. Born into a Jewish family, he moved to New York when he was 18 to join two of his brothers who had opened a dry goods business in the city.

In 1853 after he had moved to Louisville, Kentucky, where he sold his brothers' supplies, Strauss became a US citizen. The Strauss family made a decision to open a new store of their business in California and Levi was selected to run the operation. He arrived in San Francisco in March 1853 during the California Gold Rush, and he opened Levi Strauss & Co, a dry goods business selling imported products including purses, combs and clothing. One of his customers, Jacob Davis joined forces with Levi Strauss to produce blue jeans and on 20 May 1873 they received a patent for 'improvements in fastening pocket openings'.

Davis, who had emigrated to America from Riga in the Russian Empire, was a tailor who in 1870 was requested by a customer to fashion a pair of strong trousers for her husband, a woodcutter. When these trousers were considered a success, workers on the railroad bought pairs for themselves and by 1871 they were made from denim. He had approached Strauss for financial assistance, Strauss previously being his fabric provider. As other tailors had started to copy his design, Davis stitched a double orange thread onto the back pocket of his jeans.

On 26 September 1902, Strauss died in San Francisco and as he had never married he left his booming business to his family and left bequests to a range of charitable organisations including two orphanages. At the time of his death, his fortune was claimed to be $6 million. It wasn't until 1960 that the garments were called 'jeans' and until that time were called 'waist overalls'.

HEINRICH SCHLIEMANN FINDS PRIAM'S TREASURE

For many years, the city of Troy, famously besieged by Greeks in Homer's epic poem the *Iliad*, was considered to be a mythical location. However, one man named Heinrich Schliemann, a German archaeologist, was convinced the city existed and began a quest to locate the ancient site.

In 1871, Schliemann began the excavation of a hill named Hisarlik in Anatolia, which was then part of the Ottoman Empire. When Schliemann believed he had identified Bronze Age and Roman remains, he deduced that one level was the historic Troy which he termed 'Troy II'. Priam was the King of Troy during the siege and Schliemann was certain that his hidden treasure would still be in the area. While straightening a side of a trench he was digging in on 31 May 1873, the archaeologist caught a hint of gold and had found the lost 'treasure of Priam', or so he believed. Later, an archaeologist named Carl Blegen confirmed that the layer Schliemann had discovered was a much earlier version of the city and Priam's Troy would have existed hundreds of years after.

The treasure trove included a silver vase containing two gold crowns, 8,750 gold rings, a copper shield and cauldron, goblets, vases, axes and daggers. In a daring escapade, Schliemann smuggled the treasure out of Anatolia. One myth is that Schliemann's wife Sophia helped smuggle some treasure out by hiding it in her underwear. Nevertheless, the archaeologist was banned from excavating further in the empire and was monitored closely when he began digging in Mycenae.

Schliemann decided to trade some treasure back to the Ottomans, seeking permission to return to his work at Troy. The other treasure eventually made its way to Berlin where it was kept in a bunker beneath Berlin Zoo during the Second World War. By the end of the war the treasure was missing and no one claimed to possess it. However, in 1993 the treasure appeared on display at the Pushkin Museum in Moscow and it became apparent that the Soviet Union's Red Army had looted it upon storming Berlin at the end of the war. As for Schliemann, he died after falling into a coma in Naples in 1890 having just returned from Pompeii.

1876

ALEXANDER GRAHAM BELL MAKES THE WORLD'S FIRST TELEPHONE CALL

These days, most people and many homes have a telephone, all thanks to Alexander Graham Bell, the inventor of the telephone and the first person in history to make a telephone call. Bell was born on 3 March 1847 in Edinburgh and his family background explains a lot about his motivations to create this new method of communication.

Bell's mother was deaf and his wife-to-be was also deaf, while his father was a speech teacher. He first thought of the idea for a telephone in 1874 while working as a professor in speech and vocal physiology at Boston University in America, where he and his family had relocated.

He was granted his patent for the telephone on 7 March 1876 when he outlined his idea for 'transmitting vocal or other sounds telegraphically. . .by causing electrical undulations'. His US patent 174,465 was defended over 600 times amidst claims he was not the original inventor. However, these allegations were never successful and Bell was credited as the inventor of the telephone. On 10 March 1876, Bell called Thomas Watson, an electrician who helped with the device, stating 'Mr Watson, come here, I want to see you.' He asked Watson to repeat the sentence, which he did, and then Watson read extracts from a book into the phone while Bell listened at a speaker. It was a triumph and the world was about to change.

On 14 January 1878, Bell gave a demonstration of his invention to Queen Victoria on the Isle of Wight, phoning London, Southampton and Cowes. The queen was so overwhelmed, she asked to buy a telephone. The inventor's agent established the Telephone Company Ltd in 1878, which began to sell Britain's first telephones, although Bell actually refused to have one in his study, fearing it would distract him from his work.

After his groundbreaking achievement, he additionally tested devices for detecting metal in wounds, as well as aiding the inventor Thomas Edison with his phonograph and experimenting with airplanes as early as the 1890s. He was the second president of the National Geographic Society, after his father-in-law and he campaigned for the deaf, encouraging their integration into society, with lip reading and other methods.

When Bell died on 2 August 1922 in Nova Scotia, telephone owners were urged not to make phone calls during his funeral, so as to preserve silence, in honour of the inventor.

THE BATTLE OF THE LITTLE BIGHORN

After the American Civil War in 1865, new settlements began spreading to the Territories in the west. At that time, many Native Americans still lived in North America and the U.S. Army initially agreed not to force them out of their land. However, when gold was discovered at South Dakota's Black Hills, the army confined the natives to reservations, breaking their agreement. The conflict that followed was part of the Plains Indian War and saw the Native American's greatest victory at the Battle of the Little Bighorn.

For over a decade, the chiefs of the Sioux tribe, Sitting Bull and Crazy Horse, had been resisting the US Army's efforts to force their people into reservations and the Sioux and Cheyenne people who did accept the government's terms, found that the reservations were smaller than promised. Tensions increased when gold was discovered and the land was believed to be rich, and federal troops ordered a deadline for all Native Americans to relocate to reservations, but many refused. The natives set up a camp near the Little Bighorn River in Montana Territory and numbered around 100,000.

On 17 June 1876, a first wave of US soldiers encountered the Native Americans but were beaten and turned back. Five days after, Lieutenant Colonel George Armstrong Custer, a veteran solider of the civil war, and his 7th Cavalry Regiment, was ordered to proceed into the native territory to search for the enemy. Three days later, on 25 June, Custer located the forces of Sitting Bull and Crazy Horse but rather than wait for reinforcements, Custer was more concerned about stopping the natives from escaping and attacked at midday after entering the Little Bighorn Valley. When he realised an attack was underway, Sitting Bull helped the women and children to safety while Crazy Horse rode towards Custer's troops with a large force.

Custer was overwhelmed by the size and ferocity of the Native Americans and within one hour, he and 215 of his men were dead, in what became known as Custer's Last Stand. The melee marked the biggest defeat of the US Army during the American-Indian

Wars and the government's propaganda following the defeat showed the enemy as bloodthirsty savages. Within five years, the army had restrained the tribes and restricted them to reservations. In 1877 Crazy Horse was killed while resisting arrest and in 1890 Sitting Bull was also killed.

TOMATO KETCHUP

In 1869, Henry Heinz and L. Clarence Noble founded Heinz & Noble, a food distribution company which sold bottled horseradish. As a young man, Heinz had been given a garden patch by his parents, on which the horseradish was grown. By 1875 the company had gone bankrupt and the following year it was reformed as F & J Heinz and soon after Heinz Tomato Ketchup was introduced.

English explorers who travelled to Malaysia and Singapore had discovered 'kecap' in the early 18th century, which evolved into the word 'ketchup'. Ordinarily, ketchup which is often called tomato sauce in the United Kingdom, is a sweet sauce made from tomatoes, vinegar, seasonings and spices but it was not always formed from these ingredients. In fact, in the United Kingdom in the 18th century, ketchup was made from mushrooms rather than tomatoes and for a century ketchup referred to a sauce made from mushrooms or walnuts.

As the sauce grew in popularity, it was increasingly mentioned in literature and Charles Dickens wrote of lamb chops with plenty of ketchup in *Barnaby Rudge*, while even Romantic poet Lord Byron mentioned the sauce in 1817. When Heinz launched their popular version of ketchup, the product was advertised with the slogan 'Blessed relief for Mother and the other women in the household!' and by 1907, 13 million bottles were being produced and sold across the globe.

In 1896, Henry Heinz saw a poster for a shoe company which advertised 21 styles of shoe. The image stuck in his memory and he decided to market the Heinz products under a '57 Varieties' motto even though over 60 products were being sold, as 5 was his lucky number and 7 was his wife's lucky number.

1889

THE EIFFEL TOWER IS COMPLETED

The Eiffel Tower in Paris, France was completed on 31 March 1889 and for 41 years it was the tallest man-made structure in the world until it was surpassed by New York's Chrysler Building in 1930. The construction of the 324m-tall (including aerial) wrought iron lattice tower was started in 1887, built for the 1889 Universal Exposition in Paris. Originally, it was only intended to stand for 20 years.

The 10,100 tonne tower is named after Gustave Eiffel, the engineer whose company designed and built the famous monument. Eiffel himself had an apartment on the third floor of the tower to entertain friends. In addition to this landmark, Eiffel also designed much of the interior for the Statue of Liberty in New York.

The tower is repainted every seven years and needs 60 tonnes of paint to complete the task, while there are 20,000 lightbulbs fixed on the monument to illuminate it at night. Having initially been viewed as a temporary structure, it found a new lease of life as a wireless transmitter and was used by the Allied forces during the First World War. When Nazi Germany occupied Paris, the French cut the cables which pulled the elevators, so that Adolf Hitler would have had to climb the 1,665 steps to the summit. When Hitler ordered the tower to be destroyed as the Nazis retreated in 1944, the military governor of Paris, Dietrich von Choltitz refused as he recognised the significance of the tower.

The Eiffel Tower, which shrinks six inches in cold weather has had over 250 million visitors and is the most paid-for monument in the world.

PRESTON NORTH END WIN THE FIRST 'DOUBLE'

A founding member of the Football League, Preston North End FC have not been considered one of the top teams in England in recent years and have never appeared in the Premier League but in 1889 they made football history in a feat which has yet to be matched.

In the maiden Football League season of 1888–89, Preston finished the campaign unbeaten, playing 22 matches while only drawing four games. The Lilywhites, managed by William Sudell, finished eleven points above second-placed Aston Villa. In addition to winning the twelve-team league, Preston also won the FA Cup.

Remarkably, Preston didn't even concede a goal during their FA Cup run and having beaten Bootle, Grimsby Town, Birmingham St George's and West Bromwich Albion in the route to the final, Sudell's side defeated Wolverhampton Wanderers 3–0 in the final, which was played in front of a crowd of 27,000 at the Kennington Oval with goals from Fred Dewhurst, Jimmy Ross and Sam Thomson. The FA Cup final would not be held at Wembley Stadium until 1923.

Preston had completed the first 'Double' in football and due to their unbeaten season, were dubbed 'The Invincibles'. While the Arsenal team of 2003–4 managed by Arsene Wenger, also won the Premier League undefeated and are remembered as 'The Invincibles', they were defeated in the FA Cup by Manchester United (in addition to exiting two other competitions). As of 2015, seven teams have won the 'Double' of the top English league and FA Cup.

THE MARGHERITA PIZZA IS INVENTED

Although the margherita pzza was invented in 1889, early forms of the pizza existed across the Mediterranean for centuries before. The Greek and Phoenician civilisations consumed a flatbread baked from flour and water, which the Greeks called 'plankuntos' and was cooked on a hot stone. The Greek's plankuntos fundamentally served as edible crockery and the food continued being eaten by the Romans, who brought the idea to Italy.

The word 'pizza' originated from the Latin word for flatbread – 'pinsa and by the Middle Ages, pizza was seen as an affordable food to be cooked by peasants who added olive oil and seasoning. When the Indian Water Buffalo gave the world mozzarella, the cheese was added as an essential ingredient to the evolving pizza. Although tomatoes had reached Italy in the 16th century, the fruit was believed to be poisonous and was simply used for decoration. However, by the late-18th century, peasants in Naples began using tomatoes, probably due to starvation and when they added the perfectly edible fruit to the pizza, cuisine history was made. At first, many were sceptical of the new food and still believed the tomato to be poisonous but its popularity grew and it caught on with the Italian aristocracy. In 1830 the Antica Pizzeria Port'Alba in Naples became the first designated pizzeria.

The Pizzaiolo (pizza maker) Rafaele Esposito was working in the Pizzeria di Pietro in 1889 when Queen Margherita of Savoy visited. Wishing to design a new dish for the queen, Esposito created the margherita, which contained the green, white and red of the Italian flag. For the green, the Pizzaiolo used basil, mozzarella for the white and tomatoes for red. The queen, who had never tasted pizza before, was delighted and the most popular form of the pizza was born.

1892

TCHAIKOVSKY'S *THE NUTCRACKER* PREMIERES

The Nutcracker ballet, composed by Pyotr Ilych Tchaikovsky, was first performed at the Mariinsky Theatre in St. Petersburg on 18 December 1892. The two-act ballet was choreographed by Marius Pepita and his assistant Lev Ivanov. Pepita, who had worked with Tchaikovsky on his previous ballet, *The Sleeping Beauty*, drew the story from E.T.A. Hoffman's tale *The Nutcracker the Mouse King*. It takes place on Christmas Eve, when a girl called Clara is given a nutcracker which comes to life as a handsome Prince. After defeating the wicked Mouse King, they are transported to the magical Land of Sweets, to watch dances by Russian candy canes, Spanish chocolates, and the beautiful Sugar Plum Fairy.

The original performance was not a success. The ballet was performed in a double bill with Tchaikovsky's opera *Iolanta*, which was judged as superior. Critics complained that the story was confusing, the costumes were ugly, and that Clara and her Prince were danced by children instead of adults – something that changed in later productions. However, Tchaikovsky's music was praised from the start, and described as 'beautiful, melodious, original and characteristic'. The composer had passed through Paris in 1891 while working on the score, where he discovered a new instrument called the celesta. It features in the Dance of the Sugar Plum Fairy, and has a pure, bell-like sound which perfectly matches the ballet's fairy-tale atmosphere.

Despite the failure of its first performance, *The Nutcracker* gained huge popularity in the 20th century, with famous choreographers like Rudolph Nuryev and George Balanchine creating new versions. It has become one of the most famous ballets in the world, and is performed by countless ballet companies – especially at Christmas.

GROVER CLEVELAND BECOMES THE ONLY US PRESIDENT TO SERVE NON-CONSECUTIVE TERMS

Grover Cleveland is the only President of the United States of America in history to have served two non-consecutive terms in office. Born Stephen Grover Cleveland on 18 March 1837 in New Jersey, Cleveland was a teacher, lawyer and governor of New York before he ran for his first presidency in 1885. He had actually avoided the American Civil War of 1851–1865 after paying a Polish immigrant $150 to fight in his place, which was a legal transaction.

He was the only Democrat to win a presidential election during the Republican dominance of the presidency which lasted from Abraham Lincoln's election in 1860 to the end of William Taft's presidency in 1913. During Cleveland's first spell as president, the Statue of Liberty was dedicated and the Apache Wars which had begun in 1849 were ended. On 2 June 1886, Cleveland made history by becoming the first president to get married in the White House when he wed the 21-year-old student Frances Folsom. 27 years Cleveland's junior, Folsom remains the youngest First Lady of the United States.

After his first period as president, the Republican Benjamin Harrison defeated Cleveland in the election of 1888, although the country was at peace and in a healthy economic state. However, he was persuaded to run for the presidency in the following election, defeating Harrison on 8 November 1892 and making history as the only American to be elected in a second, non-consecutive presidency, and he returned to the White House in 1893.

His second term was hit by the economic depression following the Panic of 1893 and his final term ended in 1897. He retired from politics having served as the 22nd and 24th president and died in 1908, with his last words reported to be 'I have tried so hard to do right.'

CIVIL RIGHTS ACTIVIST HOMER PLESSY IS ARRESTED

On 7 June 1892, Homer Plessy, the 30-year-old son of Creole parents, was arrested for sitting in a Whites-only compartment of an East Louisiana Railroad train. The state of Louisiana had passed a law two years previously that made it compulsory for trains to feature separate carriages for black and white people. Plessy was a member of a black civil rights organisation and planned to challenge the law in court, and so deliberately sat in a carriage that he was not allowed to travel in. Plessy was in fact light-skinned, which would have enabled him to sit in the 'Whites-only' compartment unchallenged, but the train's conductor had been informed in advance that Plessy was legally black. He was immediately arrested and imprisoned in the Orleans parish jail. A month later Plessy appeared in court, represented by his lawyer Albion Tourgée, who claimed that Plessy's civil rights, as laid out in the Thirteenth and Fourteenth Amendments to the US Constitution, had been violated. The judge, John Howard Ferguson, did not accept Tourgée's argument and ruled in favour of Louisiana's right to regulate conduct on the railways.

This incident was the subject of a landmark court case, known as Plessy v. Ferguson, in 1896, which the judge found in favour of the state of Louisiana, upholding the practice of racial segregation on public transportation. This law was only overturned in 1954 in the landmark case Brown v. The Board of Education.

1895

GEORGE HERMAN 'BABE' RUTH

George Herman Ruth Jr., known as Babe Ruth was one of the greatest baseball players of the 20th century and an American sporting legend of his profession alongside iconic figures such as Muhammad Ali and Jesse Owens. As an outfielder for the New York Yankees, Babe Ruth set several Major League Baseball (MLB) records during his career which lasted from 1914 when he signed for the Boston Red Sox to 1935 after a short spell at the Boston Braves. In addition to his sheer talent, his rise as a celebrity during the early 20th century due to his exploits off the field and cultural impact over America made him a legendary sportsman.

He was born in Baltimore on 6 February 1895 and aged seven was sent to St. Mary's Industrial School for Boys, an orphanage where he learned how to play baseball. When his talents became evident, he was signed by Jack Dunn, the owner and manager of the minor-league team Baltimore Orioles after Dunn witnessed the young Herman playing for his school team. The nickname of 'Babe' originated at this time when older players of the Orioles called the rookie player 'Dunne's Babe' but Babe was a frequently used nickname at the time in baseball, given to youthful looking players.

In 1914, the same year he was signed by Dunn, the MLB team Boston Red Sox signed Babe Ruth as a left-hand pitcher. While at the Red Sox he won three World Series' before transferring to the New York Yankees in 1920 where he won four World Series' and was a crucial part of the legendary batting line-up known as Murderer's Row. When he retired in 1935 he had set many records including career home runs, hitting 714 and making 'homers' a more common element of baseball and a slugging percentage of .690 which is still the record. In his honour, the Yankees retired his number 3 jersey and in 1936 he was one of the first five players inducted into the National Baseball Hall of Fame.

His off-field exploits such as being a heavy drinker and a reckless driver made him a celebrity not just because of his big hitting on the field. In 1921 he was even arrested for speeding (at 26 mph) and was released from jail that same day to get to Yankee Stadium. Such was his fame that during the Second World War, Japanese soldiers would shout 'To hell with Babe Ruth' at their American enemies. The American chocolate bar, the Baby Ruth, which was released in 1921 was said to be named after him, but the manufacturer, wishing to avoid a royalty deal with the slugger, claimed it was named after Ruth, the daughter of the US President Grover Cleveland. Suffering from cancer, Babe Ruth died on 16 August 1948.

SORTIE DE L'USINE LUMIÈRE DE LYON IS CONSIDERED TO BE THE FIRST MOTION PICTURE

Often considered the first-ever real motion picture ever filmed, *Workers Leaving the Lumière Factory in Lyon* was filmed and produced by Louis Lumière in 1895. The French film maker, who patented the cinematograph alongside his brother Auguste, filmed the 46-second moving image in Lyon and premiered the achievement on 28 December 1895 in Paris.

Known in the original French as *La Sortie de l'Usine Lumière de Lyon*, the black-and-white film recorded one scene of workers leaving the Lumière factory although it was staged, as three different takes were filmed, in which the workers, who are mostly female, change their clothes due to the fluctuating weather and the films were named after the number of horses which appear in each take. To film the scene, Louis Lumière used his cinematograph which also worked as a projector to be used for displaying his scenes to audiences. The silent scene took 17m of film and was recorded at a rate of 16 frames per second. To show the film, one of the brothers would hand manually hand crank the film through the projector.

Although it is discussed as the first motion picture, Louis Le Prince's *Roundhay Garden Scene*, filmed at Oakwood Grange in Leeds on 14 October 1888, actually preceded the Lumière brother's film by seven years. Lasting just two seconds, it features the filmmaker's son Adolphe, Joseph Whitley, Annie Hartley and Sarah Whitley. Sarah, who was born in 1816 died just ten days after the film was made and is the oldest person ever recorded on film.

As for the Lumière brothers, their film inspired other short films to be made including *The Arrival of a Train at a Station* and their 45-second film *L'Arroseur Arrosé* (*The Sprinkler Sprinkled*) was the first comedy film and the first film to have a story. The brother's cinematograph was toured around the world and they travelled to America, India and Argentina to exhibit their work.

ALFRED NOBEL, SWEDISH DYNAMITE INVENTOR, ESTABLISHES THE NOBEL PRIZES

The Nobel Prizes were first awarded in 1901 and were split into five categories: Physics, Chemistry, Physiology or Medicine, Literature and Peace, while a sixth prize, Economics, was first awarded in 1969. Alfred Nobel, a Swedish scientist, established the awards in his will of 1895 as he wished to be remembered for good, rather than the evil some people believed him to be.

Nobel was born on 21 October 1833 in Stockholm and by the age of 17 he spoke five languages fluently. His father was an engineer and inventor who relocated the Nobel family to Russia, to work for the royal family, after he had gone out of business. The young Nobel did have an interest in poetry but was sent abroad to study chemical engineering. Back in Sweden he devoted his time to the study of explosives and became engrossed in the safe production of nitroglycerin, an extremely unstable explosive. His brother Emil had been killed in a nitrogylcerin explosion in 1864, so when Alfred Nobel combined it with a compound called silica in 1867, he made the explosive safer and named it dynamite.

The discovery made him famous and it was used for blasting tunnels and canals and building railways. After this invention, Nobel invented a few different explosives and during the following two decades he built factories to make explosives across Europe. By the end of his life he had registered 355 patents but in 1888 he read something which changed his life.

Following the death of his brother Ludvig, some newspapers believed it was actually Alfred who had died and published obituaries which described him as a 'merchant of death' and also credited him with finding a way to kill more people faster than ever, using dynamite. As a pacifist who wished for peace, Nobel was horrified by his reputation and in 1895 he provided for the establishment of the Nobel Prize in his will, leaving a large sum to fund the awards. He died in Italy on 10 December 1896 having never married or had children.

217

In 1901 the Nobel Prize was first awarded. Famous laureates include Martin Luther King, Jr., Mother Teresa and Barack Obama for Peace; Rudyard Kipling and Winston Churchill for Literature; Ivan Pavlov for Physiology or Medicine; and Pierre and Marie Curie for Physics. Marie Curie also won the award for Chemistry and became the first woman to become a laureate and the first person to be rewarded twice.

1896

THE FIRST OLYMPIC GAMES OF THE MODERN ERA

The seeds for the first modern Olympic Games had been sown by French academic Pierre de Coubertin – considered the father of the Olympics – in 1892. He had publicly voiced the idea to the annual meeting of the USFSA, a French sports governing organisation, and had been roundly praised. In 1894 the International Olympic Committee came into existence and plans began for the first games. Athens was unanimously chosen as the venue as it was the birthplace of the ancient Olympic Games.

The 1896 Athens Olympic Games lasted from 6–15 April and featured around 280 athletes from 14 different countries (thought to be Australia, Austria, Bulgaria, Chile, Denmark, France, Germany, Great Britain, Greece, Hungary, Italy, Sweden, Switzerland and the United States) although the number of countries is disputed. There were 43 events including athletics (both track and field), cycling, fencing, gymnastics, shooting, swimming, tennis, weightlifting and wrestling. The venue for the athletics events was the Panathenaic Stadium, which had been built in 330 BC but lay in ruins. It was excavated and reconstructed using white marble in 1895 following the financial input of Greek businessman George Averoff. Unfortunately, the bends in the athletics track were so sharp that runners had to slow down before reaching them, so that they did not stray into other athletes' lanes.

The 1896 Games featured the first Marathon, which was won, fittingly, by a Greek athlete called Spyridon Louis. The German wrestler and gymnast Carl Schuhmann became the most successful athlete at the games, winning the horizontal bar, parallel bars, horse vault and wrestling events.

THE FORD QUADRICYCLE BECOMES THE FIRST VEHICLE DEVELOPED BY HENRY FORD

On 6 March 1896, American automobile pioneer Charles Brady King test drove his car, the King, which became the first gasoline-powered automobile to be driven in Detroit. His drive in the 'horseless carriage', shortly before 11pm, was watched by hundreds of spectators including Henry Ford, who rode behind on his bicycle, as King drove at seven miles per hour.

The achievement inspired Ford, chief engineer at the Edison Illuminating Company, to manufacture his own horseless carriage, able to go faster than the King. He began making the automobile in a workshop behind his house on Bagley Avenue in Detroit. Ford recruited friends, including King, to help build the new machine which he completed on 4 June 1896. Ford named his new vehicle the Quadricycle, as it was mounted on four bicycle wheels. The ethanol-powered engine was designed with a fuel tank under the seat while the car was steered by a lever at the front. Steering wheels were not to be used in America until 1899 but in Europe, steering wheels had been first used in 1894. While the King had a four-cylinder engine, Ford's light metal-frame car had a two-cylinder engine of four horsepower. The transmission of the vehicle had two gears: the first for 10 miles per hour and the second for 20 miles per hour. However, there were no brakes and no reverse gear and the car horn was just a doorbell.

When Ford tried to wheel the Quadricycle out of the workshop for its first test drive, he realised it was too wide for the door and so he picked up an axe and smashed down a wall, allowing room for the car to fit through. In the early hours of 4 June 1896, Ford test drove the Quadricycle, reaching 20 miles per hour while his assistant, James Bishop, cycled ahead to warn pedestrians of the new vehicle's approach. Besides one breakdown, the drive was a success. The vehicle is now on display at the Henry Ford museum in Michigan, alongside other historic items such as the chair Abraham Lincoln was assassinated in and Thomas Edison's laboratory.

GIACOMO PUCCINI'S OPERA *LA BOHÈME* IS PREMIERED

On 1 February 1896, the opera *La Bohème* by the Italian composer Giacomo Puccini, was performed for the first time, at the Teatro Regio in Turin, Italy.

Puccini had already written three operas, including the successful *Manon Lescaut*, and he was recognised as a rising star. The words (or 'libretto') of *La Bohème* were written by Luigi Illica and Guiseppe Giacosa, based on Henri Muger's *Scènes de la Vie de Bohème* (1845), a popular collection of stories about a group of struggling Parisian artists known as 'Bohemians'. Puccini's new opera drew inspiration from Muger's young and passionate characters: Rodolfo, the poet; Marcello, the painter; Schaunard, the musician, Colline, the philosopher, and Mimi, the romantic seamstress. The four acts follow Mimi and Rodolfo's tragic love story, and contain some of the most famous musical scenes and arias in opera.

Puccini was in competition with a rival, another composer called Ruggero Leoncavallo, who was writing his own version of the *La Bohème* story. Leoncavallo's opera, finished a year after Puccini's, was not a success and is now rarely performed. Puccini's *La Bohème*, however, quickly became a sensation and was performed across Italy before being becoming popular abroad. The first performance was conducted by the young Arturo Toscanini, and Puccini described the public's reaction as a 'splendid reception'. It is now the world's second most-performed opera after Puccini's other masterpiece, *Madama Butterfly*.

1898

RAMSAY AND TRAVERS DISCOVER NEON

William Ramsay was a Scottish chemist born in Glasgow in 1852 who discovered the noble gases. In 1904, Ramsay won the Nobel Prize in Chemistry – a year after Pierre and Marie Cure were awarded the Nobel Prize in Physics – for his discovery and research with noble gases. In 1898, alongside chemist Morris Travers, Ramsay discovered and isolated krypton, xenon and neon.

Although there are six noble gases, which also include helium, argon and radon, a new element named ununoctium, recognised as an element in December 2015, was predicted to be added to the noble gas family of the periodic table. When Ramsay was made chair of Chemistry at University College London, he attended a lecture by English physicist Lord Rayleigh. Fascinated by Rayleigh's research into the isolation of nitrogen in the air, Ramsay began his own experiments into the isolation of chemicals in air. In 1894, Ramsay wrote to the physicist to declare that he had isolated a component after removing the oxygen, carbon dioxide, water and nitrogen from the sample. Ramsay called the new element argon, which in Greek means 'lazy'. Argon was found to be the third most abundant gas in the Earth's atmosphere, 23 times more abundant than carbon dioxide.

Working alongside Morris Travers in 1898, the scientific duo made their discoveries of krypton, xenon and neon, isolating the elements for the first time. Each of the new elements were odourless, absent of colour and single-atom gases. In 1895, Ramsay had additionally isolated the noble gas helium, which had first been discovered in 1868 and became the first of the noble gases. Ramsay isolated helium by heating the mineral cleveite.

When Ramsay and Travers discovered and isolated neon, which has the symbol 'Ne' and the atomic number 10, they found the element emitted a bright orange-red glow when used in high-voltage electric fields. Its bright emission made it a familiar element to be used in advertising signs and the new element was named after the Greek word for 'new', as suggested by Ramsay's son. Neon is very rare and as it is lighter than air, it escapes from the Earth's atmosphere.

MARIE AND PIERRE CURIE DISCOVER RADIUM

The son of a doctor, Pierre Curie was born in Paris, France on 15 May 1859 and by 1882 had been appointed head of the laboratory at the School of Physics and Chemistry in the French capital. Nine years later, a Polish woman moved to Paris to study physics and mathematics at Sorbonne University. This was Maria Sklodowska, who was born on 7 November 1867 in Warsaw, Poland. Three years after moving to Paris, Marie (who had adopted the French spelling of her name) met Pierre Curie and they married the following year after falling in love and bonding over their fascination with science.

The Curies began working in a storage space at Pierre's school and studied rays emitted by the element uranium. Their laboratory was basic, with some old worktables and chairs and limited scientific apparatus but when Marie tested a sample of pitchblende – a mineral which containing uranium – in February 1898, she discovered the sample was producing unanticipated levels of radiation and by July of that year, they announced the discovery of a new element named 'polonium' while Marie used the word 'radioactivity' to describe the high-levels of radiation. The new element was named after Marie's home country.

The Curie's realised that the new element could not have solely accounted for the high-level of radiation emanating from the pitchblende and on 26 December 1898 they announced to the French Academy of Sciences that they had discovered another new element, 'radium', a strongly radioactive substance. For their discovery of the two new elements, they were awarded the 1903 Nobel Prize in Physics, alongside Henri Becquerel who had originally discovered the theory of radioactivity. Marie was the first woman to win a Nobel Prize and between 1898 and 1902 the Curies published 32 papers which revealed that tumour-forming cells were destroyed faster than healthy cells when exposed to radium, which was a major advance towards fighting cancer. To extract the tiny amounts of radium from the pitchblende, the Curie's ground, dissolved, filtered and crystallised the mineral and the work was physically strenuous. Unknown to them at the time, the work was also dangerous and the risks of radiation and radioactive materials were unfamiliar, and the Curie's began to feel sick.

Tragedy struck in 1906 when Pierre was killed after being knocked down in the street by a horse and cart but Marie carried on her pursuits in science and succeeded her late husband as Chair of the physics department at the University of Paris. In 1911 she received her second Nobel Prize, this time in Chemistry and so became the only person to win two awards in multiple sciences. Marie had continued her work with radium and produced the element as a pure metal in 1910 which proved the element's existence beyond doubt and she additionally noted the properties and compounds of radium and polonium. During the First World War, Marie and her daughter developed small X-ray units to diagnose injuries close to the front line of the trenches. The X-rays allowed surgeons to locate bullets and shrapnel.

Marie Curie died on 4 July 1934, aged 66, from aplastic anaemia, which she had developed through exposure to radiation.

THE FIRST OFFICIAL GAME RESERVE, SABI, IS ESTABLISHED

In 1895, a motion to create a game reserve in order to protect the animals of the Lowveld, was tabled by a man named Jakob Louis van Wyk in the parliament of the old South African Republic, also known as the Transvaal. The motion resulted in the declaration by Paul Kruger, the president of the country on 26 March 1898, of a new 'government wildlife park'. Until 1926, the area would be called the Sabi Game Reserve when it became part of Kruger National Park.

Sabi covered an area of 4,002 square miles but disaster struck when the Second Boer War began in 1899 and the administration of the park was delayed. The Second Boer War, also known as the South African War lasted until May 1902 when the British Empire fought and defeated the Transvaal and annexed the country alongside the southern African republic, the Orange Free State. The first warden of the Sabi Game Reserve, Captain Francis, was killed during the war in 1901 and a new warden was appointed soon after but after it transpired his tenure was a failure, the new British management appointed James Stevenson-Hamilton who served from 1902 to 1946 as the warden during the period it was expanded to form Kruger National Park. Stevenson-Hamilton found a map of the area and departed with a few provisions. He aimed to eliminate poaching in the area and declared that no shooting was to be allowed and encouraged people not to kill animals for the sake of it. When a group of policeman were caught killing a giraffe and a wildebeest by newly trained native park rangers, they were convicted and fined. Able to gain more land, the warden increased the park's territory to 14,000 square miles.

Kruger National Park is now one of the largest reserves in Africa and tourism is a major industry since the first tourists arrived at the park in 1927.

1899

CAMILLE JENATZY BECOMES THE FIRST PERSON TO DRIVE OVER 60 MILES PER HOUR

At the end of the nineteenth century, when automobiles were in their infancy, some people who could afford cars and were able to drive them began to pursue the quest to drive the fastest. One of these thrill seekers was a Belgian named Camille Jenatzy who was born in Schaerbeek in 1868. He wished to drive faster than any person before him but had a rival in the Frenchman Gaston de Chasseloup-Laubat who also wished to break the speed record.

On 17 January 1799 the two drivers took their vehicles to Acheres, France where in direct competition, Jenatzy reached a top speed of 41.42 miles per hour (mph) in his car known as a CGA Dogcart. Later the same day, Chasseloup-Laubat broke that record, when he drove at 49.93mph. Ten days after this, Jenatzy, who was known as 'La Diable Rouge' (the Red Devil) again broke the record, but in his French-built Jeantaud vehicle Chasseloup-Laubat once again topped this.

However, history was made on 29 April 1899 when Jenatzy broke the land speed record and became the first person to break the 60mph barrier when he hit 65.79mph in his electric bullet-shaped car which he had designed and called La Jamais Contente (The Never Satisfied). Jenatzy held the record until 1902 when a steam train designer named Leon Serpollet travelled at 75.06mph.

Jenatzy was to meet an ironic ending when while hunting in 1913, the Red Devil hid behind a bush and imitated a wild boar to spook his friends. When one friend, Alfred Madoux, mistook the noise for a real animal, he shot and hit Jentazy. Injured, they carried him into a car to drive to the nearest hospital, but they were too slow and Jentazy died on the way.

The current land speed record was set in 1997 by British driver Andy Green who reached a speed of 763mph in *ThrustSSC* in Black Rock Desert, USA.

GUGLIELMO MARCONI TRANSMITS THE FIRST WIRELESS COMMUNICATION ACROSS THE ENGLISH CHANNEL

The inventor Guglielmo Marconi was born in Bologna, Italy on 25 April 1874. As a young boy he was privately educated and took an interest in science, particularly in physics and electricity. Aged just 21, Marconi began experimenting with sending wireless signals, which he achieved at this father's country estate, managing to send signals over one-and-a-half miles. This success would launch Marconi as one of the pioneers of wireless communication, which would see him awarded the 1909 Nobel Prize in Physics.

After Marconi had achieved his aim of sending signals to locations over a mile away, he approached the Italian government to seek support but they were not interested. Instead, Marconi and his mother moved to England in 1896, where the British Post Office had the foresight to back the Italian innovator. It was soon after that Marconi was sending signals 12 miles away and in 1898 he built a wireless station on the Isle of Wight, enabling Queen Victoria to message her son Prince Edward, who was on board the royal yacht.

Marconi accomplished possibly his greatest breakthrough on 27 March 1899 when he transmitted wireless signals across the English Channel, at the furthest distance ever recorded. Shortly after, he demonstrated his discovery in America. Marconi was confident that he would be able to broadcast signals across the Atlantic Ocean but critics believed that the radio waves would not reach past the horizon as they travelled in straight lines. However, Marconi thought that the waves would follow the Earth's curve and on 12 December 1901, he picked up the letter 'S' in Morse Code from a transatlantic broadcast.

The Nobel Prize in Physics was awarded to Marconi in 1909 for his work with radios but other inventors claimed to have invented the radio, including Nikola Tesla and in 1943, the US Supreme Court declared that four Marconi radio patents were cancelled. Marconi was not just an inventor however, but also a lifesaver. His radio telegraphs were used in shipping and when *Titanic* began to sink on 14 April 1913, the Marconi operator on board was able to notify *Carpathia* which arrived with enough time to save 700 passengers.

Towards the end of his life, Marconi returned to Italy and became a supporter of the Fascist dictator Benito Mussolini. Marconi died in Rome on 20 July 1937 and as a mark of respect, radio broadcasts remained silent.

SOBHUZA II – THE LONGEST REIGNING MONARCH IN HISTORY

When the King of Swaziland, Ngwane V, died while dancing the traditional Swazi king's ritual dance Incwala in December 1899 having only been on the throne for four years, his son Sobhuza II became the new king. However, Sobhuza II was just four months old and so his grandmother and uncle ruled the country – which was a territory of Great Britain – in his place.

The new king's reign had technically begun on 10 December 1899 but it was not until 22 December 1921 when Sobhuza II was crowned. He would reign the country until his death on 21 August 1982 in Mbabane, the nation's capital. His reign of 82 years, 254 days (or 30,204 days) is the longest of any monarch in recorded history. There are two disputed longer reigns, those of Pepi II Neferkare in Ancient Egypt and the Korean ruler Taejo of Goguryeo, but lack of evidence means the lengths of their rules are dubious.

During Sobhuza's life, he had 70 wives and 210 children. In fact, only four men in history are alleged to have fathered more children – Genghis Khan is supposed to have had 1,000 to 2,000 descendants. At the time of his death, the Swazi king had over 1,000 grandchildren. During his reign, he gained Swaziland's independence from Great Britain in 1968, although he also attended Queen Elizabeth II's coronation in 1953. Though he is mostly remembered as a peaceful leader, in April 1973 he used a privately funded secret army to assume supreme power, ban political parties and dissolve the nation's constitution. His son Mswati III inherited the throne upon Sobhuza's death.

1903

AUTHOR OF *1984* AND *ANIMAL FARM*, GEORGE ORWELL, IS BORN

George Orwell was the pen name of Eric Arthur Blair, an English novelist, journalist and critic. He was born in India on 25 June 1903, and brought up in England, where he won a scholarship to Eton. The son of a civil servant, he was unable to afford university, and instead joined the Indian Imperial Police in Burma in 1922. Returning to Europe five years later, he lived among the poor in the cities and wrote about his experiences in *Down and Out in Paris and London* (1933). He published his first novel, *Burmese Days*, the next year, and married Eileen O'Shaughnessy in 1936.

Later that year, Orwell travelled to Spain to fight against the Fascist leader General Franco in the Spanish Civil War. Although he was badly injured and forced to flee, his encounter with political injustice helped inspire his famous book *Animal Farm* (1945), a satire set in a farm yard which criticised communism in Soviet Russia. Four years later, he published another masterpiece, *1984*, a bleak vision of a world where every aspect of life, including private thoughts, is controlled by the government. Orwell struggled with ill-health throughout his life and died of tuberculosis on 21 January 1950, soon after his final book was published.

HENRY FORD SELLS HIS FIRST CAR TO A DENTIST

At the beginning of the 20th century, the Ford Motor Company was almost broke. In fact, it had spent nearly all its $28,000 of investment funds and had just $223.65 remaining. At that time, automobiles, or 'horseless carriages' were considered to be toys for the rich and the founder of the Ford Motor Company, Henry Ford was believed to have made an error in believing the concept of a motor vehicle would catch on. However, on 15 July 1903, the company sold its first car and changed the course of history.

It just so happened that a dentist by the name of Ernst Pfenning from Chicago had seen Ford's new *Model A* advertised and wished to purchase the vehicle. Paying $850 and theoretically saving the company before it had really begun, Pfenning received the car just over one week after he placed the order. Although it was described by

Ford as the 'most reliable machine in the world' it did have some engineering issues including overheating. However, the dentist was delighted with the car which allowed two passengers to sit side-by-side and had a backseat. The car was designed by Ford's assistant, C. Harold Wills and built at the Ford plant on Mack Street in Detroit, a city which would become famed for its motor industry.

The red-painted car had no roof but did have a two-cylinder engine, which was the most powerful automobile engine in a passenger car at that time, able to reach speeds of 30 miles per hour. Within two months, Ford had sold 215 cars and by the end of 1903 the company had sold over 1,000 vehicles. Although the *Model A* had kept the company afloat and gained them success, it was the *Model T* car of 1908 which made Ford's fortune and propelled him to the summit of the motor industry.

LE TOUR DE FRANCE BEGINS

The biggest cycling race in the world, Le Tour de France, began in 1903 as a six stage competition over 1,509 miles. The idea originated from Henri Desgrange, a former cyclist and the editor of the newspaper *L'Auto* which had a small but dedicated readership. Realising he needed a big event to keep the paper profitable, alongside a young worker Géo Levèfre, he came up with the idea for the Tour. What followed was a great success and while the Tour continues to this day, *L'Auto* became the major French newspaper *L'Equipe*.

The Tour de France of 1903 began on 1 July when 60 cyclists started the race at the Café au Reveil Matin, having each paid an entrance fee of 10 francs. Of the 60, only 21 would go on to finish the Tour which travelled around France from Paris to Lyon, down to Marseille, across to Toulouse and then Bordeaux, up to Nantes and finally back to Paris on 19 July.

The average stage distance of the 1903 Tour was over 250 miles and sometimes the cyclists raced through the night to cover the distance. With no support teams and no helmets, riders were expected to make their own repairs and some wore extra tires around their torsos. The leader of the general classification wore a green armband, as the yellow jersey was not introduced until a later race. For each stage, the fastest eight cyclists were awarded between 50 to 1,500 francs and the overall winner of the Tour collected 3,000 francs.

The winner of the Tour was the 32-year-old Italian-born French cyclist Maurice Garin, who was known as 'the Little Chimney-sweep' owing to his previous employment. He was the pre-race favourite having successfully competed in several cycling road races and won the first and last two stages of the Tour. He eventually finished 2 hours 59 minutes and 21 seconds ahead of second placed Lucien Pothier, which is still the biggest winning margin in the Tour's general classification.

However, after winning the next Tour, Garin was stripped of his title and disqualified together with 11 other cyclists that finished the race after they were found to have used cars and trains instead of cycling! Although disqualified he kept his prize money from the previous year and used it to open a gas station where he worked until he died in 1957.

THE WRIGHT BROTHERS TAKE FLIGHT

Wilbur and Orville Wright were American inventors and pioneers of aviation. On 17 December 1903, they successfully carried out first sustained human flight in the powered aircraft they had designed and built.

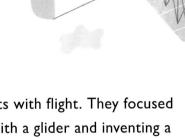

Wilbur and Orville were two of seven children, and were brought up in Indiana and Ohio. Wilbur was the older by four years, and their early obsession with flying was sparked by a toy 'helicopter' their father gave them, made from paper, bamboo and a rubber band. Neither of the brothers attended college, but instead opened a printing business, followed by a bike shop in 1892, where they sold their own design. They followed the research of German aviator Otto Lilienthal, eventually deciding to begin their own experiments with flight. They focused on finding a method for controlling the aircraft, practising with a glider and inventing a moveable rudder that made safer flight possible.

Wilbur flew their invention for 59 seconds over a distance of 260m, near the town of Kitty Hawk, North Carolina. By 1905, just two years later, the brothers had developed their flying machine into the first practical aircraft. Although at first their achievement was not widely recognised, they travelled abroad and gradually gained widespread recognition. By 1909, they had become celebrities and businessmen, selling their planes in Europe and the United States. Today, Wilbur and Orville Wright are seen as the fathers of modern aviation.

1910

THE DEATH OF LEO TOLSTOY

Regarded as one of the greatest authors of all time, Leo Tolstoy was born into an aristocratic Russian family but by the end of his life he had renounced his aristocratic heritage and his ideas about nonviolent action would inspire figures such as Mahatma Gandhi and Martin Luther King. Tolstoy's most famous novels *War and Peace* and *Anna Karenina* have remained continuously popular since their publications and have been adapted for the stage and screen numerous times.

Born as Count Lev Nikolayevich Tolstoy on 9 September 1828 at his family's estate, the young Tolstoy suffered the loss of his mother, Princess Volkonskaya and father Count Nikolay Tolstoy before he was even ten. When he began to fall behind at university and built up gambling debts, his older brother Nikolay convinced Leo to join him in the army, where he served as a second lieutenant during the Crimean War and wrote his *Sevastopol Sketches*, based on his experiences as a soldier. This work earned him praise and he drew on his experiences in battle for his first major novel *War and Peace* which was published in 1869. Originally named *The Year 1805*, the epic novel describes Napoleon's invasion of Russia and its effect on Russian aristocratic families. The novel is frequently ranked in lists of the greatest books in history, alongside Tolstoy's next major work, *Anna Karenina*, which was first published in 1878. As Tolstoy himself did not declare *War and Peace* to be a novel, he described *Anna Karenina*, which depicts Russian society in the late 19th century, as his first novel.

Tolstoy was a pacifist, having witnessed the horrors of war in the Crimea, and following his success as an author, he suffered a spiritual dilemma. He turned to the Russian Orthodox Church but believed that Christian churches were corrupt and began to develop his own beliefs. He had married his wife Sophia in 1862 and together they had 13 children but only eight survived infancy. When Tolstoy began to give away his money, Sophia objected and also grew jealous of Tolstoy's new status as a moral and religious leader. To appease Sophia, he granted her the copyrights to his novels.

In October 1910, Tolstoy left his home in the middle of the night, hoping to escape from his wife and his aristocratic heritage. By this stage, he was 82-years-old and he had been speaking and writing about his death. When he reached Astapovo train station, he died of pneumonia on 20 November. The stationmaster had brought the great author into his home and he was given morphine but it was too late. The station and settlement were renamed Lev Tolstoy in 1932 in his honour. As the author of many great works of fiction, thousands of people attended his funeral.

THE MEXICAN REVOLUTION BEGINS

The Mexican Revolution was a long and bloody conflict which evolved into a civil war and one of the biggest national transformations of the 20th century. It began on 20 November 1910 and lasted until 1920 but some historians argue that the war lasted for many years afterwards as uprisings and power struggles continued. It debatably began in 1862 at the Battle of Puebla and would lead to the deaths of over 1 million Mexicans.

Porfirio Díaz was a Mexican soldier during the French Intervention in Mexico, which had commenced in 1861. He became a hero at the Battle of Puebla on 5 May 1862, where a small Mexican army defeated French forces. The battle is celebrated annually in Mexico as Cinco de Mayo. When Díaz subsequently failed to win the Mexican presidential election democratically, he seized power in a coup of 1876. He would hold the title of president for seven terms and would serve in the role until 1911 during a period known as the Porfiriato. During the start of his rule, Mexico experienced a fairly successful era, with a boost in the economy and an increase in infrastructure and modernisation of the country. However, it was clear that the elite enjoyed the power and owned much of the land.

When the economy suffered a dip in 1907, Díaz began to lose support, especially from the upper-classes. Francisco Madero, a wealthy democratic advocate challenged Díaz for the presidency in 1910 but was imprisoned when he began to amass supporters. Madero fled to Texas and cried out for the Mexican people to rise up against the dictatorial government on 20 November 1910. Although the revolution was slow to develop, rebels gained territories in the north, including the state of Chihuahua, as Díaz began to lose the initiative. In May 1911, Díaz escaped Mexico and died in exile in France four years later.

Meanwhile in Mexico, Madero became president in November 1911 but he himself was deposed in 1913 by his general, Victoriano Huerta, who had Madero executed. Huerta was even more tyrannical than Díaz and used political assassinations as a cruel method to grasp power. As other revolutionary figures including Emiliano Zapata, Francisco Villa, Venustiano Carranza and Alvaro Obregon, joined forces, they ousted Huerta from power, who died while exiled in Texas in 1916. The revolutionaries, who had little in common besides the hatred of Huerta, were embroiled in a civil war which had many similarities to the battlefields of Europe during the concurrent First World War, as trench warfare commenced.

In 1917, a new Mexican Constitution was ratified, which included terms for a redistribution of land and a minimum wage. The president by this time was Carranza but in 1920 he was assassinated while fleeing from Mexico City. As Zapata was killed in an ambush in 1919 and Villa assassinated in 1923, the only other surviving revolutionary leader, Obregon – who served as president from 1920 to 1924 – was assassinated shortly before beginning his second term as president in 1928.

The Mexican Revolution, which repeatedly altered the course of the country's future, was also heavily influenced by US involvement as they sought to ensure their best interests through their neighbouring country's conflict. The war saw the deaths of many presidents, rebel leaders and millions of Mexicans in addition to almost 200,000 refugees escaping the country.

1911

MACHU PICCHU IS REDISCOVERED BY HIRAM BINGHAM

Hiram Bingham III was an American academic, explorer and later in life, a United States Senator. It was his discovery in 1911 of the long-lost Incan Empire site of Machu Picchu which made him famous and instigated the world's obsession with the Peruvian World Heirtage Site, which is visited by 300,000 people every year. Bingham studied Latin American history at Harvard University and pursued his dream of exploring South America, funded by his wife Alfreda Mitchell who was the heiress of the New York jewellery company Tiffany & Co. Following expeditions in 1906 and 1909 to Venezuela, Columbia and Argentina, Bingham travelled to Peru in 1911, in search of the lost city of Vilcabamba which was thought to be the final refuge of the Incan Manco Capac II who had fought against Spanish Conquistadors in the 1530s.

Near Aguas Calientes in the Ades Mountains, Peru, Bingham's small expedition came across a local farmer named Melchor Arteaga who, through a translator, informed Bingham that the ruins the explorer was seeking were in the nearby mountains, which Arteaga called Machu Picchu – 'Old Mountain'. The three men climbed the mountain for two hours in the rain and on 24 July 1911 they located, as described by Bingham 'a great flight of beautifully constructed stone terraces, perhaps a hundred of them' which were overgrown with trees and vines but which 'took my breath away'. However, this was not Vilcabamba, which was later discovered by Gene Savoy in 1964. Bingham revealed the discovery to the world and soon returned to the Incan site to take thousands of photographs and collect thousands of objects for study. His return to Peru in 1912, 1914 and 1915 was supported by the National Geographic Society, although many people claimed Bingham was not a serious archaeologist and had limited knowledge. It is thought that the character of Indiana Jones was loosely based on Bingham.

The Spanish Conquistadors of South America never saw Machu Picchu themselves and only a handful of people had discovered it before Bingham, although none of them publicised their encounter. Machu Picchu is now believed to be the mountain retreat of the Inca Emperor Pachacutec which was abandoned after he died in 1472. In 2007 it was revealed as one of the New7Wonders of the World.

RMS *OLYMPIC* REACHES NEW YORK ON HER MAIDEN VOYAGE

The RMS *Titanic* is one of the most renowned ships in history, made infamous by her dramatic sinking during the maiden voyage in 1912. Because of the extraordinary incident, *Titanic's* sister ships, the RMS *Olympic* and HMHS *Britannic* have been lost in history. While the *Britannic* would also sink with loss of life, the *Olympic* was the most successful liner of the three, with a 24-year career for which she acquired the title 'Old Reliable'.

Olympic was the lead ship of the trio of Olympic-class liners, owned by the White Star Line. From 1911 to 1913 she was the largest ocean liner in the world, besides when briefly being surpassed by *Titanic*, which was heavier than *Olympic* despite both ships having the same dimensions. In 1913 the German Empire completed SS *Imperator* which became the largest ocean liner until being exceeded by SS *Vaterland* in the same year. *Olympic* was built by the Belfast shipbuilders Harland and Wolff, who built the doomed *Titanic* shortly after. She was 10 decks high and 269m in length with the capacity to carry 950 crew members and almost 2,500 passengers.

Designed in a similar style to *Titanic*, she was created to be a luxury ship with cabins for first-class passengers, in addition to second-class and third-class facilities. *Olympic's* maiden voyage began on 14 June 1911, departing from Southampton and sailing via Cherbourg and Queenstown before successfully reaching New York on 21 June. The captain of the ship during the voyage was Edward Smith, who would perish a year later as the captain of the *Titanic*. On the ship's fifth voyage, with Smith still serving as captain, she collided with the cruiser HMS *Hawke* near the Isle of Wight and sustained damage but did not sink, which emphasised the claim that she was 'unsinkable' – an assertion also given to *Titanic*.

When the First World War started, *Olympic* served as a troopship and after the war reverted to an ocean liner but when the Great Depression followed, the ship became unprofitable and by the time she had retired in 1935, *Olympic* had finished 257 round trips across the Atlantic.

1911

The third ship of the White Star Line trio, *Britannic*, was launched in 1914 but struck a mine in the Mediterranean during the First World War and sunk on 21 November 1916, killing 30 of the 1,065 people on board. It was the largest ship lost during the war and is still the largest passenger ship to lay wrecked at the bottom of the sea. Incredibly, two people, Violet Jessop and Arthur John Priest, not only survived the collision on board *Olympic* but also the sinking of the *Titanic* and *Britannic*.

1912

ALAN TURING, HERO OF THE SECOND WORLD WAR

Alan Turing was born on 23 June 1912 in Maida Vale, England. Alan attended Sherborne School before winning a scholarship to King's College, Cambridge to study Mathematics in 1931. Aged just 22, he was elected a fellow of King's and in 1936, he published a paper that is now recognised as the foundation of computer science.

In 1939, following two years at Princeton University in the USA, Turing returned to Britain and joined the government's code-breaking department. During the Second World War, Turing worked at Bletchley Park, Britain's codebreaking centre. In September 1939 Turing led Hut 8, where he was responsible for developing the 'Bombe' machine, capable of deciphering the messages encoded by the Enigma machine for the German Navy. This was arguably his most important work as it enabled the Allies to read the intercepted German messages, defeating the Nazis and, it has been estimated, shortening the war in Europe by at least two years.

After the war Turing worked at the National Physical Laboratory (NPL) where, in March 1946, he produced a detailed design for what was later called the Automatic Computing Engine (ACE). This was essentially a digital computer which was able to store programs in its memory.

In 1950, Turing published a paper which included the idea of an 'imitation game' for comparing human and machine outputs. This is now called the 'Turing Test' and was a key contribution to the field of Artificial Intelligence. In 1951 Turing was elected a Fellow of the Royal Society for his work.

In 1952, Turing was convicted of 'gross indecency' with another man – homosexuality was illegal in Britain until 1967. Following his criminal conviction Turing was treated rather severely by the authorities who revoked his security clearance, ending his ongoing work with the government code-breaking department, and placed him under police surveillance.

On 8 June 1954, aged just 41, Alan Turing was found dead. The coroner's verdict was suicide by cyanide poisoning. In December 2013 Alan Turing was granted a posthumous royal pardon, formally annulling his criminal conviction.

CAPTAIN SCOTT AND THE TERRA NOVA EXPEDITION

Captain Robert Falcon Scott was an explorer and British naval officer who died, along with the members of his expedition, on the return journey after reaching the South Pole.

Scott embarked on his second Antarctic expedition, known as the Terra Nova Expedition, in June 1910, with the aim to reach the South Pole 'and to secure for the British Empire the honour of this achievement'. Upon arriving at Melbourne, Australia in October 1910, Scott learned that the Norwegian explorer Roald Amundsen was also attempting to reach the South Pole.

Scott and his team began the overland journey to the pole on 24 October 1911. By the end of the year, seven members had returned to the base, leaving the remaining team – Scott; Edward Wilson, the chief scientist; Lt. Henry Bowers; Captain Lawrence Oates; and Lt. Edward Evans – to press onwards. They reached the South Pole on 17 January 1912, but had spotted Amundsen's flag the previous day, so their final approach to the pole was marred by disappointment. Amundsen had in fact beaten them by over a month.

Their homeward journey was blighted by terrible weather. One day's respite allowed Wilson to unearth fossilized plant samples, which would go on to help prove the theory of Continental Drift. Shortly afterwards, Evans's health began to deteriorate and he died on 17 February 1912. Captain Oates had been suffering from frostbite and could barely walk, so he voluntarily sacrificed himself on 17 March 1912. His famous last words before crawling out into a blizzard were 'I am just going outside and may be some time'.

The three remaining members of the expedition desperately struggled on but were halted by a strong blizzard and confined to their tent. Scott's final diary entry was marked 29 March, the date that Scott, Wilson and Bowers are believed to have died. Their bodies were found on 12 November 1912, but not before Scott and his team had been lauded by the nation for their courage and determination.

THE *TITANIC* SINKS ON HER MAIDEN VOYAGE

The RMS *Titanic* was a luxury ocean liner that sank approximately 370 miles southeast of Newfoundland after striking an iceberg on its maiden voyage from Southampton to New York City.

Construction began on the *Titanic* in 1909 at the Harland and Wolff shipyard in Belfast. When it entered service, it was the largest ship afloat, with a gross tonnage of 46,328 tons. It was 269m long and 28.2m wide at its widest point. It set sail from Southampton on 10 April 1912, and after picking up passengers in Cherbourg, France and Queenstown, Ireland, it began its journey across the Atlantic. There were thought to be 2,224 people on board, including 885 crewmembers.

The *Titanic* was regarded as 'unsinkable' because it featured 16 watertight compartments, which were believed to contain leaking water if the hull suffered a breach. However, the ship would only continue to stay afloat if a maximum of four of these containers were filled. The damage inflicted by the iceberg penetrated six of these compartments and so the ship's fate was sealed. The ship only carried 20 lifeboats – enough for around half of the passengers and crew on board – and the crew had not been properly trained to evacuate the ship or to properly load the lifeboats. Many of the lifeboats were therefore launched half-full.

The first ship to arrive on the scene, three hours after receiving the *Titanic's* distress signals, was the SS *Carpathia*, but by this time, over 1,500 people had perished. Many of the third-class passengers were trapped in the lower decks as the ship filled with water, with only 174 out of 710 third-class passengers surviving. In all, 710 people are believed to have survived the sinking, in what was one of the worst maritime disasters in modern history.

1914

ARCHDUKE FRANZ FERDINAND IS ASSASSINATED

On the morning of Sunday 28 June 1914, Austrian Archduke Franz Ferdinand, nephew of Emperor Franz Josef and heir to the Austro-Hungarian Empire, was shot dead along with his wife by a Serbian nationalist in Sarajevo, Bosnia. The event is widely acknowledged to have sparked the outbreak of the First World War.

The eldest son of Archduke Charles Louis, Franz Ferdinand was married to Sophie, countess of Chotek, a former lady-in-waiting. Despite a difficult relationship with his uncle Franz Josef, he took on an important military role within the empire, and in 1913 became inspector general of the army. He was visiting Sarajevo to inspect the imperial armed forces in Bosnia and the Balkan countries which had come under Austro-Hungarian control in 1908 – causing bitterness among Serb nationalists, who fought for an independent Serbian nation.

The Archduke and his wife were touring the country in an open-top car, and had endured an earlier failed attack on the day of the assassination, when a nationalist threw a bomb at the vehicle, which rolled off and wounded bystanders including an officer. It was on their way to visit those injured that their car took a wrong turn, and the assassin, 19-year-old Serbian nationalist Gavrilo Princep, who happened to be sitting in a nearby cafe, seized his opportunity and fired on the couple at close range. They died before reaching the hospital. The assassination set off a rapid chain of events; Austria-Hungary blamed the Serbian government for the attack, and used the incident as a justification for declaring war. While the Russians backed Serbia, Germany agreed to support Austria-Hungary; within a month of the Archduke's death, peace in Europe was at an end.

THE FIRST WORLD WAR BEGINS

Following the assassination of the heir to the throne of the Austro-Hungarian Empire, Archduke Franz Ferdinand, in Sarajevo on 28 June 1914 by Serbian nationalist Gavrilo Princip events moved swiftly towards war.

The speed of the escalation was due to the treaty system at the time: Russia was bound by agreement to protect Serbia in the event of attack and the Dual Alliance between Germany and Austria-Hungary stated that if either found itself at war with Russia the other would provide assistance. Similarly, the Franco-Russian Military Convention of 1892 provided for French assistance should Russia find itself at war with either Germany or Austria-Hungary. Britain was, as the result of a number of agreements, bound to aid France should Germany invade and also, as agreed at the 1839 Treaty of London, to guarantee Belgian neutrality.

Austria-Hungary issued an ultimatum to Serbia on 23 July. Serbia consented to virtually all of Austria-Hungary's demand, however Austria-Hungary seized on Serbia's rejection of some of the minor terms and formally declared war on Serbia on 28 July.

On 30 July Russia and Austria-Hungary mobilised their armies. On 31 July Germany demanded both Russia's immediate demobilisation and a declaration of neutrality from France.

Russia failed to respond to Germany's ultimatum and on 1 August 1914 Germany declared war on Russia. Germany then delivered an ultimatum to Belgium on the evening of 2 August, requiring that Belgium remain neutral while German troops used the country as a corridor to invade France. On 3 August the Belgian King Albert I, rejected Germany's ultimatum and Germany officially declared war with France. The following day – 4 August – German troops entered Belgium. Britain demanded an explanation from Germany, when this was not forthcoming at the appointed hour, Britain completed the European line-up by declaring a state of war with Germany that same day.

THE FIRST ELECTRIC TRAFFIC LIGHTS

One week after the First World War commenced to become one of the largest wars in history, a new technical innovation was installed in Ohio, USA. It was there, on the corner of Euclid Avenue and East 105th Street in the city of Cleveland, that the world's first electric traffic light system was set up.

As horseless-carriages became more commonplace in Europe and America and roads began to fill with vehicles, pedestrians and cyclists, getting around started to become dangerous. With people in various modes of transport unsure who owned the right of way, or where in the road to be, new safety measures were gradually conceived. These included the first traffic island being built in San Francisco in 1907 and the first central dividing lines on roads in 1911 which were painted in Michigan.

Although a device in London had used a system which signalled 'stop' and 'caution' on two mechanical arms, as early as 1868, the first red and green signals were designed in 1912 by a police officer named Lester Wire in 1912. His invention, used in Salt Lake City, comprised a wooden box fixed on a pole with the two colours indicating 'stop' and 'go'.

James Hodge then designed the 'Municipal Traffic Control System' which was installed in Cleveland on 5 August 1914 and is cited as the first true electric traffic light system. In 1918, Hodge received a patent for his design which was four pairs of red and green lights, each fixed on a corner post. Hodge constructed the lights so that it was not possible to have clashing lights showing and allowed for police and fire services to control the signals. Though electric traffic lights have changed in design since, Hodge's idea was a major development in regulating traffic.

1918

THE RUSSIAN ROYAL FAMILY ARE EXECUTED

The Romanov dynasty were the rulers of Russia, who reigned from 1613 until the forced abdication of Tsar Nicholas II during the February Revolution of 1917. Nicholas was the last Tsar (ruler) of Russia.

The Tsar's immediate family was put under house arrest following his abdication. Despite being treated well to begin with by the Kerensky Provisional Government, the Romanov's living conditions deteriorated after the Bolshevik Party took over the country during the October Revolution of 1917. The Tsar's family were moved to Yekaterinburg's Ipatiev House, which was codenamed 'The House of Special Purpose'. With the success of the Czechoslovak Legion, who were fighting against the Bolsheviks, fear grew of an attempt to free the Romanovs. The local Bolshevik leaders, after discussing the matter with the Moscow leadership, decided to kill the Tsar, his wife Tsarina Alexandra and their five children. The family was informed that they would be transported to a safe location following reports of civil unrest in the city. They were instead ordered into a basement room and were executed in the early hours of 17 July 1918. Other members of the Tsar's family were also executed the same day.

A large memorial church, officially called the 'Church on Blood in Honour of All Saints Resplendent in the Russian Land' was completed in 2003. The remains of the family were found in 1979 and kept hidden until the collapse of Communism in what was then the Soviet Union. In 1998, the Romanov family's bodies were buried with state honours in the St. Peter and Paul Cathedral in St. Petersburg, the traditional resting place of Russian tsars since the time of Peter the Great.

SOLDIER AND POET WILFRED OWEN DIES ONE WEEK BEFORE THE ARMISTICE

Wilfred Owen was an English poet who enlisted in the British army in 1915. He became well-known for conveying the brutal realities of trench warfare using potent imagery and mournful language that highlighted the futility of war. Owen is often considered the greatest poet of the First World War.

Owen was injured by a mortar blast in June 1917 and spent a number of days lying unconscious on an embankment among the remains of one of his fellow officers. Owen was diagnosed with neurasthenia (shell shock) and sent to Craiglockhart War Hospital in Edinburgh to recuperate. It was here that he met fellow poet Siegfried Sassoon, who would have a profound impact on both Owen's life and his writing style. It was at Craiglockhart that Owen would write his most famous poems, including *Dulce et Decorum est*, a stark condemnation of war, and *Anthem for Doomed Youth*, a mournful lament for the generation of young men who were slaughtered in the trenches.

In July 1918, Owen returned to active duty in France and was awarded the Military Cross for his gallantry in leading units of the 2nd Battalion of the Manchester Regiment to resist a sustained counter attack before capturing a German machine gun and using it to inflict significant casualties on the enemy. Owen was killed in action on 4 November 1918 in the process of a British attack on the Sambre-Oise Canal. His death came exactly a week before the Armistice was signed that ended the war. Owen's single volume of poems was published after his death by Sassoon, his friend and mentor.

THE FIRST WORLD WAR ENDS

The First World War was formally ended by the Armistice of 11 November 1918, which took effect from 11am, later becoming known as 'the eleventh hour of the eleventh day of the eleventh month'.

Over 8.5 million combatants had been killed in over four years of air, land and sea warfare that had changed the landscape of Europe forever. Three of the world's imperial dynasties – Germany, Austria-Hungary and the Ottoman Empire – collapsed in the war's aftermath, with revolutions and intense civil unrest occurring in many other European nations. Russia's imperial government had been overthrown in the revolutions of 1917, which installed the Bolshevik Party in power, who were later forced to accept the terms of the Treaty of Brest-Litovsk with Germany.

The conflict was marked by trench warfare, with attempts to gain ground often resulting in huge numbers of casualties, such as the 57,470 British killed and wounded on 1 July 1916 – the first day of the Battle of the Somme. In total, more than one million people were killed or wounded at the Battle of the Somme and approximately three-quarters of a million at the Battle of Verdun. This was a war fought on an unprecedented scale and wiped out a generation of young men. In years to come, governments faced heavy criticism for sending thousands of men to certain death without hope of significant territorial gains.

It took six months for peace treaties to be negotiated with the Central Powers, culminating in the Paris Peace Conference of 1919. The most famous of these was the Treaty of Versailles, signed between Germany and the Allied Powers, which forced Germany and her allies to accept responsibility for the entire loss and damage suffered during the war. It also compelled Germany to cede territory, disarm and pay significant costs, called reparations. The Paris Peace Conference also led to the formation of the League of Nations, whose principal aim was to ensure that such a conflict never happened again.

WOMEN GET THE VOTE

The Representation of the People Act reformed the electoral system in the UK. It is most famous for giving British women the vote, although they had to be over 30 years of age and had to meet one of three qualifications. They had to either be a member or be married to a member of the Local Government Register; a property owner; or a university graduate voting in one of the handful of constituencies that represented a university.

However, the granting of women the vote was not the principal motive for the Act. The Act was deemed essential because without this change in legislation, soldiers returning from war would not have been entitled to vote on account of the existing property and residential qualifications. The Act changed the law so that all men over 21 could vote in the specific constituency they resided in, regardless of whether they owned a home or not. The Act also introduced the policy of holding an election on one day, which still stands today.

These changes led to the size of the electorate tripling from 7.7 million to 21.4 million people, with women accounting for 43 per cent of the total electorate. Shortly after this

1918

Act became law, the Parliament (Qualification of Women) Act 1918 was passed, allowing women to be elected as Members of Parliament.

However, it would not be until the Representation of the People (Equal Franchise) Act 1928 that women became politically equal to men. This Act allowed both men and women over 21 allowed to vote, without any property stipulations.

1922

JOSEPH STALIN IS APPOINTED GENERAL SECRETARY OF THE SOVIET COMMUNIST PARTY

Iosif Dzhugashvili (later known as Joseph Stalin) was born on 18 December 1879, in the Russian village of Gori, Georgia. The son of a cobbler and a washerwoman, Joseph gained a scholarship to Tiflis Theological Seminary in 1894. Soon after he came in contact with a secret organisation that supported Georgian independence from Russia. Some of the members were socialists who introduced him to the writings of Karl Marx and Vladimir Lenin.

Joseph left the seminary school in 1899, but stayed in Tiflis, remaining involved in the revolutionary movement and, in 1901, he joined the Russian Social-Democratic Workers' Party (the 'Bolsheviks'). In 1902, he was arrested for organising a labour strike and was exiled to Siberia. During this time Joseph adopted the name 'Stalin', which means steel in Russian. After escaping from exile, he was marked by the Tsar's secret police as a criminal and continued his revolutionary work in hiding. In 1907 Stalin was involved in the Tiflis bank robbery, which resulted in several deaths and the theft of 250,000 roubles.

In February 1917, the Russian Revolution began. By March, the Tsar had abdicated the throne and was placed under house arrest. In April, leader Vladimir Lenin urged the people to rise up and take control by seizing land and factories. By October, the revolution was complete and the Bolsheviks were in control.

On 3 April 1922, Stalin was appointed to the newly created office of General Secretary of the Communist Party, although not a significant post at the time, it gave Stalin control over all party member appointments. This enabled him to ensure that eventually nearly all members of the party's central command owed their positions to him. By the time others realised what he had done, it was too late and Lenin, who by this point was gravely ill, was helpless to regain control from Stalin. Stalin remained leader of the Soviet Union until 16 October 1952, instituting a reign of terror while also modernising Russia and helping to defeat Nazism.

THE BBC IS FORMED

The British Broadcasting Corporation (BBC) is one of the largest broadcasters in the world and is a leader of news, television, radio, sport and internet resources but when it was established as the British Broadcasting Company Ltd on 18 October 1922, technology bared little resemblance to that of the 21st century and it began as a radio station, offering a few hours of news, music, drama and 'talks' each day. By the end of 1926, the company was dissolved and the global broadcaster was born.

After the First World War ended, the airwaves were still frequently used for military communications and early live radio broadcasts which began in 1920 were unwelcome with the military but proved popular with the public who were warming to the wireless entertainment. The General Post Office, which was the licensing authority for radio waves, was compelled to ban future broadcasts but by 1922 the authority had been sent around 100 radio licence requests. The ban was lifted and the British Broadcasting Company Ltd was established, jointly owned by a conglomerate of wireless manufacturers who owned a single broadcasting licence. In December 1922, John Reith was appointed the company's first general manager.

On 14 November 1922, the BBC's first daily radio service, 2LO, began broadcasting in London. The broadcast came from Marconi House on the Strand and although it only broadcast in the capital city at first, the radio programme was soon being transmitted across the nation. The BBC's first news summary was read by Arthur Burrows, who was known as 'Uncle Arthur' by the listeners. On Christmas Eve 1922, Burrows played Father Christmas in the play *The Truth About Father Christmas*, which is considered the first ever radio drama.

While King George V became the first British monarch to broadcast on the radio, it was not until 2 November 1936 that the BBC became the first broadcaster in history to transmit a 'high definition' television programme which was beamed out from Alexandra Palace in London. Though television services were stopped during the Second World War, the BBC began broadcasting once more from Alexandra Palace on 7 June 1946.

HOWARD CARTER DISCOVERS THE TOMB OF TUTANKHAMUN

Tutankhamun was an Egyptian pharaoh of the 18th dynasty in the New Kingdom of Egypt. He is believed to have ruled from around 1332 to 1323 BC from the tender age of eight-years-old to his death aged 17. Although his reign wasn't ultimately too significant, his administration restored the old Egyptian religion of polytheism which his father had rejected and he additionally moved the capital city from Akhetaten back to Thebes. During his reign, repairs began on the temple of Amun which had been badly damaged during his father's reign and importantly, 'King Tut' as he is referred to informally, constructed his own tomb in the Valley of the Kings which lay undisturbed for thousands of years after his death, until 1922.

Howard Carter was born on 9 May 1874 in Kensington, London. As a young man he had developed an interest in Egyptology after his father had painted a renowned Egyptologist. In 1891, aged 17 – the same age Tutankhamun was at his death – Carter began his archaeological work in Egypt after his father had obtained him a position as an artist aiding an archaeologist. Carter's search for Tutankhamun's tomb, who at the turn of the 20th century was an unknown pharaoh, was financed by a man named Lord Carnarvon who as an eager amateur was prepared to supply Carter with the funds and equipment required.

On 6 November 1922, Carter discovered the tomb of Tutankhamun, which was the only untouched tomb in the Valley of the Kings. A little over three months later, Carter opened the pharaoh's burial chamber and beheld Tutankhamun's sarcophagus. Writing in his notebook shortly after the discovery, Carter wrote 'the first impressions suggested the property-room of an opera of a vanished civilisation'. *The Times* newspaper paid Lord Carnarvon £5,000 for exclusive access to the tomb and permission to supply the press with news and photographs. With new technology such as the telegram and film, the discovery made headline news around the world and fascination with the Ancient Egyptians intensified.

Among the 5,398 artefacts discovered by Carter were shrines, caskets, vases and gilded chariots. He also discovered ceremonial beds and a golden throne and it took Carter ten years to complete the cataloguing of all the treasures and artefacts upon which point he retired to become a collector. He died in 1939 aged 64. The death mask of Tutankhamun which Carter discovered in 1925, is probably the best-known object from Egyptian history and is housed in the Egyptian Museum in Cairo.

1927

THE CARVING OF MOUNT RUSHMORE BEGINS

One of the most celebrated monuments in the United States of America, Mount Rushmore, the mountain sculpture in South Dakota, which features the 18m-high heads of four US presidents, was originally not intended to depict any presidents at all. Instead, Doane Robinson, a South Dakotan historian wished to have Western icons such as the Native American leader Red Cloud and showman Buffalo Bill carved for posterity.

Chosen for the task of the historic carving was the sculptor Gutzon Borglum who decided that a national focus would be more fitting for the size of the mission and it was agreed that the profiles of George Washington, Thomas Jefferson, Theodore Roosevelt and Abraham Lincoln would be carved into the granite face of Mount Rushmore in the Black Hills in Keystone, South Dakota. The project began in 1927 and would take 14 years to complete, during which time 400 labourers, many of them miners, worked on the job of carving the 18m-high sculptures of the presidential heads. The early concept was that the four presidents would be carved from head to waist but a lack of funding made the task unfeasible.

450,000 tons of rock were blasted off the mountain during construction which used dynamite to blow sections off the mountain away, followed by jackhammering and chiselling to craft the presidential depictions. Despite the dangers of the operation, no workers were reported to have died during the construction but sadly in 1941, shortly before the completion of the Mount Rushmore National Memorial, Gutzon Borglum died and the project was overtaken by his son Lincoln. One myth is that the notion of a coffee break was originated during the construction when cold workers were discovered by Borglum taking time out from their jobs with some hot beverages.

Mount Rushmore, which welcomes over 2 million people annually, is a popular setting in television and film and most famously was the climactic scene of Alfred Hitchcock's *North by Northwest*, while South Dakota's state flag features the line 'The Mount Rushmore State'.

CHARLES LINDBERGH'S HISTORIC FLIGHT

Perhaps the most famous pilot in history, Charles Lindbergh is known for being the first person to fly non-stop across the Atlantic Ocean, flying from New York to Paris on 20 May 1927. However, he wasn't the first person to complete a non-stop transatlantic crossing as in 1919, two British aviators, John Alcock and Arthur Brown flew non-stop from Newfoundland, Canada to Ireland in a Vickers Vimy biplane. Lindbergh was the first person, however, to complete the crossing solo and the first to fly between two major cities. Lindbergh had learned to fly at the Nebraska Aircraft Corporation and had spent 2 years as an aerial daredevil, performing stunts including wing-walking, parachuting and mid-air plane transfers. As a test pilot with the U.S. Army he had survived four plane crashes by parachuting to safety and was known as 'Lucky Lindy'. When the hotelier Raymond Orteig announced a challenge to fly from New York to Paris (or vice versa) non-stop with a $25,000 reward, Lindbergh accepted and despite the dangers involved, and the deaths of competitors who first accepted the challenge, the 'Lone Eagle' Lindbergh began his flight, aged 25, on 20 May 1927. In the history-making single engine monoplane *Spirit of St. Louis*, he took off bound for Paris on a 33.5 hour journey. One of Lindbergh's major challenges was simply to stay awake during the 3,610 mile journey, as he went for around 55 hours in total without sleep. In fact he stated that during the trip he began to hallucinate and had to skim the ocean to let the spray keep him awake.

When the 'Lone Eagle' landed in Paris he was met by 150,000 jubilant supporters and his life was never the same, riding in thousands of miles of parades and being awarded the Medal of Honour.

However, his life after the experience was not always happy. In 1932, Lindbergh's 20-month-old son was kidnapped and murdered in what was dubbed 'The Crime of the Century'. The notorious gangster Al Capone had even offered a reward for help finding the child, but it was to prove futile. Apart from a career in flying, Lindbergh helped design and develop a glass pump, acknowledged with making future heart surgery possible and was also a supporter of space travel.

He was not always a popular figure and opposed American involvement in the Second World War, being classed by some as a traitor. However, 'Lucky Lindy' flew around 50 combat missions in the Pacific as a civilian. After spending his later life campaigning to protect endangered species, Lindbergh died in Hawaii in 1974.

COLUMBIAN AUTHOR GABRIEL GARCÍA MÁRQUEZ

One of the most important writers of the 20th century and arguably the greatest author of Latin America, Gabriel García Márquez was described as 'the greatest Colombian who ever lived' by the country's president after the writer died in April 2015 aged 87. The author of some of the century's most treasured novels, in addition to many short stories, upon receiving the 1982 Nobel Prize in Literature, Márquez remarked his award was a way of praising all the literature of Latin America.

Gabriel Jose de la Concordia García Márquez, but who was known by friends as Gabito, was born on 6 March 1927 in Aracataca, which is believed to have been the setting for Márquez's fictional town Macondo, first mentioned in his short story *Leaf Storm* and then becoming the central location and focus of the 1967 masterpiece *One Hundred Years of Solitude*. After becoming a journalist, Márquez began writing stories and after the publication of his 1967 novel, his fame grew. Due to the success of his literature, he even acted as a negotiator between the Colombian government and guerrilla factions and became friends with the Cuban president Fidel Castro. For a long time, Márquez was denied entry to the USA, possibly due to his friendship with Castro but also because of his perceptions of American imperialism. However, president Bill Clinton stated *One Hundred Years of Solitude* was his favourite novel and had the ban lifted.

Márquez's 1985 novel *Love in the Time of Cholera* increased the author's popularity and became another well-loved story. The author is considered to be master of the concept of magical realism in which reality is prominent in the author's world but an element of magic is accepted. He continued to write into his old age, even after becoming ill with cancer.

255

1928

PHARMACOLOGIST ALEXANDER FLEMING ACCIDENTALLY DISCOVERS PENICILLIN

In September 1928, Alexander Fleming, a Scottish scientist, returned to his laboratory after a month's holiday to find that that a dish of *staphylococcus* bacteria he had left out had become contaminated with mould. He noticed that area around the mould was empty of bacteria. Investigating further, he discovered that the substance, which he first called 'mould juice' was an antibiotic – a substance capable of killing bacteria. He named it 'penicillin', after the mould that produced it. It was a discovery that revolutionised modern medicine.

Alexander Fleming was born in 1881, the son of a farmer. He studied medicine in London, entering the new field of bacteriology (the study of bacteria) and he was able to research wound infections while serving as an army doctor during the First World War. By 1927, he was investigating the properties of *staphylococcus*, and his accidental discovery was partly the result of his untidy lab. Fleming published his discovery in 1929, but it was not until 1940 that a team of scientists from Oxford University, led by Howard Florey and his co-worker, Ernest Chain, discovered how to purify penicillin so that it could be used as a drug to treat infections. The three men shared the Nobel Prize for Medicine in 1945, by which time penicillin was being mass-produced and had already helped to save countless lives.

THE FIRST COLOUR TELEVISION TRANSMISSION

John Logie Baird was born on 14 August 1888 in Helensburgh on the west coast of Scotland, the son of a clergyman. He was in poor health for most of his life. As a child he rigged up a telephone exchange to connect his bedroom to those of his friends across the street. He went on to study at the Glasgow and West of Scotland Technical College, but his studies were interrupted by the outbreak of the First World War. Rejected as unfit for the forces, he served as superintendent engineer of the Clyde Valley Electrical Power Company.

When the war ended Baird moved to the south coast of England and decided to create a television. His first crude apparatus was made of odds and ends, but by 1924 he managed to transmit a flickering image across a short distance. On 26 January 1926 he gave the world's first demonstration of proper television before 50 scientists in central London. In 1927, his television was demonstrated over 438 miles of telephone line between London and Glasgow. Later that year he set up the Baird Television Development Company (BTDC).

In 1928, the BTDC achieved the first transatlantic television transmission between London and New York and the first transmission to a ship in the middle of the Atlantic Ocean. This was followed by the first colour transmission and then later the same year the first stereoscopic transmission, which made the images look more solid.

In 1929, the German post office gave Baird the facilities to develop an experimental television service based on his mechanical system. Sound and vision were initially sent alternately and only began to be transmitted together from 1930.

JOSEPH STALIN LAUNCHES THE FIRST SOVIET UNION FIVE-YEAR PLAN

In 1928, Joseph Stalin, leader of the Soviet Union, was told by his advisers that the country required an extra 250,000 tractors in order to modernise farming, oil fields needed to be developed to provide the necessary fuel to drive the machines and power stations needed to be built to supply the farms with electricity. Since the Russian Revolution in October 1917, industrial progress had been slow in the Soviet Union and it was not until 1927 that production had reached the levels achieved before the start of the First World War.

The first Five-Year Plan, introduced in 1928, concentrated on the development of iron and steel, machine-tools, electric power, coal and transport. The workers were set high targets. Stalin demanded a 110% increase in coal production, 200% increase in iron production and 335% increase in electric power. Every factory had large boards which showed the output of individual workers. Those that failed to reach the required targets were publicity criticised and humiliated. Some workers could not cope with this pressure and missed work. This led to even stricter measures being introduced. There was no recourse for the workers: strikers were shot, and wreckers (slow workers) was accused of trying to sabotage the Five-Year Plan and if found guilty would be executed, imprisoned or sent to work as forced (slave) labour.

Some keen young Communists, called Pioneers, went into barren areas and set up new towns and industries from nothing. Education schemes to train skilled, literate workers were introduced and large crèches to care for young children were set-up so that women could also work.

Rapid industrialisation of the country as a whole was the focus and essential resources and government funding were rerouted to the cause. This redistribution came at the expense of the people: basic goods, including food, became scarce, housing and wages were terrible and thousands died from starvation and cold.

But the improvements in industrial production during the first Five-Year Plan were phenomenal: coal, iron, oil and electricity production increased massively and the first plan was deemed such a success that it finished one-year early having achieved its industrial targets.

1930

THE CHRYSLER BUILDING IN NEW YORK BECOMES THE FIRST STRUCTURE OVER 1,000 FEET

Located in the East Side of Midtown Manhattan in New York City, the Chrysler Building became the first structure in the world to stand over 1,000 feet tall. The construction of the Chrysler Building began in 1928 during intense competition in New York to build the world's tallest skyscraper. The project was financed by Walter Chrysler, an automotive industry executive from Kansas, who founded the Chrysler Corporation. Upon completion on 27 May 1930, the Chrysler Building stood at 319m tall, becoming the tallest building in the world.

Although it is still the tallest brick building in the world, it was surpassed in height after only 11 months when the Empire State Building was completed in New York – the centre of the skyscraper race. The Chrysler Building was designed by the architect William Van Alen and is a famous example of Art Deco architecture, famed for its terraced crown, comprised of seven terraced arches in a radiating sunbeam pattern. The construction of the skyscraper was frantic as it competed with a rival building, the Bank of Manhattan Trust Building, and four floors were built per week. In fact, the Bank of Manhattan Trust Building was completed before the Chrysler but it's height of 928m was surpassed by Van Alen's design with its crown and spire. No workers died during the construction of the Chrysler Building whereas a recorded five people died making the Empire State Building.

Today, the Chrysler Building, which is the fourth tallest skyscraper in New York following the completion of One World Trade Center, is considered one of the finest buildings in New York, and a classic design. The 3,862-windowed tower was declared a National Historic Landmark in 1976.

AMY JOHNSON BECOMES THE FIRST WOMAN TO FLY SOLO FROM ENGLAND TO AUSTRALIA

On 5 May 1930, 'aviatrix' Amy Johnson took flight from Croydon in south London to begin her journey as the first female pilot to fly solo from England to Australia. Her records in aviation though were overshadowed by her death in suspicious circumstances during the Second World War. Having set many aviation records, she is undoubtedly one of Britain's greatest pilots.

Johnson was born on 1 July 1903 in Kingston-upon-Hull and was introduced to flying as a hobby during the comparatively early days of aviation. In July 1929 she obtained her pilot's 'A' licence at the London Aeroplane Club. After purchasing a second-hand de Havilland DH.60 Gipsy Moth plane in 1930 which she named *Jason*, she set her mind to setting and breaking aviation records.

She set off from Croydon on 5 May 1930 as the solo pilot of Jason and reached Darwin, Northern Territory, Australia on 24 May, having flown over 11,000 miles. For her achievement, Johnson was awarded a CBE and the Harmon Trophy which recognised accomplishments in aviation. This wasn't the end to Johnson's feats and in July 1931, alongside co-pilot Jack Humphreys, she flew from London to Moscow in 21 hours – the first time it had ever been completed in one day. From Moscow, the duo continued in her second plane *Jason II* to Tokyo, setting a new time for a flight from Britain to Japan.

In 1932 she married pilot Jim Mollison when he proposed to her just eight hours after meeting. Together they continued to break records until their divorce in 1938. When the Second World War broke out, Johnson joined the Air Transport Auxiliary but on 5 January 1941 disaster struck when her Airspeed Oxford went off course in bad conditions while on a routine mission. Plunging down, Johnson escaped from the plane and parachuted into the Thames Estuary. Seeing her, the crew of HMS *Haslemere* attempted to rescue her. The commander of the ship, Lt. Cdr Walter Fletcher dived in to rescue her but failed in his attempt and later died. A surge took the ship close to Johnson but the stern crashed down on her, sucking her into the propellers. Her body was never recovered.

Circumstances surrounding her death are still disputed. While it has been claimed there was a third person in the water, other sources have stated Johnson's plane was shot down in friendly fire after she failed to give a correct identification code but upon realising the error, the crew of HMS *Haslemere* were sworn to secrecy.

DON BRADMAN SCORES 309 RUNS IN ONE DAY

Commonly alluded to as the finest Test batsman of all time, Sir Donald 'The Don' Bradman made cricket history in 1930 and set a record which to this day has not been broken. While his Test batting average of 99.94 runs is the highest ever, set between 1928 and 1948, it was Bradman's first day innings during the 1930 Ashes Test in England which is arguably his greatest achievement.

Bradman was born in Cootamundra, New South Wales, Australia on 27 August 1908 and the legend of him practising the sport with just a golf ball and cricket stump in his garden is a part of Australian history.

In 1928, Bradman was selected for his first Test match in the 1928–29 Ashes series against the old foe, England. However, following a poor First Test, Bradman was dropped to twelfth man. In fact, that Test in Brisbane saw England win by 675 runs, which is still the biggest winning margin in Ashes history. Nevertheless, he was recalled into the side and improved as the series continued, but England won 4–1.

The year 1930 began well for 'The Don' when he set a world record innings of 452 not out for New South Wales against Queensland in Australia and was selected for the year's Ashes series in England. The editor of *Wisden Cricketers' Almanack*, Charles Stewart Caine, believed England's victorious team would comprehensively retain the Ashes urn and many people believed Bradman was too young and out of his comfort zone to be a real threat. He was to prove them wrong.

Having only featured in four Test matches before arriving in England, Bradman took to the field with his bat on 11 July 1930, in the third Test of the series at Headingley in Leeds. Bradman stated that he couldn't fathom the idea of waiting to bat while warming himself next to a fire but any doubts about his ability were going to be almost literally hit for six.

By 12.50pm he had scored a century to become only the third person at that time to have hit a Test match 100 before lunch on the first day. By tea he had hit 30 boundaries and scored 219 runs. The final ball of the day saw his 42nd boundary as he made 309, a feat unmatched to this day. No other player has ever scored 300 runs in a single day's innings, with the next best score being 295 from England's Wally Hammond against New Zealand in 1933. The following day, Bradman continued his batting but was caught off the bowling of Maurice Tate on 334 runs from 448 balls. He had been at the crease for six hours and twenty three minutes. The Test actually ended in a draw but Australia won the series 2–1 to reclaim the Ashes.

THE FIRST FOOTBALL WORLD CUP

The first FIFA (Federation Internationale de Football Association) World Cup was staged in 1930. A number of teams put forward their bid to host the tournament but it was decided to be awarded to Uruguay, who were the reigning Olympic football champions and who, in 1930, would be celebrating their centenary of independence.

The tournament was conceived by the French president of FIFA, Jules Rimet, who the trophy was actually named after. The World Cup, held a year after the 1929 Wall Street Crash, was seen as a great triumph, which is evident in its expansion to becoming one of the biggest sports events of the 21st century.

Only 13 nations competed at the World Cup, nine of which were South American. None of the Home Nations competed, as they had withdrawn from FIFA following a dispute, with England becoming the first British team to play at a World Cup when they travelled to Brazil for the 1950 tournament.

Lucien Laurent made history when he became the first person to score in a World Cup, netting for France against Mexico and 69 more goals would be scored before the tournament's final whistle. After the World Cup, when the Second World War broke out, Laurent was called up to the army and after being captured, spent three years as a German prisoner of war. Laurent was the only member of the 1930 France squad who lived to see his country win their first and only World Cup in 1998.

King Carol II of Romania personally selected his nation's squad for the tournament but they failed to progress past the group stage. Instead, the hosts Uruguay met rivals

Argentina in the first World Cup final which was played at the aptly name Centenario Stadium in the capital city, Montevideo in front of 68,346 fans. As there was no official match ball and neither team could agree on which ball to use, it was decided that one ball provided by each team would be used in either half. Some people suggest this is where the term 'a game of two halves' originates. Uruguay ran out 4–2 winners to cement their place as the first World Cup champions in history.

Francisco Varallo, who played as a forward for Argentina in the tournament, was the last surviving player from the 1930 World Cup. He died at the age of 100 in 2010.

1931

AMERICAN GANGSTER AL CAPONE IS ARRESTED FOR TAX EVASION

Al Capone is one of the most renowned gangster in American history who rose to prominence during the Prohibition era and the founder of the Chicago Mob. At one time a popular figure in society, as an illegal distributor of alcohol, Capone's command of the St Valentine's Day Massacre damaged his reputation and made him Chicago's 'Public Enemy Number One'. Having been unable to imprison Capone for his crimes, the FBI prosecuted him for tax evasion in 1931 and he was jailed until his death in 1947.

Born to Italian immigrants in Brooklyn, New York on 17 January 1899, Alphonse Gabriel 'Al' Capone was a member of the Five Points Gang before moving to Chicago and becoming a lieutenant in the Colosimo mob. With the introduction of Prohibition, which banned the sale, production, importation and transportation of alcohol, gangsters saw beer and liquor as industries to make money and Capone's influence grew during this period. In 1925 he became the boss of the Colosimo mob when the previous boss Johnny Torrio was seriously injured in an assassination attempt. As Capone's reputation of brutality against other gangs grew, he began to dominate the Chicago racketeering scene. Under Capone, the Chicago Outfit, also known as the Chicago Mob or The Organisation eliminated many other mobs in Chicago. Capone had once insulted a woman while working in a Brooklyn night club and her brother had slashed Capone in the face, which lead to a nickname of Scarface. Gallucio, who had wounded Capone, was later hired as his bodyguard.

The St Valentine's Day Massacre of 14 February 1929, which was organised by Capone, resulted in the executions in broad delight of seven members of the 'Bugs' Moran mob, when they were gunned down by gangsters posing as police. For this act, Capone was vilified and the Bureau of Investigation dedicated their efforts to arresting Capone. On 16 June 1931 'Scarface' was arrested for tax evasion and Prohibition charges. In October he was sentenced to eleven years in prison and heavily fined. Capone was sent to Atlanta Penitentiary before being relocated to the famous Alcatraz Island where he became ill. He was released in 1939 but had become gravely sick with syphilis and retired from public life. Capone died following a stroke on 25 January 1947.

Capone is the archetypal gangster for the Prohibition era and the ideas of gangsters wearing pin-striped suits and fedoras were based on photographs of Capone. He has been portrayed numerous times in film, television and literature.

THE EMPIRE STATE BUILDING IS COMPLETED

The Empire State Building was officially opened on 1 May 1931, when American President Herbert Hoover pressed a button from the White House to turn on the building's famous lights. Construction had started in March 1930, as a result of a competition between Walter Chrysler and John Jakob Raskob of General Motors, to see who could build the taller skyscraper. Raskob hired the architecture firm Shreve, Lamb & Harmon Associates to design the Art Deco Empire State Building, located on 5th Avenue and 33rd Street in Manhattan, New York.

It was completed ahead of schedule in just over a year, and at some stages of construction, the framework rose by four-and-a-half stories a week. It provided employment to 3,400 workers-a-day during the Depression era, as well as a much-needed sense of national pride.

The building stands a total of 381m-high, or 443m including its antenna spire. It remained the world's tallest building for almost 40 years, from its completion until the construction of the original World Trade Center's North Tower in 1970. It is still the fifth-tallest skyscraper in the United States and the 29th-tallest in the world. The building has been called an American icon, and named one of the Seven Wonders of the Modern World.

THE FIRST NON-STOP FLIGHT ACROSS THE PACIFIC

When the Japanese newspaper *Asahi Shimbun* offered a $25,000 to the first person able to fly from Japan to the USA, across the Pacific on a non-stop flight, Clyde 'Upside-Down' Pangborn accepted the challenge and made history when he accomplished the historic exploit in 1931.

Pangborn, who was born in 1895 in Washington, USA and was a flying instructor for the US Air Service during the First World War, where he learned to fly with his plane upside-down, hence his nickname of 'Upside-Down' Pangborn. When the war finished, Pangborn joined Gates Flying Circus, performing plane stunts and acrobatics as a 'barnstormer', but when the Great Depression stunned the world, Gates Flying Circus, in addition to many other stunt shows, went bankrupt and Pangborn turned his attention to world record attempts.

When the Pacific challenge arose, Pangborn, alongside Hugh Herndon, Jr. flew from Siberia to Japan in the red Bellanca J-300 plane *Miss Veedol* to prepare for the long journey. From there, the duo began the challenge of flying across the Pacific to America.

They took off from Sabishiro Beach in Misawa, Japan on 4 October 1931, destined for Seattle, USA, which was approximately 5,500 miles away, around 2,000 miles further than Charles Lindbergh's historic flight from New York to Paris. Three hours into the journey, Pangborn had to go onto the wing supports at over 4,200m in the air, to fix the planes landing gear which had jammed. A further incident nearly ended the attempt, and the pair's lives, when Herndon let the fuel tanks run dry, at which point the engine failed and Pangborn daringly flew the plane down to 426m and then pulled up to restart the engine. It worked and the flight continued.

Approaching their destination, in heavy fog, the plane almost hit Mount Rainier, the highest mountain in Washington but they avoided it and then belly-landed *Miss Veedol* in a field in Wenatchee, Washington. The perilous flight had taken 41 hours and 13 minutes.

Pangborn did not receive much of the prize money as Herndon had funded the journey and when the Second World War broke out, he joined the Royal Air Force and then when America entered the war in 1941, he joined the US Air Force. When he died in 1958 he was awarded military honours, having logged over 24,000 flight hours.

1936

EDWARD VIII BECOMES KING

Edward VIII became King of the United Kingdom on 20 January 1936, following the death of his father King George V. He was the elder of two brothers, the younger brother later becoming George VI, known informally as 'Bertie'.

In the 1920s and early 1930s, Edward had gained a reputation for his reckless behaviour, inappropriate interference in politics and frequent breaking of royal protocol. He had courted controversy by conducting affairs with married women, which his father strongly disapproved of.

He fell in love with the divorced American socialite Wallis Simpson in 1934 and it became apparent that Edward was considering marrying her. At the time, Mrs Simpson was seeking a divorce from her second husband. The prospect of a twice-divorced woman with two living ex-husbands as queen consort was too much for the British establishment. It was also problematic from a religious standpoint, as remarriage after divorce was opposed by the Church of England, of which Edward was the Supreme Governor.

Edward took the unprecedented decision to abdicate the throne on 10 December 1936 so that he would be free to marry Mrs Simpson. The following evening, he announced in a radio broadcast that: 'I have found it impossible to carry the heavy burden of responsibility and to discharge my duties as King as I would wish to do without the help and support of the woman I love.'

JESSE OWENS STARS AT THE BERLIN OLYMPIC GAMES

Jesse Owens was an African-American athlete who caused a sensation at the 1936 Berlin Olympic Games. The previous year, aged just 21, he broke three world records in a single day at the Western Conference track-and-field athletics meet at the University of Michigan and equalled the world record for the 100-yard dash.

At the 1936 Berlin Olympics, Owens won the 100m in an Olympic record time of 10.3 seconds, the 200m in a world record time of 20.7 seconds and the long jump with a leap of 8.06m. He also was part of the gold medal-winning team who won the 4 × 100m relay. This was an immensely symbolic moment in the context of the time as Adolf Hitler, then the Chancellor of Germany, had hoped to showcase the superiority of the Aryan race at the Berlin Olympics. Jesse Owens' performance had effectively crushed that theory on an international stage.

A popular myth emerged that Hitler refused to shake Owens' hand because he was black, and this 'snub' was reported in the American press. The truth was that Hitler had congratulated only a few German and Finnish medal winners the previous day (the opening day of the Games), which prompted the International Olympic Committee President to insist that Hitler congratulate all the winners or none of them. Hitler decided on the latter before Owens had competed.

SERGEI PROKOFIEV'S *PETER AND THE WOLF* DEBUTS

Peter and the Wolf is a short children's story written by Russian composer Sergei Prokofiev in 1936. The story is spoken by a narrator and accompanied by a number of orchestral instruments. Prokofiev hoped that his composition would help to shape musical tastes in children from an early age.

It is based on a Russian folk tale, which tells the story of how a young boy, who lives in his grandfather's house in the middle of a forest, manages to cleverly catch a wolf. There are four animals that play roles in the tale: a duck, a bird a cat and the wolf. Each of these characters is represented by a different musical instrument: the duck is identified with an oboe, the bird with a flute, the cat with a clarinet and the wolf with French horns. Peter's grandfather is signified with a bassoon, while the hunters are denoted with a woodwind and trumpet theme, with the timpani and bass drum providing the sound of gunshots. Peter himself is revealed through a number of different string instruments, including the violin, viola, cello and double bass.

Despite a disappointing opening night in 1936, which attracted a small audience, *Peter and the Wolf* became popular quickly, and it has been adapted a number of times, including an animated version of the tale produced by Walt Disney in 1946.

THE HOOVER DAM

The Hoover Dam is situated in the Black Canyon of the Colorado River on the border between the states of Arizona and Nevada in the USA. It was built between 1930 and 1936 to control flooding, produce hydroelectric power and to provide water for irrigation. The dam was named after US President Herbert Hoover, whose efforts as Secretary of Commerce in the 1920s enabled the project to get off the ground. The project was a considerable feat of engineering, and in preparation for work to begin on the dam, the Colorado River had to be diverted and the canyon walls blasted.

Around 21,000 workers helped to build the dam. Working conditions at the construction site were perilous and a total of 112 people died. This figure does not include workers who were recorded as dying from 'pneumonia', which was more likely carbon monoxide poisoning arising from working in confined and dusty spaces at temperatures over 60°C (140°F).

The dam encloses Lake Mead, which at approximately 115 miles long is one of the largest manmade lakes in the world. At the time of its completion, the Hoover Dam was the largest dam in the world. It stands at 726m high and 379m long (measured from the crest of the dam). The dam's 17 turbines generate sufficient energy to fuel 1.3 million homes, many of which are located in Los Angeles.

269

1940

THE BATTLE OF BRITAIN

After Adolf Hitler had invaded France and forced their surrender on 22 June 1940, he imagined the British would agree to sue for peace. Surrender was not something that Prime Minister Winston Churchill was willing to consider, and so Hitler approved plans to invade Britain, codenamed Operation Sea Lion.

Hitler's plan was to first achieve air superiority over the Royal Air Force (RAF) by initiating a campaign of air raids by the German Air Force (Luftwaffe). This campaign, which took place between 10 July and 31 October 1940 became known as the Battle of Britain.

German bombers attacked British shipping before concentrating on RAF Fighter Command's air bases and radar stations. However, by the middle of September, RAF fighters were destroying German bombers quicker than the Germans could manufacture replacements. The British had superior radar equipment that could warn them of attacks, but also superior fighters, most notably the Supermarine Spitfire and Hawker Hurricane. Encountering heavy losses, the Luftwaffe changed their focus in early September 1940 to a night-time bombing campaign of London and other industrial cities and ports, dubbed the 'Blitz'. By the end of October, the Germans had lost nearly 1,999 aircraft compared with 1,550 British losses. Although the Blitz would continue until May 1941, Hitler soon cancelled Operation Sea Lion. The British had won the Battle of Britain and delivered the first major military setback to Hitler's Germany.

THE FIRST MCDONALD'S RESTAURANT OPENS

In 2015 it was the fourth largest employer in the world with 1.9 million employees. Only the United States Department of Defence, the People's Liberation Army of China and the American supermarket chain Walmart had more employees than the fast food restaurant McDonald's. The restaurant chain, which now has more than 36,000 locations worldwide, first opened as the McDonald's Bar-B-Que on 15 May 1940 by two brothers named Maurice and Richard McDonald. The first restaurant was on Fourteenth and E in San Bernardino, California and offered 25 menu items. The brothers offered a carhop service whereby waiters or waitresses would bring the food to the customers in their cars, often travelling between the kitchen and the cars on roller skates.

By 1948, the restaurant had started to evolve into a more modern self-service diner. The 25 items offered in 1940 were reduced to nine with the most popular being the 15 cent hamburger. One year later, French fries replaced potato chips as one of the key items sold by the fast food company.

As the restaurants gained in popularity, a salesman named Ray Kroc, who sold milkshake machines, visited the San Bernardino site and saw an opportunity to expand the business. He inspired the brothers to open new restaurants across the country and the first under the name McDonald's was opened on 15 April 1955 in Des Plaines, Illinois. By 1958, McDonald's had sold 100 million hamburgers.

The first McDonald's in the United Kingdom opened in Woolwich, London in 1974 and is now the largest private-sector employer in the UK. Nowadays, the chain sells 75 hamburgers worldwide every single second and with 70 million customers being served daily, the number of people who frequent McDonald's is higher than the population of France.

FOOD RATIONING BEGINS IN BRITAIN

Before the Second World War broke out, Great Britain was heavily reliant on imported goods and food, including roughly 70 per cent of its cheese and sugar, 50 per cent of its meat, approximately 80 per cent of fruits and around 70 per cent of cereals and fats. It proved especially difficult to maintain these imports following the outbreak of the Second World War. The Germans adopted a policy of attacking merchant shipping on their way to Britain in order to starve the country into surrender and reduce the country's industrial output. In order to manage food shortages, food rationing was introduced in 1940 and was overseen by Lord Woolton, the newly appointed Minister of Food. People were required to register at shops and were each given a ration book containing coupons. Everyone had a certain number of points per month, which they could 'spend' however they chose.

The first items of food to be rationed were bacon, butter and sugar. This was later followed by rationing for meat, cheese, eggs, milk, lard, tea, jam, biscuits, breakfast cereals and canned and dried fruit.

Rationing continued after the end of the Second World War. Bread rationing actually began in 1946 after persistent rain damaged Britain's wheat crop, and didn't end until 1948, while confectionery rationing ceased in February 1953. Sugar rationing ended in September 1953, but it wasn't until 4 July 1954 that meat and other rationing was suspended. The rationing experiment was widely regarded as a major success, in spite of the hardship it inflicted. Lord Woolton became popular and lent his name to the 'Woolton Pie' – a cheap, nutritious meatless pie that he popularised.

1948

ALBERT I BECOMES THE FIRST MONKEY IN SPACE

Wernher von Braun was a German aerospace engineer who invented the V-2 rocket for Nazi Germany in the early 1940s. The V-2 was the first long-range guided ballistic missile, and it became the first manmade object to cross the boundary of space with a test launch on 20 June 1944. As the Allies invaded Germany in spring of 1945, they sought to capture sites and recruit scientists working on Nazi Germany's technology programmes. Wernher von Braun surrendered to the Americans in June 1945 and was transferred to the USA, where he later began working for the US Air Force.

Von Braun was involved in the US Air Force's rocket development programme, codenamed Project Blossom. On 11 June 1948, V-2 number 37 rocket, was launched from a base at White Sands, New Mexico. Aboard was a rhesus monkey named Albert I, who is believed to be the first animal astronaut. At the time, it was theorised that humans may not survive extended periods of weightlessness and so animals were routinely used to test whether it was possible to survive in space. Albert's small capsule reached a height of 39 miles but he is thought to have perished in-flight as a result of breathing difficulties. The apparatus conveying his respiratory movements failed to function. The flight lasted around six minutes and crashed into the desert sands. The next launch was almost exactly a year later, with another rhesus monkey, Albert II, used as an astronaut. Sadly, difficulties with the parachute meant that he did not survive the impact, although he remained alive until that moment.

The Albert flights provided valuable information about an animal's response to space flight and specifically, that a long period of weightlessness did not pose danger to human life.

THE BERLIN AIRLIFT BEGINS

The Potsdam Conference, which took place from 17 July to 2 August 1945, decided the fate of post-war Germany. The ensuing Potsdam Agreement divided occupied Germany into four zones, controlled by the Soviets, Americans, British and French respectively. Situated around 100 miles inside the Soviet zone was the German capital Berlin, which was also divided into four zones. The Western Allies controlled three portions of West Berlin, while the Soviets controlled the eastern sector.

In March 1948, the French, British and Americans combined their Berlin zones in order to form a single economic area. The Soviets responded by restricting access between the British, French and American occupation zones in the west of Germany and their respective sectors in Berlin. The Western Allies' introduction of a new Deutsche mark currency for West Berlin was deemed by the Soviets to be a violation of their postwar agreement, so they instituted a blockade of all road, rail and canal access between Berlin and the western occupation zones.

On 24 June the Soviets declared that the four-zone agreement in Berlin was at an end. The Western Allies responded by instigating what became known as the 'Berlin Airlift' to supply the people of West Berlin. This was a successful operation, involving the delivery of around 8,900 tonnes of vital supplies each day to Tempelhof Airport. The Soviets decided not to intervene, apprehensive that such an action might escalate into open conflict.

By spring 1949, Allied countermeasures against the Soviets, including embargoing exports from East Germany, had their desired effect. The Soviets lifted the blockade on 12 May 1949 and a British convoy immediately set off for West Berlin by road. The Berlin Airlift continued until 30 September as a precautionary measure to build up supplies should the Soviets institute another blockade. By that time, an estimated 2,323,738 tons of food, fuel and other essential supplies had been delivered.

MAHATMA GANDHI IS ASSASSINATED

Mohandas Karamchand Gandhi (1869–1948), later known by his honorific title 'Mahatma' (meaning 'Great Soul'), was the leader of the Indian Independence movement, who opposed British rule in India. His non-violent campaign of civil disobedience helped to lead India to independence in 1947, although not under the terms Gandhi had campaigned for. Gandhi had hoped for a united, free India but the British had resolved to partition the country into two: Hindu-dominated India and the newly created Pakistan, formed from the north-western portion of the country, which contained a Muslim majority.

After the partition, Gandhi attempted to heal the scars of the religious violence that had blighted the area. When he was unable to mediate between the two sides, he turned to fasting, which halted rioting in the city of Calcutta in September 1947. He also successfully encouraged the authorities to a communal truce in Delhi in January 1948. However, in the climate of mutual suspicion and anger, Indian and Pakistani partisans blamed Gandhi, both believing him to be taking the other's side. One such man, a Hindu fanatic named Nathuram Godse, plotted Gandhi's assassination with six fellow conspirators.

On 30 January 1948, Gandhi was assassinated by Godse while walking to a prayer meeting in the garden of the Birla family's house, where Gandhi had been staying. Godse approached and shot Gandhi three times with a pistol. The bullets had struck his chest, stomach and groin and he died shortly afterwards.

In India, a state of mourning was observed for 13 days and messages of sympathy flooded in from around the world. Gandhi had touched millions of people across the world and continues to inspire civil rights campaigners. He is widely regarded as the Father of the Indian nation, and his birthday, 2 October, is commemorated as a public holiday.

1953

THE SUMMIT OF MOUNT EVEREST IS REACHED

When the height of the highest mountain in the world was published in 1856 it was known as Peak XV and was measured at 8,840m. Its named was changed to Everest in 1865 by the Royal Geographical Society when a change of name was recommended by Andrew Waugh, who was the British Surveyor General of India. Waugh named the mountain after his predecessor, Sir George Everest.

The summit of Mount Everest, which is in the Himalayas (meaning 'abode of snow), lies between Nepal and China and since its discovery, humans have risked their lives to reach it. In fact, many people do not survive the challenge of reaching the summit and as of 2016 approximately 200 corpses were on the mountain and some are even used as markers for climbers. Even though it was first reached in 1953, mountaineers still attempt the challenge regularly and 2015 became the first year since 1974 in which the summit was not reached.

The most mysterious failed climb was an expedition of June 1924 when two English mountaineers, George Mallory and Andrew Irvine, attempted to succeed in getting to the summit via the Northeast Ridge. However, although they were spotted near the summit, they were lost and never returned. It was in 1999 when Mallory's body was discovered on the mountain and while Irvine was never found, it remains unknown whether the two were successful in their attempt before they perished.

In 1953, Edmund Hillary of New Zealand, alongside Nepalese Sherpa, Tenzing Norgay, became the first to reach the summit, making history at around 11.30 on the morning of 29 May. Financed by the Joint Himalayan Committee and led by Colonel John Hunt, the two men had reached Base Camp at 5.5km altitude on 12 April and after a route was established through the Khumbu Icefall – one of the most perilous stages of the climb – the two set off alongside other members of the expedition, who gradually turned back. On 27 May the duo began the final ascent to the summit on the South Col route. When they arrived at the top, Hillary took photographs of the scenery while Tenzing buried sweets and biscuits in the snow as a Buddhist offering. Hillary described the view as 'a symmetrical, beautiful snow cone summit.'

276

When the news reached home, the achievement was overshadowed as it coincided with the coronation of Queen Elizabeth II on 2 June. However, Hillary was knighted while Tenzing was awarded the George Medal. Edmund Hillary died aged 88 in 2008 while Tenzing Norgay passed away in 1986, aged 71.

THE CORONATION OF QUEEN ELIZABETH II, THE UNITED KINGDOM'S LONGEST REIGNING MONARCH

Queen Elizabeth II was formally crowned monarch of the United Kingdom on 2 June 1953. The coronation ceremony took place at Westminster Abbey in London in front of over 8,000 guests, including heads of state from across the Commonwealth.

Born in 1926, Elizabeth was the first-born child of King George VI. After his death on 6 February 1952, the 25-year-old princess was immediately proclaimed queen, although she remained in mourning and out of the public eye for the first three months of her reign.

The coronation ceremony took 16 months to organise and was an event of great splendour. Clothed in magnificently embroidered white dress and velvet cloak, Elizabeth took the Coronation Oath, swearing to serve her people throughout her reign. The Archbishop of Canterbury handed her the symbols of royal authority, including the orb and sceptre, before placing the crown on her head. An estimated three million people filled London's street to watch her procession from the Cathedral.

The event was filmed by the BBC and was the first coronation to be shown on live television. It was broadcast in 44 different languages and watched by over 20 million people in the UK and across the world. People held street parties throughout Britain, and there were grand coronation celebrations all over the Commonwealth. On 9 September 2015, Elizabeth II became Britain's longest reigning monarch, after over 63 years as queen.

IAN FLEMING'S FIRST JAMES BOND NOVEL IS PUBLISHED

The first James Bond novel, *Casino Royale*, was published in the UK on 13 April 1953. It was the first in a series of books by Ian Fleming which followed the adventures of the British secret agent, also known as 007.

In *Casino Royale*, Bond is sent by MI6 to gamble against a member of the Russian secret service known as Le Chiffre. He is supported by the alluring British agent Vesper Lynd, as well as the American CIA man Felix Leiter. The story, which features international espionage, violent action and clever gadgets, introduced audiences to the now-famous character of Bond, with his love of fast cars, vodka martinis ('shaken, not stirred'), and beautiful women.

Fleming had written the first draft of the book in 1952, finishing it in just two months while staying at his Goldeneye estate in Jamaica. Fleming himself had worked for British intelligence services during the Second World War, and the novel is inspired by many of his own experiences. The cold and ruthless character of Bond was supposedly based on the many secret agents he had encountered in his career.

Casino Royale sold out within a month of being published, and Fleming went on to write a further 11 novels and two short story collections about the daring 007. The novel was one of the last Bond books to be made into a film, which was released in 2008 with Daniel Craig in the starring role.

1954

ROGER BANNISTER BECOMES THE FIRST PERSON TO RUN A SUB-4 MINUTE MILE

On 6 May 1954, the English medical student Roger Bannister crossed the finish-line of a mile-long race with a record-breaking time of 3 minutes and 59.4 seconds. It was a moment that made sporting history.

Roger Bannister was born in Middlesex in 1929 and studied medicine at Oxford. He competed in the 1952 Olympics in Helsinki, and in 1954 he won the British Championships in the mile run for the third time, as well as the European title for the 1,500m event.

Later that year, Bannister set out to run a mile in under four minutes – a feat which many believed was impossible. He had limited time for training, since he was now studying at St. Mary's Hospital Medical School in London. Despite this, on 6 May, he swept to victory at a race at the Iffley Road Track in Oxford, watched by around 3,000 spectators. He was representing the British Amateur Athletic Association in an event against Oxford University, sprinting the last 200 yards to break the four-minute barrier.

Once Bannister had proved it could be done, many other runners went on to run the four-minute mile, and his record was broken just 46 days later by the Australian John Landy. Bannister completed his medical degree in 1954, and became an important neurologist before being knighted in 1975.

THE FIRST HYDROGEN BOMB TEST IS CARRIED OUT

On 1 March 1954, the United States tested its first hydrogen bomb at Bikini Atoll in the Marshall Islands, located approximately halfway between Hawaii and Australia. At 15 megatons, the blast was the largest man-made explosion in history until the USSR tested a 50-megaton device in 1961. The explosion was much larger than expected, overwhelming the measuring instruments. It was thought to be 1,000 times more powerful than the atomic bombs dropped on Hiroshima and Nagasaki, to devastating effect in 1945.

The codename for the 1954 test was Castle Bravo and the device itself was known as 'Shrimp'. When it was detonated, the bomb created a fireball almost four-and-a-half miles wide within a single second. The characteristic mushroom cloud, so-called on account of its mushroom-shape, extended up to a height of 40km and spanned approximately 100km across within 10 minutes. The impact of the explosion created a crater 2,000m across and 76m deep.

The fallout – the radioactive particles that are propelled into the upper atmosphere and then fall back down to earth after the shock wave has subsided – reached the inhabited Rongelap and Rongerik atolls, which had to be evacuated. Traces even reached Europe and the United States. A Japanese fishing boat, Daigo Fukuryū Maru (Lucky Dragon Number 5) was within 80 miles of the blast zone at the time, and the crew came into contact with the fallout. Many of the crew suffered from radiation sickness and one died from a secondary infection, prompting an international outcry against testing thermonuclear devices. The US government compensated the Japanese government with $15.3 million.

THE JAPANESE MONSTER GODZILLA FIRST APPEARS

The 'king of the monsters' Godzilla is one of the most feared and cherished beasts in this history of cinema. Godzilla, whose name originates from the Japanese words for gorilla (gorira) and whale (kujira) was originally pronounced 'Gojira' in its home country. So famous that he has had a star on the Hollywood Walk of Fame since 2004, his prestige as a ferocious city-destroying monster has even seen him fight the Avengers and Fantastic Four in a series of Marvel comics in 1977.

First appearing in the 1954 film *Godzilla*, directed by Ishiro Honda, two actors were actually used to play the monster in a special costume, as the special effects of stop motion animation were too expensive to use. Since the 1954 film, Godzilla has featured in almost 30 films produced by Toho productions in Japan and has also starred in several American films during which time he has fought numerous enemies including King Kong, SpaceGodzilla and of course humans. During his career, there have been a mixture of scenarios in which Godzilla has been the saviour of human civilisation but at other times a bringer of destruction and it is not definite whether Godzilla is good or bad.

Debuting only nine years after the American atomic bomb attacks on Hiroshima and Nagasaki in Japan during the Second World War, Godzilla was perceived as a metaphor for destruction, nuclear weapons and the threat of a dangerous enemy. The physical appearance of Godzilla has been argued to be a representation of the horrors of nuclear war but over the years his roles in films, video games, literature and even adverts, have seen his features vary, as have his abilities, such as being able to fly in the 1974 film *Godzilla vs. Hedorah.*

In 1997, a real dinosaur, *Gojirasaurus quayi*, was even named after Godzilla when it was discovered in New Mexico. The 6.5m-long theropod lived 210 million years ago.

1963

MARTIN LUTHER KING JR DELIVERS HIS 'I HAVE A DREAM' SPEECH

On 28 August 1963, Martin Luther King Jr, an African-American Baptist preacher, addressed a crowd of over 200,000 people gathered on the steps of Lincoln Memorial in Washington D.C. The demonstrators – rich and poor, black and white – had come together as part of the March on Washington for Jobs and Freedom, gathering to demand equal voting rights and equal opportunities for African-Americans, and appeal for an end to racial discrimination.

Martin Luther King Jr was the last speaker at the peaceful rally, which was the largest demonstration ever to take place in the US capital. He used the speech-making abilities he had developed as a preacher to show how the 'Negro is still not free', discussing the importance of non-violent protest in the struggle that lay ahead. As he came to the end of his prepared speech, he began to improvise, swept up in the moment's emotion. This section of the speech is one of the most famous in world history. 'I have a dream', he declared: 'I have a dream that my four little children will one day live in a nation where they will not be judged by the colour of their skin but by the content of their character. I have a dream today.'

The iconic speech helped to shape the course of American history. The following year, the Civil Rights Act of 1964 was passed, outlawing racial segregation and discrimination in employment and education.

THE GREAT TRAIN ROBBERY

It is one of the most infamous crimes in British history which resulted in the theft of £2.6 million and the arrests and convictions of many of the gang members. The Great Train Robbery continues to fascinate people over 50 years since the crime was committed by at least 15 men. Renowned for the scope and audacity of the operation, the incident has been recreated many times in literature, film and television.

Originally known as the Cheddington Mail Van Raid, the robbery occurred just after 3 in the morning on 8 August 1963 at Bridego Railway Bridge. The gang, led by the operation's mastermind, Bruce Reynolds, intercepted a Royal Mail train travelling from Glasgow Central Station to Euston Station in London. The gang had been informed about the amount of money regularly transported on the train and as there had a been a bank holiday weekend in Scotland, the usual amount of £300,000 carried on the High Value Packages coach behind the train's engine, was estimated to be significantly more. The gang tampered with the signal light at Sears Crossing in Ledburn, between Leighton Buzzard and Cheddington and the driver, Jack Mills, stopped the train. The gang had covered the green light and attached a battery to the red light and when the train's second crew-member stepped off the train to telephone the signalman, he was overpowered by gang members. Meanwhile, Jack Mills, awaiting a green light, was struck on the head with a club and he lost consciousness. He never fully recovered from the attack and died in 1970.

The gang removed 120 of the sacks from the carriage, loaded them onto a waiting truck in 20 minutes and then made their getaway to a hideout at Leatherslade Farm which was 27 miles from the robbery. Back at the hideout, the gang counted and split the money, most of which was never recovered. When the gang learned that the police were getting close to the farm, they fled. The police investigation eventually tracked down many of the gang members, whose fingerprints had been found at the farm including on a Monopoly board which the gang had used while hiding but had played with real stolen money.

After their capture, a trial took place beginning in 1964 and lasting 51 days. Seven of the robbers were given 30-year sentences while other members faced varying spells in prison. However, some of the gang members were never named or caught. The story didn't end there as two of the prisoners escaped from jail and became fugitives, the most famous of these was Ronnie Biggs who moved to Brazil until he voluntarily returned to the UK in 2001 where he was returned to prison. He died in 2013. Only £400,000 was ever recovered from the robbery.

ALCATRAZ SHUTS DOWN

Alcatraz prison, formally known as the Alcatraz Federal Penitentiary, was one of the most notorious and expensive prisons in the world. It was located on Alcatraz Island, 1.25 miles off the coast of San Francisco, USA. The island was originally built as a military citadel in 1859 and functioned as a battery, featuring 111 guns, during the American Civil War. It was officially designated as a military prison on 27 August 1861 but did not operate as a Federal prison until 1934.

Alcatraz was regarded as a maximum-security prison and was deemed to be escape-proof. It housed 1,576 inmates during the 29 years of its operation, including infamous criminals Al Capone, Robert Franklin Stroud, known as the 'Birdman of Alcatraz', and George Francis Barnes Jr., better known as 'Machine Gun' Kelly. Despite the high security and the island's position, surrounded by the strong, turbulent waters of San Francisco Bay, a number of audacious escape attempts were devised. In all, 36 prisoners tried to escape, with 23 caught, six shot and killed, two drowned, and five presumed to have drowned, although their bodies were never recovered. The most famous escape attempt occurred in June 1962, involving prisoners Frank Morris, Clarence Anglin and John Anglin. They had chiselled away at damaged walls and escaped through a fan vent. They had also constructed a raft made from stolen raincoats and positioned papier-mâché figures in their beds. Although an official report concluded that the three men had drowned, their bodies were never retrieved and the US Marshals Service still lists them as wanted fugitives.

Alcatraz prison closed the following year, on 21 March 1963. It now operates as a hugely popular tourist attraction, with approximately 1.5 million people visiting the site each year.

PRESIDENT JOHN F. KENNEDY IS ASSASSINATED

On 22 November 1963, John Fitzgerald Kennedy, the 35th President of the United States, was assassinated while driving through Dallas, Texas in an open-top car.

The president, who was in Texas on a fundraising trip, had given a speech that morning and was being driven with his wife Jacqueline to their next stop. An estimated 200,000 people lined the ten-mile route taken by their open limousine. At 12.30pm, as the car passed the Texas School Book Depository, shots were fired from the sixth floor, fatally wounding Kennedy and seriously injuring Texas Governor John Connally, sitting in the front seat. One bullet pierced the president's neck, while a second struck the back of his head. He was rushed to Dallas' Parkland Hospital, where he was declared dead 30 minutes later.

The killer is believed to have been Lee Harvey Oswald, an ex-US Marine with Soviet sympathies. He was arrested less than two hours after the assassination, and charged with murder, but was shot by Dallas inhabitant Jack Ruby before his case could come to trial.

At 2.39pm on the day of the killing, US Vice President Lyndon Johnson was sworn in as president, immediately before the presidential jet took off for Washington with Kennedy's body. The news stunned the nation, Americans cried in the streets, and the next day was one of national mourning. Kennedy's casket lay in state in the US Capitol, where hundreds of thousands gathered to pay their respects. On 25 November, a parade carried the casket through the capital for a state funeral which was attended by representatives from over 90 countries.

1969

MAN WALKS ON THE MOON

In 1961, the US President John F. Kennedy set a goal of landing a man on the Moon and returning him safely to Earth in the 20th century. In July 1969, an estimated 600 million people around the world watched live on television as the Apollo 11 mission successfully fulfilled Kennedy's ambition.

Commander Neil Armstrong, Lunar Module Pilot Edwin 'Buzz' Aldrin and Command Module Pilot Michael Collins were the crew of the Apollo 11 mission which took off from the Kennedy Space Centre in Florida on 16 July 1969, launched by a Saturn V rocket. The 240,000 mile journey to the Moon took 76 hours before Armstrong and Aldrin guided the lunar module *Eagle* to the Sea of Tranquillity on the lunar surface while Collins orbited above in the command and service module *Columbia*.

The *Eagle* landed on 20 July 1969 but it wasn't until the next day, six hours after touchdown, that Armstrong became the first human on the moon and voiced the famous quote 'That's one small step for [a] man, one giant leap for mankind' – it is uncertain whether Armstrong said 'a man' as was intended. And it wasn't actually too small a step as the leap from the *Eagle* to the Moon was four foot.

Armstrong and Aldrin spent two-and-a-half hours outside the spacecraft collecting 21.5kg of lunar material. Buzz Aldrin took Communion and the astronauts left a plaque which read: *Here men from the planet Earth first set foot upon the Moon, July 1969 AD. We came in peace for all mankind.*

While they were on the Moon, a Soviet unmanned spacecraft *Luna 15* actually crashed on the Moon during an unsuccessful landing. The duo planted an American flag but this was blasted away when they launched the *Eagle* to return back to the awaiting Collins. Dust from the Moon which had gathered in the astronaut's space suits was described as smelling like gunpowder while Armstrong said it smelled of wet ashes.

The journey back to Earth began and the astronauts splashed down in the Pacific Ocean on 24 July and were taken to Hawaii, where they had to sign a customs and declarations form. They were also kept in quarantine for 21 days but soon were to be applauded in parades and celebrations across the planet.

In 2012, Neil Armstrong was the first of the crew to pass away. Despite Apollo missions landing men on the Moon again in 1969 and four more times in the years after, no human has set foot on the Moon since 1972.

THE BEATLES' LAST PUBLIC PERFORMANCE

On 30 January 1969, the Beatles, the most popular band in the world, played their final gig – an impromptu performance on the roof of their Apple headquarters, at 3 Savile Row in London. Prior to this, the last official concert had been 29 August 1966 at Candlestick Park in San Francisco, USA. However, on a cold Thursday lunchtime, the four Beatles – John Lennon, Paul McCartney, George Harrison and Ringo Starr – played a 42-minute set which ended when the Metropolitan Police, who were concerned about noise levels and traffic issues, ascended to the roof and stopped the performance. Alongside the 'Fab Four', the keyboardist Billy Preston played nine takes of five songs including 'Don't Let Me  Down', 'One After 909' and 'I've Got a Feeling', while their last track was 'Get Back'. At the end of this track John Lennon famously said 'I'd like to say thank you on behalf of the group and ourselves and I hope we've passed the audition.'

Director Michael Lindsay-Hogg filmed the concert from several points of view including at street-level where passers-by were stunned by the lunchtime performance as they made their way around the city. As news of the gig spread, people made their way onto rooftops and the crowds in the streets grew, which caused the police to stop the performance. The footage was used in the documentary film *Let It Be*. Although the Beatles went on to release one final album, *Abbey Road*, in September 1969, this was their last public performance and the end of a musical era.

THE BOEING 747 AIRPLANE MAKES ITS FIRST FLIGHT

The Boeing 747, commonly known as the 'Jumbo Jet', was at the time the largest and heaviest passenger aircraft ever constructed. It was conceived partly as a result of pressure from Juan Trippe, the President of the airline Pan American (Pan Am), to build a considerably larger version of the successful Boeing 707. The resulting 747 could carry up to two-and-a-half times the weight of the 707. It had a total length of 70m, a wingspan of 59m and a top speed of 594 mph. The four-engine plane is very distinctive-looking, with its pronounced 'hump' in the front portion of its upper deck, containing the cockpit and First Class or Business Class seating, although early models featured an upstairs lounge.

Its first flight was carried out on 9 February 1969, flown by Jack Waddell, Brien Wygle and Jess Wallick. Aside from a minor technical problem with one of the flaps, the test flight was a success. The first 747 entered service with Pan Am on 22 January 1970 and was christened by the First Lady of the United States, Pat Nixon.

As at the end of March 2016, 1,520 Boeing 747s had been built. Its formidable carrying capacity was only bettered by the arrival of the Airbus A-380 in 2008. A modified 747 famously serves as the official plane of the President of the United States, which is known by the call-sign Air Force One when it is carrying the President. The first Presidential 747 was delivered during the tenure of George Bush in 1990.

1973

THE SPANISH PAINTER PABLO PICASSO DIES

Picasso was one of the greatest and most influential artists of the 20th century: a painter, sculptor, ceramicist, printmaker and designer. Born in Spain in 1881, he was an artistic child prodigy and went to art school in Barcelona and Madrid. He travelled to Paris in 1900, where he met other important artists and patrons, from Henri Matisse to Gertrude Stein. He experimented with different styles, from the sombre colours of his Blue Period (1901–4), to the warm oranges and pink tones of his Rose Period (1904–6).

He settled permanently in Paris in 1904, and in 1907, he painted the famous *Les Demoiselles d'Avignon*, a depiction of five nude women with mask-like faces which was influenced by African tribal art. The work caused a scandal, and its abstract, distorted figures helped to inspire Cubism, the art movement founded by Picasso and his friend, the painter Georges Braque. Cubism was seen as a revolutionary art movement, using collage-like effects to fragment objects into geometric shapes seen from multiple viewpoints. Later, Picasso was deeply affected by the violence of the Second World War and the Spanish Civil War. His Surrealist 1937 painting *Guernica* showed the inhumanity and destruction of conflict, depicting the anguish and terror caused by the German bombing of the Basque town of Guernica that year.

As he got older and became a celebrity, his painting style became more childlike, using simple imagery and crude lines. He continued to create art all the way up to his death, superstitiously believing that work would keep him alive. On 8 April 1973, Picasso died aged 91, at Mougins in France. His influence is still felt today, and he continues to be celebrated for his creativity, technical skill and revolutionary ideas.

THE WATERGATE SCANDAL AND THE RESIGNATION OF THE PRESIDENT

On 17 June 1972, several trespassers were arrested inside the headquarters of the Democratic National Committee in the Watergate complex in Washington, DC. The intruders were from the Committee to Re-Elect the President (CREEP) and were associated with the American Republican President Richard Nixon's campaign for re-election. Police had caught the burglars stealing copies of top-secret files and bugging the office's telephones. The scandal led to Nixon's eventual resignation on 9 August 1974 – the only president to resign from the office – but it is debated whether Nixon knew of the surveillance mission before it took place. However, his role in attempting to cover up the sabotage led to his demise.

Having lost a presidential campaign against John F. Kennedy in 1960, Richard Nixon was elected as the 37th President of the United States in 1969, presiding over the Moon landings and helping bring the Vietnam War to an end and safeguarding the return of American prisoners of war. However, it was the Watergate Scandal and his resignation from office before certain impeachment that he is infamously remembered for.

Shortly after the break-in and the arrests of the intruders, Nixon gave a speech in which he promised neither he or his staff were involved in the operation. Most people believed him and in fact he won the presidential election that November by a landslide, receiving nearly 18 million more popular votes than his Democratic counterpart George McGovern, which is the biggest-ever margin of any US presidential election. It is important to understand Nixon's popularity to comprehend his downfall and the trust lost in the president's office by the American nation.

It was in 1973 that the fallout from Watergate began to gather momentum and in January two people were convicted of charges relating to the scandal. It came to light that Nixon had arranged for large payments to be made to the burglars and had attempted to block the investigation of the incident by the FBI. When it was revealed Nixon taped conversations which took place in the Oval Office – the president's office – prosecutors requested their release so they could examine what exactly the president knew. However, Nixon refused to hand over the tapes during the summer of 1973 but eventually he surrendered some tapes. When the House of Representatives voted to impeach the president for several counts including abuse of power and criminal cover-up, Nixon released all the tapes and it was confirmed that he had been involved in the scandal. Rather than face impeachment, Nixon resigned and when Gerald Ford, Nixon's vice-president, succeeded the disgraced president, he pardoned Nixon for his crimes. Nixon died in 1994 aged 81.

THE SYDNEY OPERA HOUSE OPENS

The Sydney Opera House is one of the most recognisable landmarks in the world and a frequently used emblem of Australia. Standing on Bennelong Point in Sydney Harbour, close to Sydney Harbour Bridge, the performing arts centre is distinguished by its remarkable white roof with its shell-shaped sails standing 65m high. Designed by the Danish architect Jorn Utzon, the construction of the Sydney Opera House was not always a smooth affair but in June 2007 it was designated as a UNESCO World Heritage Site and has been spoken of as one of the new Wonders of the World.

The Syndey Opera House was opened by Queen Elizabeth II on 20 October 1973 with a large crowd in attendance, fireworks and a performance of Beethoven's Symphony No. 9, all broadcast on television. However, Utzon was not there and had not even been invited. After a disagreement between the designer and the New South Wales government responsible for the project over cost and design and with Utzon unpaid, he resigned and left Australia, never to see his finished creation. He had won an international design competition in 1957 and construction of the venue began two years later but was scheduled to be completed in 1963.

When it was completed in 1973, it had cost 102 million Australian dollars which was about 1,450 per cent over budget. However, the 185m-long home to ballet, opera, theatre and symphony orchestra welcomes over 1 million visitors a year, and the project is considered a great achievement of architecture.

1989

THE TIANANMEN SQUARE PROTESTS

The Tiananmen Square protests of 1989 were a series of public demonstrations in Beijing, China following the death of Hu Yaobang, the former Communist Party General Secretary. Hu had been a liberal voice in the party, initiating political and economic reforms and claiming that members of his party were corrupt. This antagonised more radical members of the party, who forced him to resign in 1987, after blaming him for widespread student protests. After his death, university students congregated in Tiananmen Square to pay their respects and to call for democratic reforms.

By the middle of May 1989, protests had spread to over 400 cities in China and the Communist Party authorities responded by declaring martial law, mobilising over a quarter-of-a-million troops. By June, troops and tanks moved towards Tiananmen Square, opening fire on protesters blocking their path. By the following morning, most of the protesters had been forcibly removed but pockets of resistance remained. The following day, 5 June, a lone protester positioned himself in front of an advancing column of tanks. The front tank attempted to move around him, but the protestor maneuvered himself back into the tank's path. He continued to stand there, with television cameras filming the iconic scene. He then climbed onto the front tank to talk to the crew inside but soon returned to his position in the road where he was eventually pulled aside by two men dressed in blue.

Not much is known about the fate of the protester, widely known as the 'Tank man'. The *Sunday Express* named him as 19-year-old student Wang Weilin, but the Chinese Communist Party refuted this claim. The Chinese authorities did all they could to confiscate and destroy the film taken by the international press. Even now, commemoration of the incident is officially prohibited in China.

THE FALL OF THE BERLIN WALL

The Berlin Wall was built by the government of the German Democratic Republic (GDR) to encircle West Berlin, an area administered by the Western Allies of World War II. The wall not only physically separated West Berlin from East Berlin, but also separated West Berlin from East Germany.

Berlin had been separated into four separate zones in 1945. The areas controlled by the Western Allies formed West Berlin, and the Soviets controlled the eastern portion, which became East Berlin. Between 1949 and 1961 approximately 2.5 million people fled from East Germany to West Germany, including many skilled young workers and intellectuals. This mass migration placed economic and political strains on East Germany, so the GDR resolved to construct a wall to prevent further movement. The GDR concealed the real reason for constructing the wall, instead claiming that it was erected as an 'anti-fascist protective rampart' to discourage Western aggression.

The construction of the wall began on 13 August 1961. It was over 87 miles long, containing numerous guard towers, anti-vehicle trenches and nine border crossings. The most famous of these was on the corner of Friedrichstraße and Zimmerstraße, nicknamed Checkpoint Charlie. In the 38 years that the wall stood, approximately 5,000 people were captured by East German soldiers and 191 were killed trying to cross the wall.

A tide of democratisation washed through Eastern Europe in 1989. When Hungary began to dismantle its fortified border fence, thousands of East Germans emigrated through the border, fleeing to West Germany and Austria. On 9 November 1989, shortly after its communist leadership was ousted, the new East German authorities announced that its borders would open. That evening, guards stationed at border crossings allowed the East Germans to cross. West Berliners greeted them, offering flowers and Champagne and the two groups of people danced and celebrated together. Television cameras captured iconic images of German citizens tearing down the wall and cheering on the bulldozers. The following year, Germany was reunified, and in 1991, the USSR was officially dissolved on 26 December 1991, signalling the end of the Cold War.

1989

TIM BERNERS-LEE AND THE INTERNET

The World Wide Web is a revolutionary information space that can be accessed via the internet. It was invented by English computer scientist Tim Berners-Lee in 1989 while he was working as a fellow at CERN, the European Organisation for Nuclear Research. Berners-Lee had become a software engineer at CERN shortly after graduating with a first-class degree in physics from Oxford University. Scientists and technicians travel from all over the world to CERN in Geneva to use their particle accelerator complex, but they were encountering difficulties in sharing their research. Different information was stored on many different computers, which often required learning a new program in order to retrieve the information. Berners-Lee started working at a solution to this problem. In 1989, he put together a document entitled *Information Management: A Proposal* to outline his vision for what would later become familiar world-wide as the Web. Berners-Lee began to make his vision a reality using a NeXT computer, an early product developed by Steve Jobs.

It wasn't until October 1990 that Berners-Lee had developed the crucial components of the Web: the HyperText Transfer Protocol (HTTP), which allows the retrieval of linked resources from across the Web; the first HTTP server software; Hypertext Markup Language (HTML), the special formatting language used for the Web; the Uniform Resource Identifier (also known as a Uniform Resource Locator, or URL), a unique address use to identify different resources on the Web; and the first Web page editor and browser. The first web page appeared on the open internet before Christmas 1990 and on 6 August 1991, Berners-Lee's Web became a publicly available service.

The creation of the Web was a critical moment in the Information Age and in the history of communication. It is what we use to interact on the internet, and it is used by billions of people every day.